WEB PROJECT MANAGEMENT

Delivering Successful Commercial Web Sites

WEB PROJECT MANAGEMENT

Delivering Successful Commercial Web Sites

Ashley Friedlein

Wheel

MORGAN KAUFMANN PUBLISHERS

AN IMPRINT OF ACADEMIC PRESS
A Harcourt Science and Technology Company

SAN FRANCISCO   SAN DIEGO   NEW YORK   BOSTON
LONDON   SYDNEY   TOKYO

Senior Editor	Jennifer Mann
Senior Production Editor	Edward Wade
Editorial Coordinator	Karyn Johnson
Cover Design	Yvo Riezebos Design
Text Design, Composition, and Technical Illustration	Mark Ong, Susan Riley/Side By Side Studios
Copyeditor	Daril Bentley
Proofreader	Jennifer McClain
Indexer	Steve Rath
Printer	Courier Corporation

Designations used by companies to distinguish their products are often claimed as trademarks or registered trademarks. In all instances where Morgan Kaufmann Publishers is aware of a claim, the product names appear in initial capital or all capital letters. Readers, however, should contact the appropriate companies for more complete information regarding trademarks and registration.

ACADEMIC PRESS
A Harcourt Science and Technology Company
525 B Street, Suite 1900, San Diego, CA 92101-4495, USA
http://www.academicpress.com

Academic Press
Harcourt Place, 32 Jamestown Road, London, NW1 7BY, United Kingdom
http://www.academicpress.com

Morgan Kaufmann Publishers
340 Pine Street, Sixth Floor, San Francisco, CA 94104-3205, USA
http://www.mkp.com

05 04 03 02 01   5 4 3

Library of Congress Cataloging-in-Publication Data

Friedlein, Ashley.
    Web project management : delivering successful commercial Web sites / Ashley Friedlein
        p. cm.
    Includes index.
    ISBN 1-55860-678-5
    1. Web sites--Management. I. Title: Web project management. II. Title: Commercial Web sites. III. Title.

TK5105.888 .F73 2001
650'.0285'4628--dc21

00-043827

This book is printed on acid-free paper.

Contents

Preface

I still haven't worked out a simple way of explaining what I do. "Internet producer" just gets blank looks, and "Web project manager" fares little better. It's a funny thing, really, because "film producer" or "TV producer" are usually greeted with an impressed "Oh, really!," with appropriate raising of the eyebrows and yet, when pressed, the layperson really doesn't know what these jobs entail either.

I started off working for a TV production company, working my way up to producer. I was first drawn to becoming a TV producer because unlike other more narrowly focused jobs, it required creative, commercial, and technical skills. You needed to have an idea for a show, you needed to be able to justify why it would work commercially, and you needed to understand how it would be made. You really had the chance to create and own something for which you would also then see the results. Working as part of a team toward creating a product that could get such immediate feedback seemed ideal.

I moved from TV to multimedia to video on demand. At the time (1996), the video-on-demand project I was working on used such bleeding-edge technology that it ended up hemorrhaging to an early death. I decided to go "narrow band." The Internet looked liked it was going to take off, and surely it couldn't be as complicated as developing a proprietary interactive digital video system . . . ?

The Internet as a delivery medium was just too tempting not to get into. Here was a medium that required all of the same creative, commercial, and technical skills of a producer, but in a field that was still such virgin territory. Anyone could publish his or her "show" on the Web, which would receive even more tangible and immediate feedback than television production, and your show could run 24 hours a day worldwide. Now that's what I call empowerment.

Since taking up this new challenge, I have found that it has lived up to everything I had hoped for. I have to admit that not all that long ago the terms *computers* and *project manager*, particularly when used anywhere near each other, would have conjured up images of supreme dullness. How wrong. The Internet, enabled by computer technology, is a medium in which to communicate, create, and trade that is more quickly and radically changing the way we live than any other technological revolution before it. As a Web project manager, you have the opportunity to be a part of forming and informing this evolving world.

How This Book Can Help You

There seem to be a lot of books on the market that fall among general introductory "dummies" guides to the Internet, specialist programming and design tutorials, or the esoteric strategic musings of a Web guru. However, there seems to be very little that helps explain exactly how to make it all happen. There are books that tell you how to put together your own home pages, but not a full-scale commercial site. This book will tell you how to bring the various elements together so that you can "walk the talk" and actually deliver Web sites that are as successful in the process of their implementation as they are in then delivering real commercial benefit.

In most jobs there is no substitute for experience. This is certainly true of Web project management. The more practical experience you have had, the better. This book distills the many hard-earned lessons that I, and others, have undergone so that you can benefit from them. However, the nature of the new media industry is such that no one can be completely "experienced," as the industry itself is yet to fully mature and continues to change and evolve at a terrific pace. This means that core skills such as people and project management are as vitally important as ever. Much of this book is based on standard project management principles and techniques, but always in the context of online projects and the specific challenges they present.

This book is written with larger-scale commercial Web sites in mind. This is because such sites are increasingly common, and if you are not already involved on projects of this scope, you probably soon will be, and the book will prepare you for that transition. This book relates the best practices from the higher end of the market, which can be used to the benefit of those working on smaller projects.

If you are working on an intranet, you will also have a lot to gain from the book. The development of an intranet has many similarities to Internet site development, particularly in the fundamental processes and methods applied. However, with an intranet, the technical environment can usually be better controlled, and there are likely to be more business process issues, more internal staff training, and more of an emphasis on applications than brand communication and sales. In this way, a business-to-business Web site will have more similarities with an intranet development than a business-to-consumer site. Nevertheless, the fundamental lessons this book communicates are applicable to all online projects. Indeed, many of the fundamentals would apply to any project.

Audience

Whatever the job name or description a person might hold, this book is for those responsible for making a Web site happen, for delivering a site, and for seeing the job through. This could be someone in-house at an organization, or a project manager or producer who is part of a contracted Web development team.

Many other areas and job roles are touched upon (e.g., design, programming, marketing, and strategy) that the project manager comes into contact with and needs to understand. This book is also useful to any member of a Web development team, whatever the role, who needs to get a better understanding of how to work with a project manager.

This book refers to *clients* and to the *Web development team*. The *client* could be internal or external. The client is the person or group that commissions the building of the Web site. If your project is internal, your client might be your line manager, the marketing director, the information systems (IS) department, or the CEO of the company. If the client is external, it is probably because you work for a Web development agency, or freelance, and sell your services to clients who need your expertise.

Approach

The core of this book is the Web project management method put forward in Part II. This method was developed at pres.co, the United Kingdom's largest new media agency, over many years of Web development, and is specifically designed for delivering media to large-scale commercial Web sites.

The method consists of eight work stages. These work stages take you from the beginning of a project—through its design, construction, and launch—to what happens after the site is launched, focused on in the last two work stages.

Far too often, people only think about the actual design and creation of a site. However, if design and creation are to be successful, you first need to clearly define what you are going to do and why. Equally, the maintenance and evaluation of a Web site post launch is often not properly addressed. In reality, this is usually the most expensive and important part of the site.

Fundamental to the approach represented by this method is recognition of the fact that planning, specification, and site maintenance and evaluation are just as important as design and creation. Web development is an ongoing process, and this method shows very clearly how that process should evolve.

The eight work stages of the method are presented in considerable detail so that you can see the hands-on practicalities of what is involved at each stage. The case-study material is kept separate to make it clear that this method can be applied to any Web project and, as a method, will not date nearly as fast as the specifics of a case study.

It is hoped that you will pick up a lot of practical tips as you read through the book, but most importantly you can take this eight-stage methodological framework and use it to give your projects more structure, more robustness, more professionalism, and more control. All of these factors help minimize the difficulties encountered on Web projects, and improve the quality and accountability of what you deliver—which, ultimately, is what your clients will most admire you for.

Content

This book consists of four parts. Part I looks in detail at the world of Web project management, and what that entails for the Web project manager. What is it about Web project management that makes it different from other forms of project management? What are the roles, responsibilities, qualities, and rewards associated with being a Web project manager? Who will you be working with the most, and what are their roles?

Part II, Method, represents the framework you can use and adapt to create your own Web project method. This part is about workflow and process; it is about the steps you should go through, largely in chronological order, to create your site. This method is intended to be applicable to any Web project, and therefore the text does not go into the minute details of particular example projects. This should mean that the method will remain a valuable reference for you even when Internet technologies have advanced well beyond current status.

However, as much detail as possible fleshes out the framework, to make it as "practical" a guide as possible. Often (e.g., with technical specification) "the devil is in the detail," and the success (or otherwise) of a project can hinge on a few words, a specification detail, or an assumption that may have been omitted. Therefore, the level of detail seeks to avoid these situations. There is also supporting example documentation on the companion Web site (*www.e-consultancy.com/book*) that should further help you on a practical front.

TIP   **Look out for the tips**

Throughout Part II you will see tips such as this. These are practical tips that are not necessarily part of the theoretical or methodological framework but are hints, suggestions, and resources that have proved useful in the past.

Watch out for the cartoons that appear periodically in the book. One of the qualities Web project managers need to have is a sense of humor. Arguably, there is a useful message behind each cartoon, but they are there more to enliven what might otherwise seem a little dry, to share some common insights into the Web project management experience, and (as one friend rather unkindly, but correctly, pointed out) to serve as visual book-marks to get where you want in the book more quickly.

Part III contains an extended case study and comments from other industry professionals on Web project management. The case study intends to show how the theory actually looks in practice, as we all know that the two are never quite as close as we might hope.

Rather than go into less detail on several sites, Part III concentrates on one example so that you can really get a feel for the process; as it were, to live and breathe what practicing what you preach can become. The example maps out the creation of a Web site set against the project method of Part II. There will no doubt be many elements you recognize as you read it. Hopefully you will enjoy reading about the trials and tribulations of someone else for once.

The comments from other industry players will also help give you a further taste of the reality of Web project management. These comments come from around the world and provide a valuable insight into Web project management as viewed not just by the project managers themselves but by clients and by other members of a Web development team. Again, you will see how other people in a similar position to you have fared, and how Web project managers are perceived by those they work with and for.

Appendix A provides further resources. These are centered around the companion Web site that supports this book, found at *www.e-consultancy .com/book*. See Appendix A for more detailed information of what is available in the book and on the companion Web site. Appendix B provides recommended reading.

Acknowledgments

Most of all I would like to thank my wife Annabel for her support in the writing of this book. Not only did she put up with the loss of a lot of time that we would otherwise have spent together, but I also refused to let her read any of the manuscript as I was writing it. I have far too high a respect for her own writing abilities to have let her see my own efforts. I hope she likes it.

This book would not have been half as good without the dedication of my editorial team. Jennifer Mann, Senior Editor, was remorselessly correct in her observations and yet made the process remarkably painless with her encouragement and enthusiasm. Karyn Johnson was equally helpful, particularly in lining up an excellent panel of reviewers and chasing them for their invaluable feedback.

This book would not have been possible at all without the generous support of my employer, Wheel. Particular thanks to Phil Redding for making it possible, and to Matt Flynn for all the wisdom and help I have taken from him and incorporated into the book. Thanks also to all the clients and colleagues from whom I have learned so much, in particular the marketing team at Channel 5: David Bainbridge, Elin Parry, and Toby Dabek.

Special thanks to Paul Tinsley of Wheel for the design of the companion Web site at *www.e-consultancy.com/book*, and Matthew O'Riordan of Thinc! Digital Media for all of the programming behind the site.

Many other individuals have helped shape this book, though some may not realize it. Thanks to Lester Milbank of Cambridge Film and TV for inspiring me with the powers of creativity, enthusiasm, and good communication. Thanks to Ian Foley for forcing me to learn Microsoft Project and to create my first project specification.

One thing you learn very quickly with Web sites is that users have a lot of very helpful, if sometimes rather blunt, suggestions about how the site could be improved. I have been lucky enough to get invaluable feedback and suggestions from reviewers in the process of writing this book—all of them experts in their fields and several successful authors in their own right. In particular, I would like to thank Mike Stone, Jay Goldbach, Brett Lorenzen, Kiril Iossifov Iliarionov, Jerry Altman, Jerrie Andreas, Mark Samis, and Philip Greenspun for their contributions at the proposal stage of the book, and Mike Stone, Morgan Everett, Dave Robertson, Dan Owsen, and Adam Safran for their reviews and suggestions throughout the writing process.

Finally, I must thank the Internet itself. Without it I would not be where I am today, and I certainly wouldn't have been in a position to write a book. I wouldn't have been able to research IT publishers and email my proposal directly to numerous editors around the world. I wouldn't have been able to communicate nearly as effectively with a publisher on the other side of the world and in a different time zone. It's easy to criticize the Internet, but it is a truly remarkable phenomenon, and one that only improves with further acquaintance.

THE WORLD OF
THE WEB PROJECT
MANAGER

1

Setting the Scene

Successful project management is about ensuring the right blend of diverse skill sets and cultures needed to produce a truly great Web site. Bringing together, in one team, people with art and technology degrees can be difficult in having them understand each other's point of view. The project manager must be a skilled translator between the creative push of "this is what we could do" against the technologist view of "this is what we can do," especially if back-end legacy systems are involved.

—Andrew Bibby, Director of Projects, Razorfish, USA

I t wasn't that long ago that the majority of Web sites consisted of static HTML pages containing text and graphics, and incorporating some basic functionality, such as online forms for collecting feedback, rollovers, and search functions. I know enough HTML, and enough about Photoshop and file optimization (and can "borrow" standard JavaScript and Perl scripts), so that I have the tools to create a basic Web site. However, I wouldn't say I possessed anything like the depth of skills and experience in any one of these areas to create a Web site of real quality, even a basic one, on my own. Not that this has stopped me from trying, mind you, to the arguable benefit of various friends and relatives.

The fact that one person can create Web pages with relative ease often means people find it difficult to see why a large team can be needed to create a Web site, or why it can cost as much as it does. The speed of development in the Internet industry, the insatiable demand from users for new features and functionality (coupled with very high expectations of service levels), and clients' demands for the fastest possible development times all mean that it is impossible, and not sensible, for a single person with a broad but thin knowledge base to attempt to create a commercial Web site.

Thus was born the need for dedicated Web project managers. Once a Web project gets to a certain size, it becomes very difficult for a designer, or programmer or other developer, with a specialist skill set to manage the project and its resources in addition to performing their specialist work. Web project management requires its own set of specialist skills, and it is a full-time job.

As the name implies, a project manager manages projects. However, he or she also manages people as a vital component of any project. This book will help you steer the team of people necessary to the development of commercial-grade Web sites as professionally and productively as possible.

It is important to create standards and processes to which your team can work. For a team to form quickly—and then perform successfully in delivering quality, and delivering on time and within budget—it helps enormously if all work to a single structure and system. This structure will not stifle creativity but infuse confidence in the project and the team, promoting rather than inhibiting calculated risk taking, innovation, and creative excellence— within the controlling parameters you establish and monitor.

This book provides you with such a framework, based on many collective years of Web development experience, which has been proven to work effectively. Use it to help establish the processes and environments that work best for your particular circumstances. However, before we look at this framework and before we look at you, the *Web* project manager, it is worth considering the discipline of project management itself.

1.1 Project Management Principles

General project management principles state that the following are the three key elements that underpin any project.

▶ *Cost:* This includes not just money actually spent, but costs such as management time, opportunity cost, or other monetary value expended or created as part of the project.

▶ *Time:* This is not necessarily the number of days between the start and end points but the total number of man-hours or days spent on the project.

▶ *Quality:* This is difficult to define. You will need to establish for your project what represents quality. It might mean meeting the required specification, it might mean creating a commercial success, or it might mean leading the way through innovation. It might mean all of these.

The principles further state that if any one of these three factors is affected, it will have an impact on the other two. This might seem fairly obvious if you stop to think about it. However, the notion that one thing *cannot* change without there being a consequent effect is an important mind-set and approach that becomes very helpful when applied to a Web project, which has exactly the same pressures and constraints. It is all the more helpful in that this way of thinking has the authority and approval stamp of history: it may be obvious to you but it may be less obvious to your client until explained and couched in terms of professional standards.

It is the responsibility of the project manager to maintain the best possible balance among these three key elements. Any adverse impact on any one of these elements needs to be communicated to the appropriate project stakeholders by the project manager, along with a suggested method of proceeding.

1.1.1   The Force of Change on the Web

These project management principles are just as valid for a Web project. However, what is not clear from this simplified overview is just how slippery and changeable a fish a Web project is. At one extreme you have the assembly line. Here, every step has been laid out in advance, and personnel do exactly the same thing at each stage of the process, over and over again. The goal is consistency achieved through repetition: every action, and every product, should be as much like the previous as possible.

At the other extreme you have Web projects, where no two projects are ever exactly the same. Change is fundamental to the nature of Web development. The Web itself is hardly controlled; it is growing organically in all directions at a terrific pace and in a manner that quite deliberately, and quite refreshingly, defies the structure and order that project management implies. This is very exciting and you would not want to stifle the energy and dynamism that inherent change and volatility bring, but these can cause trouble when it comes to implementation. To get things done in a sensible fashion, you need to develop working practices that can contain and control change (to make sure projects don't spin out of control) but at the same time embrace change as one of the very life forces of the Web.

TIP   **A change for the better**

One way to understand the process of managing Web projects is to see it as the management of innovation. This encompasses the elements of change, uncharted waters, creativity, and volatility that are hallmarks of most Web projects.

You need to create boundaries within which you can work and manage the shifting sands. From a strategic point of view you can, and should, think big and with high aspirations. From an implementation point of view, success by the inch is much more prudent than success by the mile. That is not to say that your inches should not be innovative and inspired.

1.1.2   Parallel Development on Web Projects

What is also unique about Web development is its parallel development style. Multidisciplinary teams (e.g., including the programming, creative, and commercial areas) have to work in parallel to meet aggressive development schedules and to embrace the changes that inevitably occur. Controlling this process has been described as more like being an orchestra conductor than a traditional project manager.

Despite parallel work, there are tasks that cannot begin before another task is complete. Such sequential dependencies cannot be avoided. However, there is a lot of pressure on the Web project manager to find ways of breaking down any strict linearity of development toward compressing schedules as much as possible. Doing this requires a very clear awareness of what can be developed in parallel and what must remain sequential. For example, you can usually buy time for creative research efforts by running them in parallel to longer items in the critical path.

1.1.3   Broader Skill Set Needed for Web Work

Web project management requires a particularly broad set of skills. To create a successful Web site, the project team needs to combine the skills and techniques involved in the following:

▶ Software development
▶ Magazine production and publishing
▶ Creating a work of art
▶ Producing a live TV show
▶ Planning and running a commercial venture

There is a host of further knowledge in areas such as marketing, contract law, worldwide tax and value-added tax (VAT) regulations, security, and privacy that the team will also need to call on. This requires a team that contributes a diverse set of skills. Uniting these disparate skills and the different types of people involved requires that the Web project manager be able to "speak different languages" and interpret as necessary. You need to be able to facilitate effective communication between parties coming from widely varying areas and levels of knowledge, and who are quite probably very different types of people with different priorities and motivations.

As a project manager, you will spend a lot of time with designers, programmers, and clients. It is dangerous to generalize, but it is probably fair to say that these three parties are usually quite diverse. You need to understand and communicate with each to be able to reinterpret the message of one to another. Table 1.1 summarizes some of the key differences between a typical Web project and an assembly-line-style project.

1.2   Roles and Responsibilities of the Web Project Manager

As we have seen, the traditional definition of the project manager's role is still valid in broad terms: to control the progress of the project against any detrimental influences on the time, cost, and quality involved in regard to the client, the place of work, market forces, other external influences, and the development team.

We have also seen that there are many other issues involved in a Web project that make this a complicated and intricate role to fulfill. The following is

Table 1.1 A summary of the key differences between Web projects and other projects.

Project elements	Web project	Assembly-line project
Development schedules	Tends to be shorter and more aggressive	Tends to be more set in stone, and to take longer
Development style	Tends toward parallel development streams and iterative development	Tends to be more linear; fewer, more rigid product releases
Project manager skill set	Needs to be broad, including a range of disciplines and skills as applied to the Web	Can be more confined to time, cost, and quality management; less involved with implementation
Communication	More interpretation and education needed	Lines and terms of communication more clearly defined
Tools and technology	Often "cutting edge," with little proven track record or support	More industry standards to follow that are tested and proven
Pricing	No standard pricing models for Web projects; each is costed ad hoc	More accepted and recognized pricing structures; more case studies to refer to
Standards	Fewer industry standards; likely to change; often driven by market demand rather than governing bodies	More standards; industry driven; more fixed points of reference
Clients	Understand the medium and its parameters less well	Are more used to working on these projects so can quickly understand issues involved
Team roles	Team members often perform multiple tasks and roles; project manager is not always the main point of client contact	Skills and roles of team members more closely defined; project manager is usually main client contact
Innovation	As the Web is still a comparatively new way of doing business, finding newer and better ways of exploiting its potential is a key objective for any Web project	It is not necessarily innovation that is paramount; consistency in production might be more important
Change	Is endemic; is likely to continue happening at all stages of project life cycle; is part of the raison d'être of the medium	Is more formally controlled; is often not possible at many stages of a project; having to embrace a great deal of change is more likely to lead to a separate new product or none at all

an overview of the areas of responsibility of the Web project manager organized in five key component categories.

1.2.1   Knowledge

The key component area of knowledge requires the following.

▶ Understanding of the industry and of the company's capabilities.
▶ Understanding of business disciplines and skills (commercial, marketing, editorial, creative, technical, and so on), as well as how they apply to the Web and how they will contribute to and enhance the project.

1.2.2   Communications

The key component area of communications requires the following.

▶ Liaison with and management of any external agencies and contracted parties or specialist contributors (e.g., copywriters, researchers, illustrators, strategists)
▶ Effective briefing of resources, management of meetings, and team leadership
▶ Communication of project progress to client(s), including any slippage, and actions taken to remedy it; change control; monitoring of other factors affecting progress of project; and risk management
▶ Management of and compliance with deadlines and milestones for the development team and the client
▶ Project review to assess where the project was conducted well and how the process could be improved next time

1.2.3   Documentation

The key component area of documentation requires the following.

▶ Consultation with the client to produce a mutually acceptable project specification (see Part II for details on what this contains), ensuring parameters of team's involvement are clear and success criteria are defined

▶ Input to further project documentation and work, as required (e.g., testing strategy, service-level agreements (SLAs), nondisclosure agreements (NDAs), contracts, market research, and strategy)

▶ Documentation of project's progress, including storing emails, contact reports, all versions of documents, ensuring product is signed off at agreed stages, and so on

▶ Archive of project, including documentation, assets, content elements, and return of material to the client and other sources

1.2.4 Quality Control

The key component area of quality control requires the following.

▶ Ensure product is tested, as agreed, before release

▶ Ensure each component part of the project is produced to the agreed technical and functional specification

1.2.5 Development

The key component area of development requires the following.

▶ Developing personal skills and making sure that other team members are given the chance to develop theirs

▶ Looking for new opportunities and new business, and seeking to improve working practices and build team knowledge and expertise

Section 1.4 looks in more detail at some of these skill areas to see what constitutes the attributes of a really good Web project manager. First, however, we need to explore where your job begins and ends.

1.3 Where Do the Project Manager's Responsibilities Begin and End?

On the face of it, it would seem clear that the project manager's responsibilities begin at the outset of a project and end at the conclusion of a project. However, a Web site is a living and evolving "creature," with no end and, once born, living, we should hope, longer than any of those who initially created it. Increasingly—as Web sites become larger, more expensive, and more busi-

ness critical—the project manager is not necessarily involved at project inception. It is often the case that a commercial and strategic team will have already done a fair amount of work on the project (defining business goals, long-term objectives, partnering strategies, financial models, and so on) before the Web project manager is brought in to handle the implementation phase.

In the situation of launching a completely new site, or starting from scratch in order to relaunch an existing site, it is clear where the product "begins." However, the work involved is often a matter of evolving and enhancing an existing project, including adding new features, content, and functionality.

What this means is that the project manager's *involvement* begins when he or she is asked to work on the project. The project manager's *responsibilities* begin and end as defined and agreed upon with the client. It is up to the project manager to ensure that these boundaries are adequately defined. Experience will help you judge what excess time you should budget over and above the agreed time span. A budget for maintenance and ongoing development work (see Part II for details) will also allow you time, after the main implementation phase, for continuing work on the project.

1.4   Attributes of a Good Project Manager

If pushed to choose one skill that, above all, defines a good project manager, most Web professionals seem to agree it would be the ability to communicate well. The way you communicate can vary enormously, and there are no completely right or wrong ways of doing it. Some practical guidelines for establishing good communication are presented in Part II. The deft ("soft") people skills are more difficult to learn and to define. A really good communicator will be able to mould the way he or she communicates to suit the audience, so that it can understand and absorb the required message.

The second most important asset a Web project manager possesses, which is less innate than an ability to communicate, is his or her knowledge—with all of the connotations of experience, wisdom, and breadth of information this implies.

TIP   Do It Yourself (DIY) accelerated learning

I believe one of the best ways to learn Web project management, or to increase your knowledge, is to create an entire site yourself. Do everything from A to Z: the idea, the strategy, the costing, the design, the programming, the testing, and the updating. It doesn't have to be a complicated site at all; it could revolve around a hobby or interest of yours. You will find you learn an awful lot about the challenges your Web team members face, learn new terminology, see why some things take longer than others, learn the joys of cross-browser compatibility at first hand, and so on. All of this will make you better at communicating with your team and client, better at planning, and better at empathizing with your team members regarding the problems they face.

With the Web industry developing as fast as it is, there is a lot to know. The more you know, the more you realize just how much you still have to learn. The knowledge you acquire is a mixture of knowing specifics (e.g., facts, figures, and details) and knowing fundamental drivers and structures (e.g., processes, models, and working practices).

A good project manager will want to increase his or her knowledge of both the details and working practices on every project with which he or she is involved. As with the project itself, it is all about knowing how to set the boundaries for yourself of what is and what is not possible, to ensure that innovation and education are maintained without sacrificing quality. The ability to come up with solutions is also key. A lot of a project manager's time is spent troubleshooting. A great deal of trouble can be averted through proper planning, allowing you in many cases to anticipate and diffuse problems before they arise. However, particularly with the Web, some issues do not have a clear and easy solution. For example, you may be working with a common piece of software when you discover a bug that was not previously known about. You and your team will need to think up a different way of doing things to get around this bug. The good project manager will take responsibility for maintaining the priorities and criteria by which the best solution is chosen in the circumstances. Table 1.2 summarizes some of the "hard" (technical, measurable) and "soft" (personal and interpersonal) skills that characterize a good Web project manager.

TIP   **No pain, no gain**

There is nothing like a good mistake or two to truly learn something. If you are not making the occasional mistake, you are not pushing yourself; and if you are not pushing yourself, you probably shouldn't be in the Web business. The best producers or project managers take responsibility for events and outcomes appropriately, admit oversights and weaknesses, and never make the same mistake twice. Ideally, running your own toy projects is a better way of learning via mistakes than on clients' projects. That is, the lower the cost of failure, the easier it is to push the limits and see what of an even more positive nature can happen.

This book cannot give you all the skills you need to be a good Web project manager, but it can impart a lot of knowledge, tips, and processes regarding the areas discussed in Table 1.2 to help you learn and progress more quickly than you might otherwise.

In Part II, Chapter 3, The Project Road Map, you will see how the project manager's competencies "map" against the evolution of a Web project. This helps you to see what skills are required at what stages of the project.

1.5   The Rewards of Being a Web Project Manager

Being a project manager in the Web industry can be a tough job. There is so much pressure (time to market, seizing the opportunity, getting ahead of the competition, building critical mass, standing out from the crowd, and so on) from all sides to get things done yesterday, yet better, faster, and for less money than anything previously done. As many clients do not feel entirely at

Table 1.2 "Hard" skills and "soft" skills that characterize a good Web project manager.

"Hard" skills

Project management and production experience; especially Web, software, film, TV, and multimedia

Rigorous understanding of scheduling, budgeting, and resource allocation

Risk management

Testing

Superior written and verbal communication skills

Ability to lead effective meetings

Change control

Sufficient level of technical knowledge

Understanding of key business disciplines and activities

Knowledge of legal issues: contracts, data protection, copyright, and so on

"Soft" skills

Good communicator and educator

A team player, leads by example, hands-on mentality

Ability to empathize

Enthusiasm for the Web

Good sense of humor; ability to stay calm under pressure

Ability to fight your own battles; grit and determination

Good at handling relationships; recognition of emotional credits and debits for use with client and team to steer project forward

Ability to take responsibility and learn from own mistakes

Attention to detail

Pragmatism—a strong grip on reality

Solution oriented

home with e-business, they can mask their ignorance and their fear of being taken for a ride by being unusually aggressive and demanding.

Furthermore, you are often working with tools, technologies, and even resources that are not as tried and true as you would like. You have to be an ambitious, inquisitive, and resilient character to continue to survive and thrive on Web project management. So why do we do it?

In the Preface, I touched upon some of the reasons I got into the Web business. From discussions with others, it seems there are some common benefits that draw Web producers to their role, and that continue to motivate them. A discussion of these benefits follows.

Doing business creatively: One of the things that enticed me to become a TV producer originally was that it seemed to mix creative and commercial skills in a way that was not possible in most other jobs. The TV producer is usually the person that comes up with the idea for a show and then attempts to sell that idea to a programming executive. This requires creative vision and an understanding of the marketplace. The producer then needs to steer the production to commercial success by making sure the correct resources are put to work on the project, and schedules and budgets are adhered to.

The Web is similar. Your client has a business need or a problem to be solved, and you get to supply the need or help solve the problem as creatively as possible. *Creative* does not necessarily mean wacky ideas and original designs; it means creative business thinking, coming up with novel and better ways of doing business using the Web.

A TV program is linear and fixed once created, and only really has purpose if it is actually broadcast (and even then there is a limited audience). The Web's worldwide, dynamic, networked nature, which allows virtually anyone to publish content, is truly mind expanding and exciting. The more you know about it, the more you recognize the Web's power to transform the way we live and work. Being in a position to know how to do this is a great reward for me.

Empowering creative resources to come up with novel ways of communicating: It is great to work with creative people in an arena wide open to new ideas. Often creative people don't know enough about the technology to turn the "art of the possible" into reality reflecting what can be done on the Web to better communicate a message or interact with an audience. Working with both creative and technical resources allows new ideas to germinate and flourish.

Chance to learn, innovate, and motivate: Being in a fast, evolving industry means there is always the opportunity to learn and invent new ways of doing things. If you are enthusiastic about the Web, it is also a pleasure to be able to communicate that enthusiasm and knowledge to others, hopefully motivating them to also get involved.

Chance to carve your own path: An industry characterized by dynamism, change, and evolution is very stimulating if you have an entrepreneurial bent, a desire to make your own way. The industry is still young enough to offer you the opportunity to make your mark much more quickly than in many other industries.

Creating a "living, breathing," reactive product: When you launch a Web site, you create something that has a life. It is there all the time, doesn't go away, needs constant attention, and can be a constant cause of worry, just like a child.

Sometimes it seems like you have given birth to a problem child in need of some rather severe discipline to be brought into line. Most of the time you give birth to an overachieving angel, whereupon further children are demanded.

Personally I take great reward from being part of creating something that is not only "tangible" and visible but that virtually anyone can see and interact with. The feedback you get from a Web site is greater, more immediate, and more "real time" than for almost any other product.

Communicate with the world: It remains a source of wonder that what you create often gets seen and visited by people from all over the world, from completely different cultures, living in potentially any time zone. Usually you will have a defined target audience that proscribes who you are trying to reach, or even restricted access to the site, but there are still almost no physical boundaries to how the medium can work.

Potential rewards: Web fever has meant that there are unusually large potential rewards (e.g., financial, status, and career openings) for those that do well. There is still a feeling of "gold rush" and "the sky is the limit," which can be exciting and intoxicating.

Other people in the business: The Web industry tends to attract dynamic and progressive professionals. Not only are they often very talented, but tend to be passionate and driven, fascinating and challenging. Usually these people lead interesting lives outside the work setting.

Wild Wild West: It is not quite the frontier land of the Web in its earlier days, when the true pioneers took great steps into the unknown, but the Web is still a land of opportunity and uncharted waters. It is not conservative or entrenched; the boundaries are still not fully defined. If this appeals to you, working in the industry will be rewarding.

So, enthused with the joys of the Web, it is time to meet your team.

1.6   The Composition of a Web Development Team

Unless you are working on a smaller project, or are an outstandingly multi-talented person, you aren't going anywhere without a team. The next few sections look at how the changing demands of the Web industry have affected the necessary composition of a Web development team and have contributed to the broad range of roles now possible.

1.6.1   The Evolution of Web Development Teams

To understand how Web development teams have evolved and continue to evolve, it is useful to appreciate the development cycle many sites have gone through and continue to go through. Each stage requires a different team with different skills. The four phases outlined in the following material serve as an example that will not be true of every corporate site but do illustrate the various factors that affect how a site, and the team that works on it, matures.

In the first phase, the internal IS (information systems) department members have put up a corporate Web site largely because they know how and are interested in these things. The site doesn't necessarily look that good, but it does work. The rest of the business isn't really interested, as there is little commercial imperative involved and therefore it doesn't really matter what the site is like. Project management has been less of an issue at this stage.

In the second phase, the marketing department has seized the notion that the Web is to be one of their communication channels of the future. As brand stewards—and being creative, rather than technical, types—the marketing department hires an external design agency (perhaps through their existing advertising agency) to make the site "look pretty." This is duly done and some people complain that the site takes a long time to download, is difficult to update, and that some of the functions don't quite work properly in certain technical environments. Again, it doesn't matter too much, as no one that really matters knows much about the Web, or about the company Web site, and the marketing people see the site functioning in only ideal circumstances, and so are satisfied they have done their job. Project management has become more important, as budgets and schedules are not properly pinned down and tend to be very hit and miss.

In the third phase, as the Web population has continued to grow considerably and other sites have begun to make large enough headlines and amounts of money, there has been a shudder passing through the company's board that perhaps something ought to be done about the Web. Often this is the first time the board finds out the company already has a Web site. The chief financial officer (CFO) in particular is eager to know what ROI the marketing people are getting for the money they have spent on the site. Transactional sites, e-commerce, and personalization become the order of the day. The external design agency struggles to provide adequate solutions, unless they have grown their systems expertise sufficiently in the intervening time or have partnerships with more technically proficient companies that can handle database integration, application, and systems development. Poor project management has become the main reason for project failure in this phase.

In the fourth phase, the CEO and the board have become enlightened as to the Web's importance and release budgets and resources in making a real commitment to the company's Web presence. The commercial powers that be want to know what their ROI will be. Web development agencies recognize the importance of ensuring that their clients have the correct Web strategy in place before starting a project, and therefore start hiring e-business strategy consultants. Project teams grow to incorporate a much larger set of skilled members. These teams are a combination of both service-side and client-side input. Companies realize the need for in-house Web expertise for handling updates, customer relationship management, distribution and fulfillment issues, legacy system integration, and staff training and development. Project management has become critical in optimizing speed to market, maximizing quality, and controlling cost.

Ironically we have come full circle to the internal IS people, who play a vital role in integrating existing business functions with the Web front end of the business. However, in these later stages the process has been driven by commercial and strategic imperatives and has necessitated a much more diverse team, put together from in-house departmental resources, or external resources, or, most often, a combination of both. So what skills might be needed in the Web team?

1.6.2   The Necessary Skills Within a Web Development Team

The exact size and composition of your Web development team will, of course, vary, depending on a large number of factors specific to the project: scope, budget, schedules, available resources, target market, client, nature of the project (e.g., design driven or more data driven), and so on. The team's skills will invariably be expanded by what the client can contribute in terms of marketing and customer service expertise. However, there are some core skills that will be needed in developing the site. Explanations of these follow.

▶ *Strategy:* Define an Internet strategy that takes into account existing and future business objectives, the marketplace, opportunities and threats, the competition, the short- and long-term investment (financial and people) required, the likely ROI to the business, marketing needs, risk analysis, reporting structures, partnership strategies, and other business planning needs.

▶ *Project management:* Define and deliver a project on time and on budget according to an agreed-upon specification. The ability to communicate project requirements to the development team.

▶ *Architecture and design:* Interface and information design to ensure the user can navigate and interact with the site as desired. Create visual graphic designs that communicate the desired message to the target market. Optimize files for Web display.

▶ *Content:* Developing the content for the site. Creating original content, collating and editing existing content, commissioning content, sharing content with other sites, and managing content feeds.

▶ *Programming:* Data design and site architecture, technical infrastructure recommendations to meet expected demand, client- and server-side coding and scripting, creation of Web applications, integration with other systems, and database management.

Depending on the project, it may be that one person fills a role that covers more than one of these skill areas. Equally, each of these skill areas could have an entire team of its own, with extended and specialist skills contributed.

1.6.3   Team Structure

Figure 1.1 is a diagram of the people and roles that could go into forming a Web development team structured according to the skill areas discussed in the previous section. Some of the roles will not be relevant to some projects. For example, an account team is often present when there is a client/agency relationship, but not if the project is internal.

The team shown is large. You will not always need all of these people. The majority of projects require a team of about six to eight. However, Web teams are getting larger and there are roles evolving that are not shown here. For example, the figure does not include an email channel specialist, data mining specialist, or audience analyst. Covered here are all of the main roles you are likely to come across in a large team before further specialists are required.

1.6.4   Roles and Responsibilities

What are the roles and responsibilities of these various team members? In the following material you will find an explanation of the roles of each of the team members represented in Figure 1.1. If they are not all relevant to the size of team you work with, skip to the roles you feel constitute your team.

Remember, the roles outlined in the following describe the fundamental resources you might expect to call on to build a Web development team for delivering and maintaining a site of reasonable scale. Larger agencies or in-house teams will have all of these resources available, possibly with other skills on which to call, such as media planning and buying, advertising sales, market research, and so on. Smaller agencies or in-house teams will still need most of the skills described, but one person may cover several of these roles. For example, the project manager may well be the project director, producer, assistant producer, strategy consultant, and technical consultant all rolled into one.

Client

It may seem strange to give the client responsibilities, considering that they are the ones paying for the work. However, the client does have responsibili-

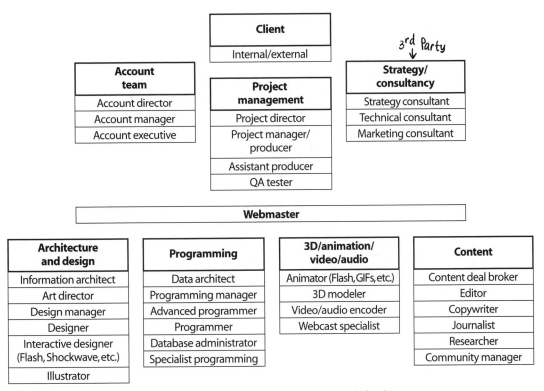

Figure 1.1 A team structure showing the roles that can constitute a large Web development team.

ties in regard to the contract, most notably involving the terms and conditions of payment if it is an external agency doing the work. These terms and conditions will probably also include details on intellectual property, termination notice, and other notices and statements to which the client is bound.

In terms of the project, the client should also ensure that the necessary internal resources are made available for the project to proceed, that those resources are committed and given the necessary authority to make the project a success. The cooperation and collaboration of the client is vital to the project's success. Making sure that sign-off and approval processes run efficiently internally is a very important part of this.

Often the client will have content responsibilities. Late delivery of content is one of the greatest headaches for the Web development team, as it throws schedules off or out. The format and structure of the content is also often a problem. The content may arrive on time, but may not be anything like the format specified. This is particularly true of databases.

Some clients will take on testing responsibilities, particularly usability testing, and many will assume a copy proofing role before sign-off. This is often to ensure that the company comes across as professional and that nothing is said that might infringe upon rights, violate any laws, or cause professional damage to the organization. Final copy sign-off should be the responsibility of the client for these reasons.

As a project manager, your relationship with your client makes a big difference in how you run the project. As the relationship with your client grows, you will find that a natural way of working evolves that suits you both. The greatest difference, at least initially, is whether your client is internal or external. Table 1.3 summarizes how project managers working with internal and external clients deal with similar issues but in slightly different contexts.

Account Team

An account team, which normally only exists when an external agency is involved in the project, can include personnel performing the roles of account director, account manager, and account executive.

Account director: Initial point of contact with the client. Responsible for winning new business and then overseeing strategic and implementation phases. Higher authority for client to go to if required. Higher authority for agency team to go to if help is needed managing the client. After CEO, or board member, the highest-level decision maker on the agency side.

Account manager: Day-to-day contact with client. Arranges meetings, logs meetings with action points, manages billings, handles purchase orders and payments, ensures client is happy with the way the project is being run, ensures compliance with client's business requirements, and monitors schedules and budgets for the client.

The account manager should know the client's business better than anyone at the agency, and should represent the client's best interests at all stages. The account manager will also help resolve any problems by understanding and communicating the issues to both client and agency.

Account executive: Depending on the size of the project, there may also be account executives involved, to assist the account manager.

Table 1.3 Internal versus external client work for Web project managers.

Issues	Internal client (in-house)	External client (agency)
Politics	Internal politics; your career development and promotion; departmental targets; bonuses; budgets	Need to understand client's political pressures and hidden agendas to steer project successfully
Justification	Need to sell value of project to management to get proper levels of internal support and commitment	Need to persuade client of value of your services over other competitors' offerings
Sign-off	Need to establish lines of communication and authority; ownership of the project	Need sign-off to protect schedule slippage and budget overages
Budgets	Need to manage expectations of project stakeholders (largely those who contribute to the budget), often across many departments	Need to ensure the budget agreed upon allows you to complete the specified project and make a profit on the work
Time	Need to manage expectations internally as to what can be done by when, and why; control management making promises that cannot be met within specified schedules	Need to ensure you can deliver the project within the time frame agreed upon, and meet milestones
Knowledge	Need to educate internal clients and project contributors on working method, schedules and budget, quality, importance of testing and planning, and so on	Need to show client knowledge of the industry and best working practices; show creative, commercial, and technical excellence, and so on, to gain trust and empower and educate client
Team	Working more often with contractors, freelancers, and external solution providers; need to manage internal client and external providers; need to ensure all parties working cohesively	Need to ensure the correct resources are working on the project and that they are clear on their roles, responsibilities, and tasks in completing the project

Strategy/Consulting Team

A strategy/consulting team can include personnel performing the roles of strategy consultant, technical consultant, and marketing consultant.

Strategy consultant: Helps client define the Web strategy. This person will have strong strategic and business planning skills, and an excellent knowledge of the Internet, including projected growth areas, statistics, market sizes and opportunities, risks, revenue possibilities, demographics, industry benchmarks, gender usage information, emerging technologies, best practices, and so on. The strategy consultant is a business strategist who can understand and help clarify the client's e-business objectives in the context of the greatest advantages and best implementations/applications of the Web.

Technical consultant: Defines the technical architecture and technical method for the project. Provides input to the testing strategy. Recommends server hardware and software. The Web development team will have a strong knowledge of general technical parameters, but the technical consultant will have a more in-depth knowledge of the specifics of a particular information technology (IT) infrastructure and how best to approach, say, the Web-enabling of an existing legacy system.

The technical consultant will be able to assess whether specialist programming or networking skills are required. He or she will also keep the development teams abreast of emerging technologies that might be employed to improve the efficiency and quality of the solution. The development team will turn to the technical consultant during the project to help overcome any specific technical hurdles.

Marketing consultant: Is a specialist in e-marketing. The marketing consultant will know how to create traffic to your site using the appropriate mix of traditional and new online and offline techniques. This could include online techniques such as search engine positioning, link exchanges, Usenet promotion, email campaigns, banner advertising, and specialist directory placings in conjunction with offline promotions, such as billboards, direct mail, flyers, TV and radio ads, and other vehicles. The marketing consultant will also know about market research, including quantitative and qualitative research, and about focus groups, panels, market segmentation, and sampling. Market research can be done online and offline, each having its own merits.

Project Management Team

A project management team can include personnel performing the roles of project director, project manager/producer, assistant producer, and QA tester. The project director often serves as, or is considered, the chief operating officer (COO).

Project director: Oversees the implementation of the project, including ensuring it is correctly resourced, planned, and specified so that it runs according to schedule and budget. The project director manages the team working on a project to ensure all is running smoothly. This involves a lot of planning ahead and troubleshooting decisions. The project director will have a lot of client contact, and therefore must be able to communicate effectively at different levels and types of knowledge and expertise. He or she will be most involved in the project at the beginning and end. Works closely with project manager and strategy/consulting services team.

Project manager/producer: Manages the day-to-day implementation of the site according to the project specification. Briefs creative and programming teams, and gathers, processes, and distributes content assets. Organizes proofing and testing, and ensures deadlines are met. Once the site goes into production, the project manager is the engine that drives the team and the project forward.

Assistant producer: Depending on the size of the project, there may be an assistant producer, who helps the project manager, particularly in sourcing and managing content, which can be a time-consuming task.

QA tester: Depending on the size of the project, and length and complexity of the testing, this may be a large, structured team, or may be only one or two testers. The QA team has the responsibility of testing the site according to the testing plan defined in the project specification, and of reporting errors and observations to the development team.

Webmaster

Webmaster as a job description is used to cover a wide range of tasks and skills. She may work on the client or the agency side. The Webmaster's role really comes into play after the main development effort, when the site needs maintenance, administration, monitoring, and updating. The Webmaster is often more of a generalist than the other roles described here, and will have basic skills in design, programming, content, and project management. The Webmaster is usually responsible for ensuring the correct functioning and uptime of the site once it is running. She is often the first line of support regarding user interaction and issues with the site.

Architecture and Design Team

An architecture and design team can include personnel performing the roles of information architect, art director, design manager, designer, interactive designer, and illustrator.

Information architect: This person will understand how to structure the content of the site in such a way that it can be easily navigated and retrieved by the user. This requires a good understanding of usability issues, the site's target market, interface protocols, and user psychology, as well as the ability to restructure information that exists offline to best suit the online medium. The way content is labeled and signposted throughout the site will also be addressed by the information architect.

Art director: The art director will come up with the creative concept and ensure that all brand guidelines are met where required. Any template styles, the overall "look and feel," and the specifics of the navigation system will all be defined by the art director, usually working with the information architect and design manager to create the core interfaces.

Design manager: In a large team, the design manager is responsible for monitoring the quality of work the design team produces, ensuring the team has the correct working environment and tools, and the necessary content, briefs, and specifications. The design manager will work with the project manager to make sure the design team is meeting its deadlines and target output for the project.

Designer: The designer implements and rolls out the design concept under the guidance of the art director. She will also be responsible for working with programmers to prepare graphics files for HTML display. Basic GIF animations are also created by the designer.

Interactive designer: There are some projects that require extended interactive design skills. Interactive designers often come from a multimedia design background and usually have more programming skills than a typical designer, in order to script the necessary interactivity. On the Web, this means working with Flash, Director, and other applications to create the desired interactivity. The interactive designer will work more closely with the programming team than the designer, particularly on interactive applications that use Java or JavaScript.

Illustrator: Not all graphic designers can create line art. Sometimes a particular illustration style is needed. In these cases, a specialist illustrator may be required.

Programming Team

A programming team can include personnel performing the roles of data architect, programming manager, advanced programmer, programmer, database administrator, and specialist programmer.

Data architect: Working with the technical consultant, the data architect maps out how the information, data, and files will be structured on the site. This often requires mapping a data-flow diagram to the content site map, as well as showing how the processes and functions of the site will integrate with "external" systems and applications. In many cases, these will not be located near the Web server but will form part of the networked structure that constitutes the Web site.

Programming manager: On larger projects, there will be a programming manager who has the same role as the design manager, with the exception that he represents the programming team.

Advanced programmer: Responsible for the integrity of the code that powers the site. He will serve as liaison with the site architect and project manager to ensure that the correct infrastructure and technical solution, as specified at the beginning of the project, is then implemented. This involves hardware and software installation and configuration.

Database and legacy system integration; advanced programming such as TCL, Perl, C, C++, Java, ASP, JSP, and servlets; and other server-side tasks and scripting will be handled directly by the advanced programmer.

Programmer: Working under the guidance of the advanced programmer, the programmer will perform the HTML, DHTML, CSS, and JavaScript (client-side) programming necessary to display content as Web pages, and to incorporate site interactivity elements, such as rollover effects and hyperlink states.

Database administrator: The database administrator will work with the advanced programmer and technical consultant to ensure that any database software is properly installed, configured, and maintained, and that the database environment is correctly specified for handling the tasks it is expected to perform. The most common databases used on the Web are MS SQL Server, Oracle, IBM, Sybase, and Informix products.

Specialist programming: Some projects may require specialist programming skills. Some applications, hardware or software, may use proprietary protocols and languages that do not form part of commonly held programming skills. In this case, you will need to add these specialist skills to the Web development team.

3D/Animation/Video/Audio Team

Animator: Some projects require advanced animation skills. This might include cell animation, 3D animation, or a frame-by-frame animated GIF. This is a skill not all designers possess. The animator is most likely to be working with the interactive designer.

3D modeler: The creation and rendering of 3D objects does not happen to a great extent on the Web, but it will be needed for some projects and could well be more commonly used in the future, with further advances in the use of vector graphics and the advent of broadband communications.

Video/audio encoder: Assuming you have the source video/audio, it will need to be encoded into a suitable format for Web playback. This might be MP3, MPEG, WAV, AU, AVI, or MOV, or streaming formats such as QuickTime, RealVideo, and NetShow. There is a skill in choosing the correct format for the target market, and then ensuring the optimal trade-off in speed of download versus quality of playback.

Webcast specialist: If you are going to have video and/or audio content that is transmitted live, or near live, to your site, you will need a Webcast specialist. This person understands both the content acquisition element (i.e., the video and audio recording and encoding methods) and content transmission parameters (i.e., the opportunities and limitations of broadcasting over the Web).

Content Team

A content team can include personnel performing the roles of content deal broker, editor, copywriter, journalist, researcher, community manager, and production service provider.

Content deal broker: This is not a likely job title but it describes what might be done by the editor, or someone in a commercial role. Often sites will need content not viably created in-house. If someone has already created the content you need, it can make more sense to strike a deal with them for use of the content on your site. Most commonly this involves such content as news, weather, stock prices, mapping, or addressing. There are many items negotiated in such a content deal that require expert knowledge, including branding issues, data capture and ownership issues, advertising conflicts of interest, revenue shares, and so on.

Editor: The editor has overall responsibility for the content on the site. She will understand the target market very well, will set the tone of the content, ensure copywriting and content standards are maintained, develop new content areas, ensure content is kept up to date, and react to user feedback, among similar duties.

Copywriter: Copywriters, not surprisingly, write and create copy for the site. They write the copy that links sections of the site, and help name the sections of the site appropriately. Depending on the site, copywriters may need to have specialist industry knowledge, and will need to follow style guidelines defined by the editor. There is a skill in writing for the Web as opposed to other media.

Journalist: A journalist is probably also a copywriter. Journalist implies more of a focus on news and feature material than the core content or linking/naming copy copywriters work on.

benchmarking standards Copyrighted →

Researcher: A researcher will not necessarily write copy but will support the journalist and editor in developing ideas, and in researching new content opportunities, potential content partners, pictures and sourcing contacts, and other material that helps develop the site's content.

Community manager: For sites that feature communities, you might well have a community manager on your team. This person will have a strong understanding of the community, including its likes and dislikes, and how the community as a whole thinks and behaves. It is the community manager's responsibility to build the community to the benefit of the site by interacting with the online community, listening and responding to its wishes, monitoring and prompting discussion, and encouraging participation. The community manager's tools will encompass research, journalistic, and copywriting skills.

Production service provider: This role is not on the team diagram, but there is a lot of work to be done surrounding a Web project that can be handled by production services. This includes file conversion (e.g., Mac to PC, and vice versa), file creation (e.g., creating PDFs), CD-ROM burning, color printing, photocopying, scanning, courier service, and so on.

1.7   Once upon a Time . . .

We have set the scene for what is expected of you and your Web development team. Now, does the following story mean anything to you?

Once upon a time there was a company and it had a Web site. The Web site was initiated by members of the IS department because they had a need for it and were the only ones who knew how to set it up. Or cared, for that matter.

All of a sudden the marketing department came along because it heard that the Internet really was going to be *the* marketing channel of the future. They pulled together the beginnings of a budget, and appointed a design agency to develop their site. They got a very pretty, heavily branded site.

Then the online rumblings began to penetrate higher levels of management, and the CFO began to wonder why the company was spending all of this money on a site and getting nothing tangible back. He called for a transactional site, ROI, and benchmarking.

At just about the same time, the CEO of the company was told by his eight-year-old daughter that his company's site was pretty lame, a view confirmed by the CEO of a rival company in the clubhouse after a particularly bad round of golf. Now, the CEO may not have been entirely aware of what the Web was, but nonetheless a storm was brewing.

All too suddenly the thunderbolt came from on high to "sort it out—yesterday." Over to you . . .

1.8   Summary

The following list contains some of the main points you should walk away with after having read Chapter 1.

▶ Cost, time, and quality are the three key factors involved in any project. Each is respectively influenced by the other two.

▶ Change and innovation make Web project management very different from assembly-line-style project management, where consistency is paramount.

▶ A good project manager is able to define his or her role in the project. He or she communicates well, has a broad understanding of the industry, and is reliable, organized, and delivers on a promise.

▶ Web development teams are becoming larger, and more specialist skills are required to meet the demands of larger-scale Web projects.

METHOD

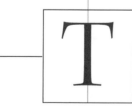

A Web Project Method

I've found on occasion that processes are sometimes left to find their own way. That's suicide. And the project manager has got to keep on bullying people to make sure the job gets done. In essence, I think a good project manager should be the "unsung hero" of the project. They don't get the glory and swank of the designer or consultant, but they're the glue that makes it all stick together. —**Sam Owens, Chief Editor,** *www.complete-skier.com,* **France/U.K.**

T his part of the book runs through a suggested Web project method. Although projects need defined boundaries, Web projects in particular tend to live past the defined implementation phases that constitute individual projects. The final two work stages in this project method are all about how to maintain and develop a site after its launch, and how to evaluate and review the project's success to feed back into a new work stage 1, where a new project is born.

This method has been formed and refined over many years of developing Web sites of all types. If you apply this framework to your project, it will help ensure the project follows a proven development path.

2.1   The Importance of Having a Method

In my earlier days as a Web project manager, we didn't have a method we worked to. We were working things out as we went along, and doing many things for the first time. This just about holds together for smaller and less complex sites. However, it soon became apparent that we needed a defined method for coping with larger, more complex sites. There is nothing like a contract with a late delivery penalty clause to focus the mind.

Once we had a method in place, it turned out to have all sorts of benefits we hadn't thought of when devising it. Summarized in Table 2.1 are some of the many benefits a Web project method affords.

One thing that should be noted about methods, however, is that they do not make for spellbinding reading, particularly if you, as the client, are more into marketing than method. You can be sure that if you include your method as part of your project proposal there will be some, quite possibly your main project sponsor or client, who will not read it.

Make sure you reinforce the key points of your method verbally. In particular, emphasize to the client those factors that are the client's responsibility, and that are most likely to cause project delays. Often these are issues surrounding sign-off and the timely provision of correctly formatted content. You need to make sure the client understands how they fit into the method, and is aware of the responsibilities this role implies.

DILBERT reprinted by permission of United Feature Syndicate, Inc.

Table 2.1 The benefits of having a defined project method.

Benefit	Comment
Checklist	Your method works as a checklist for ensuring you have gone through all of the important steps. It can be easy, particularly if you are quite new to the game, to forget something that then becomes a real problem later in the project. Having this checklist makes you feel more confident that you are progressing according to plan, as you and your team have goals and milestones.
Common focus	Having a common framework to work to gives a team focus and confidence. It ensures that everyone is heading in the same direction. It will also give the client confidence.
Justifies expenditure	If you have a method, it facilitates budgeting, and it is easier for the client to see where and how the money is being spent, as well as the amount of work that goes into the project at the various stages.
Accountability	A client can hold you to your method, and you therefore become more accountable. Again, this sets standards and infuses the client with confidence.
Competitive edge	Many new media agencies or in-house development teams, especially the smaller ones, may not have a method. If you do, it sets you apart as taking a more professional and robust approach. Some Web agencies are seen as "cowboys"; a method shows you are serious.
Facilitates progress reporting	The method creates a model against which to report progress, and highlights how change will affect the project further downstream. Creating project milestones and setting benchmarks is easier when you have a methodological framework.
Maintains professional standards	Increasingly Web development teams are dealing with software development/IS teams who are used to working to a defined method. If you can do this too, you will inspire confidence in the other team and be able to work together more easily.
Control mechanism	During a project, the method can serve as a control mechanism. You can show why you are not going to do K yet because you still have to achieve A through J, as was always understood.
Benefits new team members	If new members join the team, it is much easier for them to get up to speed quickly and pick up their role in the team if they can see the bigger picture and framework to which the team is working.

continued on next page

Table 2.1 (continued)

Benefit	Comment
Speed of development	If your Web team is used to a working practice defined by the method, you will be able to work faster, as the team has no confusion about where it is heading, how work will be organized, the steps that need to be taken, and so on.
Better scheduling, resourcing, and budgeting	If resourcing, tasks, and schedules are broken down into discrete stages by the method, it is easier to create accurate predictions and quotes for what will be needed overall. It is also possible to work a stage, or several stages, at a time. For example, you might only want to commit to scheduling, resourcing, and budgeting of the first three stages.
Facilitates project communications and handovers	If team members know the language and practice of the method, it is easier for the team to communicate quickly and effectively about the project and its elements. If someone falls ill or has to be taken off the project, it is easier to hand the project over to someone else if it is clear what has and what has not been done to date.

Recognizing the importance and role of a method is the first step to using it effectively. The next step is get a firm grasp of the key elements and stages of the method before going into the detail of each stage. This overview is provided in the following chapter.

2.2 Different Methods for Different Purposes

Methodology is a metadiscipline. It involves the study of methods. An individual project has a method, and that method is the framework for making decisions about the project. A project with a methodology has a formal system for observing and analyzing the methods used to make decisions, which is valuable in situations that involve life-critical systems such as flight control software for the space shuttle, medical equipment, and nuclear weapons manufacture. However, this would be excessive for a Web project. What this book proposes is a method that works very well for delivering medium- to large-scale commercial Web sites.

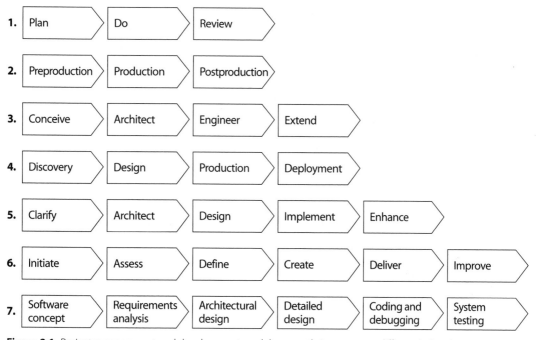

Figure 2.1 Project management and development models currently in use across different industries.

There are many project management methods employed across different industries for varying purposes. Some project management methods are quite generic, and others have very specific applications. Figure 2.1 presents a few examples of such methods.

As you can imagine, some of these methods are more suited to Web projects than others. It is not usual to talk of postproduction for a Web site, but it is absolutely the norm if you work in TV. Consultancy or strategy projects involve methods different from production projects, as the deliverables and tasks related to each are very different. Whereas a Web project method might include a "test" element, this is much more likely to be called "validation" (or something similar) for a consulting project.

As you will see in Chapter 3, the method proposed in this book consists of eight work stages. These can be categorized into four project phases. This method is designed specifically for Web projects and, more particularly, for the project manager who has to deal with all stages of a Web project. Although eight work stages may be a few too many for each to be remembered as a catchy phrase, each forms a very important, and separate, function in the delivery of a commercial-grade Web site. If you forget which work stage you should be at, use this book (in particular, Chapter 3) as a guide to where you are in the process.

2.3 Summary

The following are three main points you should have derived from this chapter.

▶ The bigger the project you work on, the more critical a project method is.
▶ Methods work best when designed to serve a particular purpose.
▶ The project method put forward in this book is designed to deliver medium- to large-scale commercial Web sites.

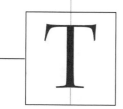

3

The Project Road Map

In my experience the project will never have a chance of success without the careful coordination of the project manager. [Key attributes are] patience, credibility, a sense of perspective, and the ability to communicate.

—Markus Schmidt, Editor, *Braunschweiger Zeitung Daily News,* **Germany**

This chapter gives you the project framework to use for successfully developing, deploying, maintaining, and evolving a commercial Web site. The following chapters then go into detail on each of the stages mapped out here.

3.1 Project Phases and Work Stages

A project can be broken down into the following eight work stages.

Work stage 1   Project clarification

Work stage 2   Solution definition

Work stage 3	Project specification
Work stage 4	Content
Work stage 5	Design and construction
Work stage 6	Testing, launch, and handover
Work stage 7	Maintenance
Work stage 8	Review and evaluation

The eight work stages can be grouped as four key project phases. These phases are very similar to the well-known three-part project approach of "Think, Do, Review." An additional stage, Maintenance, is included because it is particularly important and relevant to Web project work. The following outlines the eight work stages as four phases.

Phase 1, Preproduction: Phase 1, preproduction, consists of the following stages.

▶ Project clarification
▶ Solution definition
▶ Project specification

Phase 2, Production: Phase 2, production, consists of the following stages.

▶ Content
▶ Design and construction
▶ Testing, launch, and handover

Phase 3, Maintenance: Phase 3, maintenance, consists of the following stage.

▶ Maintenance

Phase 4, Evaluation: Phase 4, evaluation, consists of the following stage.

▶ Review and evaluation

© 1998 Ted Goff, *www.tedgoff.com.*

Phase 1			Phase 2			Phase 3	Phase 4
Preproduction			Production			Maintenance	Evaluation
Project clarification	Solution definition	Project specification	Content	Design and construction	Testing, launch, and handover	Maintenance	Review and evaluation

Figure 3.1 The four phases and eight work stages.

Figure 3.1 shows how these phases and work stages relate to each other. Let's have a look at these phases and work stages in a little more detail. The initial overview and structure presented here is then explored in more detail in the following chapters.

3.1.1   Phase 1 Overview: Preproduction

Phase 1 is also known as the planning phase or the discovery phase. Quite simply, it is the stage during which you work out what it is you want to achieve, and plan how you are going to do it.

This is the most important phase of the project. If the three most important factors in a property are location, location, and location, then the three golden rules of Web projects are plan, plan, and plan. It is at this stage that the project's success or otherwise is determined. If you get it right at this stage, the rest should, at least in theory, run smoothly. In the industry, it is increasingly widely accepted that the money spent on this phase of a Web project is the money best spent. Some agencies advocate spending as much as 50% of the project's scheduled time and budget until launch on preproduction.

For the client, spending large amounts of money on preproduction is a bitter pill to swallow. Until they actually see a product come to life, it is difficult for the client to justify the expense to themselves and, often more importantly, to others within their organization.

In in attempt to save money and speed up the development process, some clients will want to skip the planning phase of the project and jump into the production phase. When you protest that there is a need for proper planning, they say they have already done that, and know what they want and how they want to go about it. If you cannot persuade them otherwise, it is up to you whether you take on a project of this nature, though it would make me extremely nervous. You can in this situation go through your method (particularly the first three work stages) with the client. Challenge them to answer all of the questions you would want answered in the preproduction phase, ensuring that all of the bases have been covered. It will soon become clear to you and the client whether or not enough planning work has really been done.

TIP   **The baby is on its way ...**

Once you can show the client a site map and a few designs, it becomes easier to work with the client according to your method, as there is tangible evidence of work being accomplished, and the site itself has, at least conceptually, been conceived. Pictures are often worth a thousand words.

There are clear benefits in spending some time and money up front in proper planning. The following are time-tested arguments you can make that should both inform and encourage the client.

▶ *Planning will actually speed up the total delivery time.* If you know exactly what you are doing and how to do it, a team can work much faster than if there is any confusion. You also avoid duplication of effort, miscommunication, and the risk that you spend time developing something that is not part of what you want.

▶ *Planning improves overall quality.* You will get better quality and better results if you spend time in preproduction. You can ensure that you are developing a product that will meet your needs and your customers' needs much more effectively.

▶ *Planning will save money.* Yes, it can be true. Proper planning can avoid costly errors and give you the time to research and define more cost-effective solutions.

▶ *Planning will improve long-term prospects.* If more people can contribute their thoughts at the early stages of the project, they will have a greater level of buy-in, understanding, and commitment to making *their* project work, which will help build morale and ensure longterm success.

3.1.2   Phase 2 Overview: Production

Phase 2 is all about putting into action the project plan defined in the pre-production phase. The production phase exists until the launch of the Web project, at which point you enter the maintenance phase. The production phase involves the design, programming, testing, and marketing of the site for launch, as well as the subsequent handover to the site maintenance team.

Some overlap might naturally exist between the preproduction and production phases, or become necessary in an effort to maximize speed of development. This is most usually seen in the development of a working prototype of the site, which is created as part of the preproduction phase but actually involves production-phase skills. Often the prototype simply evolves as part of the process and becomes the actual site.

There is also some overlap from the production phase into the maintenance phase. This exists in part inherently in the team resources that continue to be involved across these phases, but also in some of the parallel activities, such as marketing, which typically requires a big push at site launch time and continues with promotions during the maintenance phase.

3.1.3   Phase 3 Overview: Maintenance

Once the site is launched, the work is not over, it has only just begun. The site is then available all of the time, all over the world, forever. You will have to deal with users interacting with the site, and the work this implies. Despite the best of preproduction planning, needs and issues arise during the course of ongoing work that must be factored into the project as it evolves. You will need to update the site to keep the content current and to keep users coming back. You will need to be able to scale the site's capacity to meet demand. All of these elements and more need to be taken into account, as far as possible, before the site is launched. In the rush to get something built and launched, it is easy to sideline maintenance issues as a low priority. This, however, risks undermining the good work you have done in creating the site.

There is also cleanup work to be done after the main implementation thrust, including archiving project assets, finishing any project documentation, settling bills (e.g., copyright fees and freelance resources), returning assets where necessary, and so on.

3.1.4   Phase 4 Overview: Evaluation

Evaluation of a project is currently one of the areas of Web work most poorly covered. This will change, however, as the industry and the nature of sites mature, but at the moment the majority of development teams have so much work to do in creating new sites that the focus is very much on building rather than evaluating. The more seasoned players are much better than the competition at evaluating the performance of their Web properties, in an effort to ever improve their product offering.

Proper evaluation is crucial in assessing whether you have achieved what you set out to achieve, as defined in the preproduction phase. Effectively measuring the performance of your site will enable you to accurately gauge ROI, and will inform your future decisions and strategy for evolving the site. Any business needs good management information for making intelligent decisions, and an e-business is no different.

The evaluation phase includes a review of the strengths and shortcomings not just of the final product but of the process through which it came about. That is, evaluation seeks to determine how the method worked in practice for the project and how things could be improved for the future. Figure 3.2 outlines Web project phases, work stages, and deliverables.

3.2   Individual Projects as Part of a "Virtuous" Development Spiral

The project method is designed to fit into the "virtuous" development spiral that should accompany the growth of any successful Web site. *Virtuous* as used here connotes the opposite of *vicious*: in a vicious cycle, things spiral downward, each factor contributing to the detriment of the next until the project fizzles out or self-destructs. A virtuous development spiral is one whereby each project builds on the last and contributes to the betterment of the next.

As indicated in Figure 3.3, projects should repeat and magnify themselves as the lessons of each project contribute to the objectives and vision set out in the Web strategy. The amount of initial and ongoing work associated with a project will generally vary according to the maturity of the site, typically the initial launch of a site being the most labor intensive. However,

Phase	Work stage	Deliverables
Preproduction	1. Project clarification	• Project brief: business, creative, technical, and content requirements • Outline budget, schedule, and resource plan • Full preproduction budget and schedule
	2. Solution definition	• Consultancy recommendations: business, creative, and technical
	3. Project specification	• Project specification document
Production	4. Content	• Content delivery plan • Asset tracking mechanism • Content preparation • Storyboards
	5. Design and construction	• Project milestones as defined in project specification • Change control documentation
	6. Testing, launch, and handover	• Testing as defined in project specification • Marketing initiatives • Handover briefing and documentation
Maintenance	7. Maintenance	• Maintaining plan/SLA • Training and development
Evaluation	8. Review and evaluation	• Project review • Site performance analysis: traffic, users, information, technical, and commercial

Figure 3.2 An overview of a Web project's phases, work stages, and deliverables.

as a general rule, the overall size and scope of a Web presence will grow. So too will the maintenance requirements of the site as more and more people in the offline business become woven into the online e-business, and vice versa. The resulting spiral reflects the incremental and evolutionary nature of Web development.

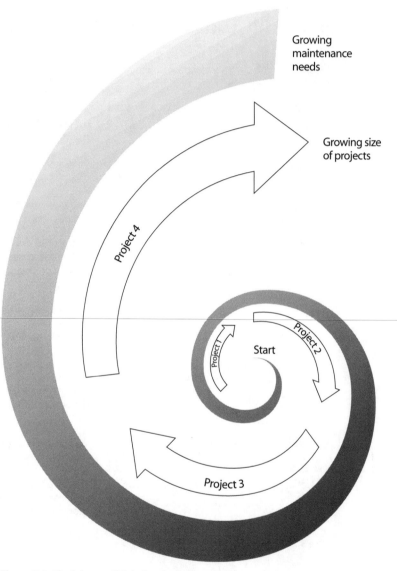

Figure 3.3 The "virtuous" Web development spiral.

3.3 Team Workflow Throughout Project Work Stages

The level of contribution and involvement of team members throughout project work stages varies. It is difficult to predict exactly the level of involvement at each stage, as this is dependent on the nature of the project. If a project is for instance particularly content heavy, design light, or programming intensive, the team makeup and the level of contribution from particular skill areas will of course need to be adjusted accordingly.

Once you have a feel for the nature of the project, obtained at the project clarification work stage, you will be in a better position to predict the required levels of commitment needed at each stage. Experience is invaluable in getting this right. As your budgeting will largely be based on resource time, being able to accurately predict budget requirements goes hand in hand with accurately assessing resource requirements.

Figures 3.4 and 3.5 present a rough indication of the levels of involvement across the life span of a typical Web project for the client, account, project management, strategy/consultancy, design, content, and programming teams. The graphs should not necessarily be read as an exact depiction of involvement over time. The content and design/construction work stages, for example, often occur simultaneously, as do the maintenance and review/evaluation stages.

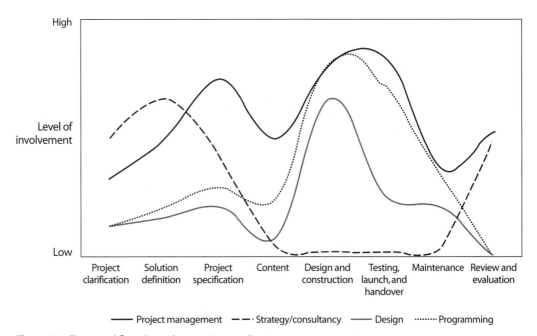

Figure 3.4 Team workflow throughout project work stages.

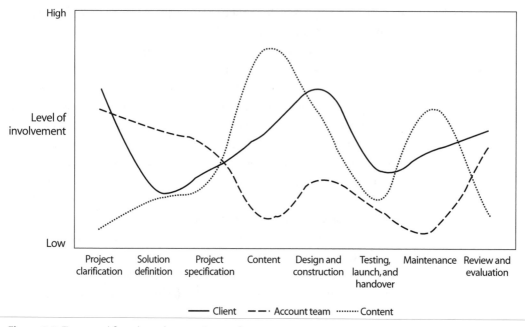

Figure 3.5 Team workflow throughout project work stages.

3.4 Project Manager Competencies and Tasks Mapped to Work Stages

In Part I we looked at the skills, roles, and responsibilities required of a Web project manager. Table 3.1 provides extensive lists of tasks and competencies required of the project manager at the eight work stages of a Web project. There is a great deal to master, as is evident from the table. These lists represent the universe of possible competencies, as opposed to those you are likely to need for any given project.

With so much to master, and so much to be thinking about, it is helpful to organize your work as manageable stages. Although you will be employing many types of skills throughout the project, if you can define task specifics and give them a structure, you will find that the wall of work and responsibility facing you can be broken through. The following chapters further define the project road map presented in this chapter, against which you can compare and break down your work into definable tasks and manageable chunks.

Table 3.1 Project manager's competencies and tasks mapped against the project's work stages.

Project work stage	Competencies and tasks for project manager
1. Project clarification	Understanding of client's operating environment and objectives, target market and user requirements, and technical issues
	Ability to interview clients/audiences
	Ability to coordinate and run effective meetings
	Ability to analyze results
	Ability to write research reports
	Ability to state business, creative, technical, and content requirements
	Ability to define and set up as necessary steering and working groups
	Ability to understand and define required levels of security
	Ability to gauge outline time and resource and budget requirements
2. Solution definition	Ability to administer creative, commercial, technical, and content briefs
	Understanding of requirements of other departments, site architecture and integration processes, the legal environment, best practices/best of breed examples and possibilities and opportunities of the Web
	Coordination of solution to security requirements
	Recognition of where cutting edge becomes "bleeding" edge
	Management of the solution definition process
3. Project specification	Coordination of technical analysis of proposed and existing systems
	Ability to write functional and technical specifications, and writing ability in general
	Analysis of risk
	Defining security procedures
	Creation of a content plan
	Generation of creative and technical quotes, including quotes for project management time
	Leadership of brainstorming sessions
	Creative thinking
	Resource planning abilities
	Collating contributions
	Budget development
	Creation of project timeline
	Definition of success criteria and reporting methods
	Stipulation of budgetary and other assumptions

continued on next page

Table 3.1 (continued)

Project work stage	Competencies and tasks for project manager
3. Project specification (continued)	Understanding of contractual issues
	Maintenance of project scope and SLAs
	Specification version control
	Management of the project specification creation, distribution, and sign-off process
4. Content	Understanding of online publishing methods, and of general content formats
	Management of assets, content providers, and the copywriting process
	Definition and integration of data feeds
	Collation of content
	Storyboarding ability
	Version control
	Definition of editorial access privileges
	Maintenance of security levels
	Development of a style guide
5. Design and construction	Resource planning abilities
	Administration of creative, commercial, and technical briefs
	Sufficient technical and design knowledge
	Team motivation
	Support of other departments
	Management of change and risk, multiple providers, code documentation, and creation of design guidelines
	Maintenance of project communication
	Version control
	Forward anticipation and resolution of issues
	Documentation of project progress and decisions
	Ensurance that sign-off procedures are followed
6. Testing, launch, and handover	Ability to write a testing plan
	Management of testing process, of changes, and of partnerships
	Scoping of time, cost, and quality impact of testing results
	Client training
	Development of a traffic strategy

Table 3.1 (continued)

Project work stage	Competencies and tasks for project manager
	Liaison with PR/ad/media agencies
	Recognition of partnership opportunities
	Collation of handover documentation
7. Maintenance	Definition of a maintenance plan and SLA
	Management of content and functionality rollout
	Resourcing of maintenance team
	Version and crisis control
	Establishment of update procedures and site access privileges
	Ongoing training and development
	Capacity planning
	Coordination of promotional activities
	Archiving and storing
8. Review and evaluation	Conducting a project review
	Reporting against success criteria
	Analysis of traffic data
	Suggestions of improvements
	Celebration of success
	Proposal of next steps

3.5 Summary

The following are significant points contained in this chapter.

▶ There are four main project phases: preproduction, production, maintenance, and evaluation

▶ The preproduction and production phases each consist of three workstages. Within the preproduction phase are the work stages project clarification, solution definition, and project specification. Within the production phase are the work stages content, design and construction, and testing, launch, and handover.

▶ The method presented in this chapter is designed as a "virtuous spiral," meaning that it does not stagnantly circle back on itself but continues to evolve, improve, and grow.

▶ The various members of a project team will be involved to varying degrees throughout the life span of a project.

▶ The role of the project manager changes as a project progresses, but he or she should be involved to some degree at all stages.

Work Stage 1:
Project Clarification

The project manager holds the key to making sure the client's expectations are both realistic (from the outset) and achievable (once the project is underway) by the team.

—**Graham Anderson, Marketing Director, Sharenet, South Africa**

Preproduction			Production			Maintenance	Evaluation
Project clarification	Solution definition	Project specification	Content	Design and construction	Testing, launch, and handover	Maintenance	Review and evaluation

T
he start of a new project can be both exciting and daunting. The project, and your involvement in it, may be clearly defined, with a definite starting point, but you may alternatively find yourself performing some or all of the Web project manager's job by default. If, for example, you work for a Web development company awarded the job of creating a company's site, you normally have a more defined start date. If you work on the client side, such responsibilities might creep up on you, until one day you realize you seem to have ended up charged with leading the progress of the company's site.

At this "take a deep breath" stage, it is particularly comforting to know two things: what your next steps should be, and who will be taking the plunge with you. This chapter, on the project clarification work stage, and indeed this entire book, hopes to make you feel more confident about what your next steps should be.

You will find more on working with a team in Chapter 8, but for now we will explore the process via a mini project kick-off meeting with some of the key team members you know you will be working with. The aim is to get a team spirit going, to begin to get the feel for a common purpose and goal, and, for your sake, to help you feel you are not alone. From a practical point of view, this type of meeting should enable the planning and implementation of the project clarification work stage as described in this chapter.

The first work stage, project clarification, is about fully understanding the client's commercial goals, and the financial, technical, creative, and resourcing context in which those commercial goals need to be set. This stage involves asking a lot of questions of the client, to gain a better understanding of their operating environment and to elicit what to this point has been the client's motivation and level of thinking behind this particular Web initiative. Often there are other agendas afoot, influencing those that might at first seem straightforward.

In simplified terms, you might view the stages of the preproduction phase as addressing the fundamental questions of why the project is being done, how it should be done, and what exactly is going to be done.

Project clarification = Why?

Solution definition = How?

Project specification = What?

It is not just about asking questions of the client, however. The first work stage is a two-way knowledge transfer process. The Web development team moves from ignorance to knowledge as to the client's business environment. The client moves from ignorance to knowledge as to the particular skills, working practices, and online expertise the Web development team brings with it.

Clearly, the level of knowledge client and Web development team have, respectively, about each other and about the Web will vary. If you are an agency and have been working for a particular client for a long time, you should be as aware of their business needs as they are. If you are a Web project manager working with an in-house team, you will already have a high level of knowledge of the client's operating environment. For the project's benefit, and for the benefit of your team, it is always worth going through the project clarification process to make sure that what you do is properly accounted for. There should be no room for later recriminations based on a perceived lack of knowledge or proper awareness of what was going on. As we saw in Chapter 3, the following are the deliverables at the project clarification work stage.

▶ A project brief that details the business, creative, technical, and content requirements
▶ An outline of a budget, schedule, and resources plan for the project
▶ A full preproduction budget, schedule, and resource plan

Once you have all of this information, and have a budget and schedule to work to, you can proceed with confidence into work stages 2 and 3, covered in the following chapters.

4.1   Where the Project Manager Fits In

Throughout this section there are references to what "you" will be doing. It is worth pointing out that depending on your level of experience as a project manager, and the structure of your organization, not all of these tasks may be performed by the day-to-day project manager.

As the preproduction phase is so crucial to the success of the project, the most experienced people should be involved at the beginning to ensure that the project gets off to a good start and follows the best possible development path. This often means that the most senior project manager (i.e., the project director or the COO) will coordinate this phase, with input from the client and from consultants across the creative, technical, and commercial disciplines.

The earlier the involvement of the project manager who will be running project implementation, the better. It is easier to understand the project and make sure it meets its higher objectives if you understand how it came into being and what it hopes to become. It also engenders a higher degree of commitment in you if you are involved and consulted at the early stages.

It is outside the scope of this book to go into minute detail of the commercial, technical, creative, and content strategies formed as a result of the work that goes on in this and the next work stage. Each could be the subject of its own book. Each also depends to a great degree on the nature of a particular project.

However, we can outline the types of questions that need to be asked and the issues that need to be addressed—for use as a guide—if you are responsible for these stages. If you are not involved until later in the project, these sections will help give you an understanding of how these elements fit into the overall process and method we are working through.

If you are responsible for coordinating and project managing these work stages, you will need the same types of skills and techniques (though additional experience and a higher degree of knowledge) as those discussed in more detail in Chapter 8.

4.2   The Importance of Getting a High-Level Project Sponsor

One of the most important aspects of any Web project is that there exist someone sufficiently high up in the organization who is prepared to champion the project on your behalf. As a successful Web site will be both a reinvention and extension of the existing business, it will be most successful if it can draw on the best of the resources that reside across potentially all departments of the company. This typically involves marketing, operations, human resources, finance, and IS.

No single department is ideally suited to take on the project alone. The two most likely candidates are the marketing and IS departments. However, the marketing department has little experience in building scalable software applications that integrate with back-end systems. The IS department, on the other hand, has little knowledge in creating an innovative site that enhances brand values, speaks to the customer, and moves the company through the customer life cycle.

To have assurance you can access departments of the company as necessary, and obtain the cooperation you need, you need the authority and support of a high-level project sponsor. This should be at least on the level of the head of a department, who has direct access to the company's board, or, preferably, a board executive. The COO would be the ideal person to get behind the project. In many cases, the project will have been authorized by the COO or someone at a similar level, which will minimize problems in getting the authority to orchestrate the efforts of all departments.

Two other reasons it is important to get high-level support for your project are to maximize speed of critical decision making and ensure budgetary control. The larger the organization, the longer it can take to get key decisions made. Late sign-off or decision making can cause major problems on a project, as you may know from having been on the painful end of a project run by "decision by committee." If you have access to a single person who has the authority to make decisions, it will greatly facilitate the project.

It is very rare that any project ends up costing less than was originally predicted. Any savvy project manager will leave room both in schedules and budgets for overrun. About 20% or more is a fairly standard buffer for a Web project. If you are going to need significant amounts of money for the project (as is increasingly the case), it is only sensible that you are communicating with someone high enough within the organization to authorize and take responsibility for the level of spending. One of the benefits of spending a large amount of money on a Web project is that it will, by virtue of the level alone, be seen as an important project and will have the full attention of the necessary high-level people.

4.3   The Opportunities at This Stage

The project is still in its early stages, and although the project may be considered very important to the business, large amounts of money and resources have yet to be committed. Therefore, it may seem as though this stage is less important, less critical to get right. Although it is true that the risk is lower and the exposure less at this stage, and deliverables and deadlines somewhat more fluid (and do not form part of a chain of critical dependencies), there exist significant opportunities and threats both to the project and to you and your development team.

There is a danger the project could get shelved. This might be for factors outside your control, such as the key project sponsor leaving the company and replaced by someone who has an entirely different agenda. If you do a poor job at these initial stages, it might also be that the project goes ahead but you are not the one to work on it. If you work in-house, this does not do your promotion chances any favors. If you are an external agency and lose the work, clearly this is of even more fundamental concern.

What are some of the opportunities this initial phase presents in getting the project off to a flying start? An overview of the opportunities is presented in Table 4.1.

Okay, so you have the authority you need to pull the project together, and expectations and anticipation are running high. What are the questions you need to be asking toward decisions on further steps, and how do you go about asking them?

4.4   Discover, Refine, Define

The early stages of the preproduction phase are also known as the discovery phase. This is because you are discovering and uncovering all available information that will inform your approach. To reach the point at which you can produce the deliverables for the project clarification work stage, you should go through the three iterations described in the following subsections.

4.4.1   Discover

Here you attempt to discover as much as possible about what it is the client thinks they want, and why. Any supporting rationale, documents, projects, and other work that has gone into the project to date should also be collated and reviewed at this stage.

What you are doing is conducting a knowledge and resource audit. You will need to conduct workshops and interviews to assess current aspirations

Table 4.1 The opportunities for the project team during the first work stage.

Project element	Opportunity
Commitment	By involving people in the project at its outset, you have the chance to build buy-in and commitment to it. You sow the seed that will start to generate momentum and enthusiasm.
Trust	If you can excel at this first stage, you will create trust between the client and you and your development team. This trust will be invaluable to upcoming work stages, where there is increased scope for friction and unexpected issues. Trust is the single most important thing to develop between the client and your team. First impressions count, so make sure you make a good start.
Relationships	This work stage helps you develop working relationships. It sets the tone for the rest of the project. There is the opportunity to build relationships with the key project stakeholders and contributors. Often you are creating new relationships and new working groups. This can be very positive within an organization if handled well. Getting to know and work with new people, seeing new faces, and doing new work is a great opportunity. If you are an agency, these relationships are key to developing new business opportunities.
Scope and budget	There will probably be an initial expected scope and budget for the project. However, this may be based on very little. During this work stage, there is an opportunity to sell the client on upgrading the project to the bigger picture, the grand vision of just what could be possible if more budget and resources were available. As you learn more about the project, the organization, and the potential of the Web, you may see opportunities others have not spotted. If you can make a strong argument for chasing these opportunities, you are likely to get what you need to make it happen. This can only be good for you, whether internal or external.
Inspiration	Once you have specified the project and are into the later work stages, the role of project manager becomes more about doing than thinking. You will no doubt have creative and commercial insight, particularly based on your implementation experience, that you would like to share. This is your opportunity to be inspired! If you are an agency that has won the work through a pitch, this is also an opportunity to *improve* on the initial pitch; that is, to overdeliver. This will inspire client confidence, trust, and admiration.

continued on next page

Table 4.1 (continued)

Project element	Opportunity
Protect yourself	This is actually a negative way of stating what is a much more positive element. It needs to be clear that the project is not just about you, and you cannot take responsibility for everything associated with it. The responsibility needs to be shared. This will lead to a much better quality end result, and will avoid the fingers of blame. The project clarification process makes it clear that you are, in terms of opportunity and responsibility, opening the project up to a wider group of people.
Education	A lot is learned during a Web project by all involved. Learning can be a very positive experience. If the client feels she has learned from the experience, she will feel empowered. You should begin the education at this stage.Open the client's eyes to the nature of the work involved, the importance of it, the opportunities it brings, and so on. Even asking the appropriate questions and giving reasons for the questions will be educational. If you are lucky, the client should perceive you as something of a guru. If you can maneuver yourself into a position of indispensability, you will command more authority and respect.
Working practices	For those involved in the project, this work stage could be the first contact they have with each other, and with you and your team. This gives you the chance to set expectations and standards in terms of working practices. It gets people used to how documents will be presented (e.g., budgets), how meetings will be run, and even such things as how formal or otherwise the dress code is for those involved. This means that as you go into the next work stages there is already a project protocol established that you can build on.

for the project. You will also need to analyze the organization's technology and business infrastructure to assess the opportunities and limitations associated with the project, and you will need to determine what personnel and other resources (e.g., office facilities) could be leveraged to the benefit of the project. To discover what you need to know, you need to ask. What you need to ask is covered in material that follows.

4.4.2   Refine

Once you are in possession of the available facts, figures, and information, you can begin to refine the proposed project by suggesting other opportunities that may not have been considered, suggesting alternative options to those proposed and investigating the assumptions made by the client. Take the best of what the client can offer and play it off against your own expertise and insight to see if you come up with something even better. Respect the fact that the client will know far more about their business than you, but see if you can add value to their ideas through your own experience. At this stage, you are not really proposing a solution (as you will do in the next work stage), but you are suggesting alternative ways of doing things to see how well the initial proposal and thoughts hold up.

TIP   **It's all about contacts**

As you talk to, and become aware, of people who will have input to the project, make sure you maintain a central contact list containing everyone's name, position, role in the project, direct telephone number, and email address. When you are putting together the final team, or need important questions answered quickly, it is very useful to have this at hand. As the team expands, and you are introducing new members to the team, such a list is also valuable to them as an overview of who is involved and who they should turn to if they have a particular question. It also makes a good impression if you can correctly remember someone's name and position!

4.4.3   Define

When you are clear on the project requirements and scope, you will be in a position to define what work is required to make it happen. At this stage, you need to be confident of putting together a budget and schedule for the next two work stages, which will complete the preproduction phase of the project. You should also have a much better feeling for how much the entire project will cost, what resources will be needed, and how long it will take.

You are not yet in a position to start building a Web site because although you are much clearer about what you want, you are not necessarily sure about the best way to do it. Nor do you have the work carefully defined enough to enter into a meaningful contract or to properly brief a team of resources to implement it. The following sections offer a framework for obtaining the information you need to reach this position, as well as some pointers on the budgeting, resourcing, and scheduling at this stage.

4.5   Commercial Requirements

Part of the next work stage, solution definition, should involve the definition of a Web strategy. This strategy will include the commercial and strategic rationale underpinning and driving what is being done on the current project in the short term, as well as what needs to be done toward longer-term ambitions and targets, which will be much more far reaching.

At this stage you want to find out as much as you can about what the client is hoping to achieve through the Web, how aligned this is to other business objectives, what the competitors are doing, what the aims of the current site are (if they have one), and other such commercial factors. Often what the client is aiming for is to be "the leading Web site in X business sector," or something equally ambitious and open ended. There's nothing wrong with shooting for the stars, but you will have to work with the client to ascertain just how achievable that is, what the costs would be in achieving that, what the risks would be, and whether it would even be profitable and in what time frame.

Sometimes the client's brief is open ended because they feel understandably unsure about what exactly they want and how it is going to happen. Other times the brief may be deliberately open ended, as the client wants to see what the development team can come up with, and does not want to impose preconceived ideas on them. As previously mentioned, much of a successful ongoing client/development team relationship can be built around the development team educating the client about what can and cannot be done, the hows and the whys, and the art of the possible. If the client feels enlightened, they will feel empowered, which tends to lead to faster and firmer decisions and larger budgets. If you can empower your client to sell the Web and its potential internally, with real commitment and understanding, you are doing yourself an enormous commercial favor.

This education and information process will be played out principally through workshops and one-on-one interviews that will answer the following types of questions in several commercial areas. In the general commercial area, you might ask the following questions.

▶ To what extent does the evaluation and development of this project form part of a larger initiative?
▶ To what extent are you interested in building relationships with other Web properties?
▶ To what extent do you wish to retain the development, rollout, and servicing of this Web project in-house versus building relationships with service providers, contractors, and other business partners?
▶ What would need to happen for you to consider the site a success?
▶ How important is it for this site to generate revenue?
▶ Do you have any products or service offerings you feel would work and/or sell particularly well over the Web?
▶ At what level of Web technology sophistication would you place your suppliers and customers?
▶ Should you be considering the business-to-business potential of the Web as well as business-to-consumer, or vice versa?
▶ Have you had approaches from business partners to be involved in a joint Web project?
▶ If you are planning to sell advertising on the site, do you have current advertisers who would be interested? Would there be conflicts of interest between online and offline advertisement?
▶ What training and development programs do you have planned for managing the new ways of doing business the Web site would entail?
▶ How prepared are you to reengineer some core business processes and systems to fit with new e-business paradigms?
▶ How much involvement do you see the various departments of the business having in the project?
▶ Who is the key project sponsor?

In the area of finance, you might ask the following questions.

▶ How self-sufficient should the Web property be? And on what schedule?
▶ What ROI are you looking for from the Web property? Is this different from other company projects?
▶ What are the key criteria for approval of a business case? Will this differ for the Web project?

▶ What financial benefits are you seeking from the Web: pure revenues, increased customer numbers, increased indirect revenues, brand building and other nontangible revenues? How would these be attributed?

▶ What is the maximum funding capability available for Web projects? How far is this dependent on the size of the business case for the specific idea?

▶ Are there other areas of funding within the business that could contribute to the Web budget?

▶ If you have e-commerce on your current site, how many sales have you made, what is the growth trend, and what reporting methods are in place?

In the area of marketing, you might ask the following questions.

▶ Who is your offline target customer?

▶ How do you see the demographics of your current customer base changing in the future?

▶ Which key demographics are you looking to target with your Web proposition?

▶ What level of interest have your customers shown in your Web presence?

▶ Do you want to focus on giving existing customers an added-value service online, or do you want to use online primarily to generate new customers?

▶ What information do you have on the users of your current Web site?

▶ How do you market your current site?

▶ Do you have any market research that could help define user requirements?

▶ How could what happens on the site be integrated with your offline offering, or vice versa?

▶ Which of your competitors' sites, or other sites, do you particularly admire, and why?

▶ What existing agencies do you use for above and below the line marketing? Do they have experience of marketing Web properties? Do they have particular areas of expertise?

▶ How do you report on the performance of your current site?

▶ Are there existing resources who have expertise or experience in Internet marketing?

▶ What responsibilities and decision-making powers does the marketing department have in entering co-marketing deals or co-branding initiatives online?

Questions such as these will begin to force the client to think more closely about what they really want out of their site. It will provide a base of information for use in forming a Web strategy with real focus and that meets the client's business objectives in the short term and in the longer term. These will be tailored online business objectives the client will feel part of and committed to because they helped form them.

It is also worth asking if you can meet and talk to any of the client's other business partners and agencies. Their advertising agency and PR agency can often give you insightful objective information on the client.

4.6   Creative Requirements

If you are an external agency and gave a pitch to win the Web site work, you may well have done a creative concept to show the client your creative skills. To do this, you might have taken their existing site, logo, brochures, and so on as a starting point for your design inspiration. As the client has chosen you to do the job, you must be going down the right track. It is worth finding out more exactly what they thought of the creative treatment, if you did one.

Certainly you should ask for any corporate design guidelines they might have, along with the corporate font(s) and colors. As HTML can only display using fonts on the user's computer and (if you are sticking to the 216 basic Web-safe colors), and as you have a limited number of colors to play with, you may well have to explain to the client why their design guidelines cannot be applied exactly to your Web design. Clients are usually prepared to see their Web site as a very separate medium to other channels, so there is rarely any problem with this.

To help the creative process, it is also worth asking the client for as much visual material as they can provide. This includes brochures, press ads, letterhead and stationery, photos, TV ads, calendars, and other marketing and PR material. This can be held together centrally with other content as it arrives. It will greatly help the designers visualize their concepts. The following are other questions you might want to ask.

▶ Who acts as your "brand guardian"? Will they be responsible for any changes in the brand positioning?
▶ How far could this site take on a life of its own versus sticking closely to existing brand/product/service offerings?

▶ What are the brand values you would seek to promote through your Web site?

▶ How would you describe a typical member of the target audience?

▶ If the target audience only remembers one thing from the work, what must it be?

▶ Do you have brand or corporate design guidelines that should be followed? Have they been designed or updated with the Web in mind?

▶ What other agencies or suppliers do you use who you would want to have input into the creative process for the Web site?

▶ What competitors' sites should be taken into account?

▶ Are there any sites you particularly like/dislike the design of, and why?

▶ Who will have sign-off concerning creative issues?

You are working toward producing a communications brief for the creative team. The communications brief forms part of the overall project brief. When you are briefing any creative resources, particularly designers, the communications brief will give them a conceptual and information base to work and think from. You should have asked the client for any available visual material and design guidelines. With these hard assets and the communications brief, the creative team has everything it needs to start work.

Information such as target audience, technical restraints, and competitor activity all form part of the brief. It is a good idea for the client to review this brief to check that you are all still thinking along the same lines and not risking shooting off at a totally inappropriate tangent. If the client likes the communications brief, they are also much more likely to approve the designs developed in the next work stage, as they can see how and why they have been developed as they have.

4.7 Technical Requirements

The Web development team is going to want to know more about the client's current server and hosting arrangements, if any. You will want to know if the client has a strong preference for a particular Internet service provider, or for particular server hardware and software, or if these parameters are to be entirely defined by you.

It is also useful to get a better picture of what Web-related skills currently exist within the client's organization. This could mean site updating and maintenance mechanisms need to be less formulated and advanced if they do not need to cater to non-Web-literate users, hence saving the client additional programming costs.

It is also worth finding out what the client's standard corporate desktop machine consists of, in particular the operating system and standard Web browser, as this may help avoid teething problems when you are creating the prototype or early versions of the site. The following are other questions you might want to ask.

▶ What database formats do you use? Any preference?
▶ Do you have a large IS team or is it outsourced? If so, who are the contractors, and in what ways will they be expected to contribute to the Web project?
▶ What level of security are you expecting of the system?
▶ Are you expecting us to devise a testing strategy? Do you want to be involved in any of the testing?
▶ What networking technology do you use? How fast are internal networks, and what is your Internet connectivity like?
▶ Do you have any minimum/maximum technical specifications you would expect a Web site to conform to?
▶ Do you have any preferred form of documentation or project method you would like to work to?
▶ Do you have any preferred applications of software systems you would like considered, such as e-commerce, content management, or customer relationship management (CRM) systems?
▶ Do you have an intranet? If so, who supports it, what functions does it serve, and so on?
▶ What technical reporting would you expect on a Web site's performance?
▶ Who will be the primary point of contact for technical matters, and who will be responsible for sign-off on technical issues?

Just as a communications brief is created for the creative team, so too should a technical brief be created that captures all of the required information for the technical consultants to then define the optimal technical solution for the project.

4.8   Content Requirements

Good content is expensive to create or to buy. In the early days of the Web, it was easier, though never legal, to get away with using content that was not strictly yours. However, with the Web now being of great commercial importance, content owners are now making sure that people do not make unlicensed use of their content. Owning content and selling it for Web use is big business. Most publishers have migrated their content to include the Web, in an effort to gain wider readership, more customers, and to exploit the potential advertising revenues.

As the earlier generation of Web sites consisted largely of "brochure ware" promoting the services and products of a company, content used to be less of an issue. It was almost assumed that the client would supply the content, and there were few rights issues and there wasn't all that much content. With larger publishers now online—and with sites having to offer increasingly deep, wide, and functionally rich content to retain their customers (who are "one click away from the competition")—content has become a much bigger issue.

This isn't the book to go into all of the ins and outs of content creation, rights issues, and content management, though many of these are touched on in as far as they affect project management in subsequent chapters. The questions that follow give you an idea of the types of questions you should be asking yourself and your client regarding content.

▶ What content do you currently have that you plan to use online?

▶ What content other than "brochure ware" could you exploit? Customer databases? Suppliers' databases? Stock and inventory databases? And so on.

▶ What rights do you have over the proposed content? Do you have worldwide rights?

▶ Are you happy to use library/stock material for some content, or would you rather create or commission original content?

▶ How important is it to you to own the intellectual property rights to any content and code created for the site?

▶ Do you have someone who would be able to broker content deals for you?

▶ How far are you prepared to compromise on your own branded content to save time and money in getting content on the site?

- ▶ Do you have, or intend to employ, an editorial team responsible for creating and updating content?
- ▶ How important is it that existing staff are able to update content on the Web site? What level of technological skills do those people currently have?
- ▶ How many content contributors do you think you will have? Where will they be located? Will there need to be varying levels of editorial control and access?
- ▶ How important is version control for your content? How important is the ability to roll back content to a former state if needed?
- ▶ In what format will the source content be?
- ▶ What types of rich media content do you envision being on the site? Animations, video, audio, virtual reality, 3D, and so on?
- ▶ What are your data protection and privacy policies concerning user data captured on the site?
- ▶ Do you propose to have user-generated content on the site? How will you monitor this content?
- ▶ Do you have a legal department to ensure the legal correctness of all content on the site and to ensure that suitable disclaimers and so on are in place?
- ▶ How do you update the content on your existing site? What works well, and what would you like improved?
- ▶ Do you have any editorial, style, or publishing guidelines we could see?
- ▶ Who will be the main point of contact for editorial decisions, and who will have final sign-off on content?

4.9 The Project Brief

The project brief summarizes the findings of the project clarification phase so that you can then get to work devising the best solutions possible, knowing that you have unearthed all you need to know, hashed out any thorny issues, and come to an agreement on the way forward.

The project brief is a milestone in itself, and can be referred to if there is any dispute at a later stage as to why particular elements of work were undertaken, or why a particular avenue was being explored.

Usually the project brief is less formal and considerably shorter than the project specification, as a contract is less likely to hinge on the brief, and therefore less detail is needed. Similar to the project specification (see Chapter 6), this document's chief purpose is to document the work that has been done and to collate the findings in such a way that it can then serve as a brief for the resources that will work on the next (solution definition) work stage.

In some cases, the project brief may not even exist as a separate and unified document. The technical, commercial, and creative resources involved on the project at this stage can work in isolation of one another to a much greater degree than at later stages of the project. More of the work is done through meetings involving fewer, more specialized people, often consultants in their particular field. Effectively, the briefs for each of the various areas are created and managed by each of the various teams. As long as these teams are clear in their minds what they are doing, and the same teams remain on the project throughout the preproduction phase—and as long as there is a central project manager who is comfortable that the various strands will pull together to form a coherent solution in the next stage—then not having an exhaustive project brief document is not the end of the world.

That said, having the client's agreement and sign-off at the end of this work stage *is* very important, so you have to be sure that the client is clear on what is being signed off and that this will "hold up in court" further down the road if necessary. A document makes this much easier. Try at least to collate and store any emails that detail what has been done and what is going to be done.

4.10   Budgets, Schedules, and Resources

Don't think that putting a budget at the back of a document is going to mean the client will look at it last. Strangely, the budget always seems to be the most interesting part of any document, and usually the client will surreptitiously flick their way through anything you hand them to ferret out the bottom-line figure, recoil in horror, and then wait for you to impress them enough to justify the expense.

After cost, schedules are, not surprisingly, the other big item of interest. In the current Internet gold rush, it is actually not uncommon for schedules to be a much bigger issue than cost. Start-ups flush with venture capital are scrambling to build market share and a large enough critical mass not to be squashed by the slower-to-move established players. Even the established players want to move quickly once they do decide to go ahead, as they are often under large shareholder pressure to make a significant mark on the Web.

TIP   **Fight the early battles to win the great victory**

With pressure on time and cost reduction, it is, unfortunately, the third constant, quality, that can be sacrificed. One of the unending and difficult tasks for the Web project manager is to fight for the time and money needed to do a good job. One thing that experience teaches you is that history will only judge you by your end product, and will forget the journey you had to go through to get there. E-business is, despite the hype, a performance-rated business like any other. Bear in mind that you will be judged, fairly or unfairly, by the results of the final site. Fight hard in early time and cost battles to gain the best chance of succeeding with the final quality of the product. Ironically, only by producing quality work will you be in a position to demand more money and set schedules.

What you need to commit to at this stage of the project is a budget and schedule for the entire preproduction phase, including the work you have done on the project clarification and the work to be done on the next two stages, solution definition and project specification. You will also be under pressure to provide at least an estimate for the likely costs for the entire project.

Sometimes, particularly on smaller projects, you may not be able to split out the budgets in this way, and will be expected at this stage to provide a fixed-price budget for the entire project. You should argue the merits of doing at least the project specification first. You can reasonably argue that this might actually lead to a lower cost than you would otherwise be forced to quote based on incomplete knowledge. If you must provide a fixed quote, make sure it includes generous "padding" and plenty of caveats and assumptions. If you are forced into a fixed quote at an early stage, you should also create a risk plan that very clearly highlights overrunning this quote as a high risk.

Unfortunately, really good budgeting skills only come with experience. This comes not just through experience of budgeting, but of budgeting for

Web projects and, even more specifically, budgeting according to the resources you have available for the project and your knowledge of how they will perform.

To learn more on how to go about budgeting, see Chapter 6, particularly the section on the budget that goes in the project specification. This tells you how to arrive at reliable quotes, how best to present the costs to the client, and how to make sure adequate assumptions are included to protect yourself.

TIP   Ballpark figures

It's always tricky providing cost estimates and ballpark figures. You know that despite your warnings people will take them as quotes and try and hold you to them. Make sure you accompany outline costs with suitable assumptions, overbudget if anything, and refer to similar projects where you can. If you want to use an external source of generic Web project pricing figures, you can find them on the Web. Try *www.netb2b.com*, for example.

Your pricing will depend on the daily rates you charge for the services of your team members, but as a rough estimate you should expect the majority of preproduction phases (for a moderate-size e-business site) to last between three and six weeks, with a team of three to eight people working on it. For larger projects, the preproduction phase can last up to six months, but as a general rule clients will get very twitchy if production cannot start within six weeks of project start-up.

Many of the larger Web development agencies are now marketing themselves on their ability to develop sites incredibly quickly. A time frame of between three and four months seems to be the norm for these aggressive development schedules. Of this time, the first three to four weeks would still be spent on preproduction, representing almost 25% of the total time spent on the project.

Once you have an approved project brief, and a preproduction budget and schedule, you have what you need to move on to the next work stage, solution definition. Whereas you have largely been asking questions and defining working practices, now you will begin to formulate answers and pin down further details of the project.

"We'd like to use technology as a cost reducer, competitive weapon, and to make us look cool."

Heuristics Search, Inc., *www.heur.com.*

4.11 Summary

The following are significant points raised in this chapter.

▶ Make sure you have a high level of support for the project.
▶ Make sure you ask enough questions to be confident you understand the commercial, creative, technical, and content requirements of the project.
▶ Create a project brief that summarizes your understanding of the project's requirements and objectives.
▶ If you are clear exactly what is required for the preproduction phase, you can agree on a fixed budget for that work, but recognize the high risks involved in committing to a fixed budget for the entire project at this stage.

chapter

5

Work Stage 2: Solution Definition

Communication is key—most clients are okay with the unpalatable truth if they are warned early enough, are made to feel involved in the process, and are not held for ransom. Remember that what we live and breathe may be alien to them, and conversely what may be technically complex for us can seem simple to them.

—Matt Flynn, Director, pres.co, U.K.

Preproduction			Production			Maintenance	Evaluation
Project clarification	Solution definition	Project specification	Content	Design and construction	Testing, launch, and handover	Maintenance	Review and evaluation

t this stage you will be coordinating the appropriate resources to define the technical, strategic, creative, and content solutions to meet the requirements of the project brief put together in the first work stage. This work stage can be quite short if the project brief does not highlight anything that merits further exploration. However, if you are working on a large project, the Web strategy in particular can take quite a while to formulate and pin down. In these cases, it would not be unusual for the first two work stages to last two to three months.

If there is no need for additional consultancy recommendations as a result of the project brief, this work stage effectively becomes rolled into the project specification stage, which comes next. This is where you pin down the details of the particular project that is to be implemented, as opposed to defining the bigger picture and longer-term objectives that can come out of the first two work stages.

As defined in Chapter 3, the deliverables for this work stage are the argued and reasoned recommendations, created in response to the project brief, that are drawn up by the project director, who coordinates a team of consultants across the key areas of commercial, creative, technical, and content. The findings of this work stage are presented to the client for their approval before being fed into the project specification, thereby casting them in stone for action by the Web development team.

5.1 The Project Manager's Role

It is likely that the same team that worked on the first work stage—where information was gathered, analyzed, challenged, and refined—will now work on defining the solution. This is the most sensible way of proceeding, as that team will have the best understanding of the client and the project brief. If you have been involved in the first work stage, it is likely you will still be involved at this work stage, performing a similar role in coordinating the team and bringing together the findings.

5.1.1 Bring In the Consultants

As a result of the project clarification process, it may have become clear that there is a need to bring in some specialist consultancy skills. It may also be clear that for the project to succeed some initial discussions and negotiations need to take place with a third party; for example, with a content provider. You will spend less time arranging interviews and running meetings with the client in this phase (you may well have worn them out with your barrage of questions in the last phase), but you will spend more time working with external specialists or potential partners, and more time ensuring that the various teams work toward a common solution.

As consultants and specialists can have strong views and opinions, borne quite fairly of experience, it can be difficult bringing the parties together to create a cohesive solution. As this stage defines the way forward for the entire project, it is understandable that each contributor wants to see his or her proposals taken very seriously. As you can imagine, and may already have experienced, the wishes of the strategists may not fit with those of the creatives, and the technologists may not feel comfortable with implementing the proposals of either.

The project should be driven by the strategy, whoever creates it. The creative treatment, content, and technology should then serve to realize the strategy. Make sure your resources are all working toward realizing the strategy and not heading off on a tangent. One way to help ensure this happens is to stagger the solution-definition work so that the strategy is defined before the creatives, technologists, or content contributors are fully involved.

As you move toward the production phase, your skills and ability in bringing people together to move the project forward will become increasingly important. Your ability to understand, empathize with, and listen to team members will need to be balanced with the requirement of ensuring that the project sticks to the deadlines and line items defined in the preproduction budget, as the culmination of the previous workstage.

5.1.2   How the Bidding Process Fits into the Preproduction Phase

If you work for an agency, you will recognize that when making a pitch you are effectively asked about, and have to carry out, at least the first two work stages, if not the project specification stage as well, all in a very condensed period of time and often for no money. This is why pitches can be so pressured and frantic. You should try to ensure that if the pitch is successful you have created enough breathing room in the budget and schedules to revisit the initial work stages you were forced to cut short and compromise when pulling out all the stops to win the business.

5.1.3   Defining How You Will Run the Project

Apart from your responsibilities in coordinating the efforts of the solution-definition team and in sticking to the preproduction deadlines and budget, you also need to be sure that you define your project management solution at this stage. Before you go into the production phase, in which you can become too busy doing to have the luxury to think and plan, you should be clear in your mind how you want to run the project. You should communicate this to the client and to your team to ensure they are happy with your proposed methods and commit to working to them.

Although you may have been following a method similar to the one proposed in this book, it may not yet have been clear to the client or your team. As discussed earlier, you may not even have been involved in the project until this stage, so this might represent your first chance to establish your role and preferred methods of working. Of course, you do not want to impose a dictator-style regime on your client and team, but the more experienced project managers will listen a lot initially, think, come up with a solution, and then be quite firm about how things should be done. This type of confidence comes with experience. Usually this confidence will come across in the communication of the project management solution, and will be much appreciated by the client and project team who look to you to "seize the bull by the horns" and drive the project forward.

5.1.4   An Opportunity to Learn

Finally, you should look at this phase of the project as an opportunity to learn. In the project clarification work stage, it can be very stimulating to learn about a new business, a new market sector, new disciplines, working practices, management styles, and business cultures. In this phase you have the chance to increase your knowledge by working with talented people who often have a great depth of knowledge in a particular field. The combined team will always have more knowledge than you can possibly master, but a lot of what they know and recommend will rub off on you, and for your own growth you should seek to leach as much out of them as you can. You will find yourself coming out with sentences and thoughts you didn't know you were capable of. One day you will wake up a Web guru!

5.2 Defining a Web Strategy

It is very important to have a Web strategy. It should communicate the strategic goals the site is aiming to achieve. It paints the bigger picture and need have less to do with the practical details of the implementation than with the commercial imperatives behind the Web initiatives. It is the commercial solution that is defined based on the findings and information gleaned during the project clarification stage.

The Web strategy will set goals that may well not be achievable in the first phase of implementation. It goes beyond the detailed confines of the project specification and, as far as the project manager is concerned, will be of little day-to-day importance once the production phase is under way. The strategy is crucial in moulding the proposed solutions and the project specification, however, so it has a large impact on what the project manager ends up doing.

With a Web strategy in place, it is much easier to come up with content ideas and design concepts, and even to make technical decisions, as there is a focus and underlying rationale against which all further decisions and work can be compared. Everything should grow from the Web strategy, so you should be able to relate everything back to it. Just as a business should have a mission statement and business plan, so should a Web site have a Web strategy.

The process of creating the Web strategy is likely to involve one or more of the following: market research; customer needs analysis; strengths, weaknesses, opportunities, threats (SWOT) analysis; risk analysis; competitor reviews; financial modeling; industry benchmarking; funding requirements; ROI projections; future growth opportunities; and so on. Depending on your experience, the size of the project, and the depth of resources you have available, the project manager will be more or less involved in these tasks. If the project is relatively small, the strategy may be very clear and can be put together among client, account manager (if there is an agency involved), and project manager. Otherwise, it is likely that e-business strategy consultants will be driving this, working in close cooperation with the project manager and client. A more in-depth strategic study might break down as described in the following sections.

5.2.1   Review of Strategic Objectives

In a review of strategic objectives, an overview should articulate the client's strategic objectives as understood in the project clarification process, setting out the nature of the market opportunity and the company's internal corporate objectives.

5.2.2   Development of a Business Case

A Web strategy should include a detailed business case and strategy for the Web property. This will involve a range of work steps, including the following:

▶ Setting out a detailed business proposition for the site, with an overview of the main business processes involved
▶ Developing a cross-media strategy for the site
▶ Reviewing the market and competitive environment, and indicating the key success factors
▶ Identifying the target customer base for the Web business, and understanding their needs
▶ Indicating the main cost and revenue areas
▶ Setting out the growth potential for the site
▶ Developing a partnership strategy (e.g., service providers for product sourcing, and for fulfillment and distribution, and Internet distribution partners)
▶ Developing a marketing strategy for the site

5.2.3   Development of a Business Model

A Web strategy should also include a business model for the site, setting out the costs and developing illustrative revenue projections for the business. This will allow the client to identify the investment requirements for establishing the site, and will indicate the potential for value creation. The business model will usually cover no more than three to five years of operations, including the period up to launch of the site. A dynamic financial model may be created with a software product such as Excel, allowing the client to see the effect of changing key projections and assumptions.

5.2.4   Development of the Web Proposition

A Web strategy also requires development of a proposition for the site, detailing the content, look and feel, and structure of the Web property, as well as details of the resources and technology required to develop and construct the property. This may also involve setting out the manner in which the Web site can be integrated with existing product promotions for maximum mutual benefit. A prototype is often developed to bring the proposition to life.

5.2.5   Implementation and Organizational Requirements

A Web strategy also sets out the main implementation and organizational requirements for the site, including staffing requirements, operational requirements, and an organizational map showing the structure of the team who will support the site. The Web strategy will usually be presented to the

Heuristics Search, Inc., *www.heur.com*.

client as a series of slides that summarize the key findings and arguments. These slides will have supporting documentation detailing the assumptions, information sources, calculations, and examples upon which the arguments are based. As the strategy is less "tangible" than the project specification, it is usually best discussed face-to-face than via the exchange of documents, which becomes more normal at the detailed specification stage.

5.2.6   A Web Strategy Example

Let's take the Web strategy for a TV broadcaster as an example. It might argue that the site is to appeal to existing viewers by giving them premium program-related content available only online. The site should also appeal to potential new viewers by appealing to the current Internet user profile with content that is original, entertaining, Web-only, and nothing immediately to do with the channel's TV content. The primary aim of the site is to be entertainment (rather than information) driven, to drive traffic from the Web to the TV, to be innovative and stand out from the competitors, and to promote the brand and personality of the channel.

The secondary aim, once sufficient traffic levels have been generated, is to use the site to create revenue through banner advertising and third-party e-commerce deals. This second phase should begin within six months of site launch. Existing TV advertisers will be given the chance to advertise on the site, as well as on TV. Data capture will be used to give the channel valuable user profiling information and afford one-to-one relationship marketing opportunities. Channel airtime will be used to promote the site and increase traffic. The airtime can also be offered to partners as a key lever in negotiating e-commerce fulfillment and distribution deals.

Within a year, the site aims to become a channel in its own right, independent of the TV content, offering each unique user a personalized online viewing experience. It is expected that the use of interactive digital TV will grow in the coming years, becoming mainstream within the next five years. As such, the site will develop to embrace and support interactive TV, both with program-related additional information (e.g., recipes to print out during cooking programs) and further e-commerce revenue streams (e.g., purchase of ingredients for the recipe). The following points describe the thinking behind this strategic overview.

▶ The current Internet user profile is one all advertisers are eager to attract and willing to pay a premium for, so an online offering will appeal to existing TV advertising clients.

▶ The competitors have only repackaged existing program support material for the Web. By creating original Web-only premium content, the site will stand out from the competitors.

▶ With the fragmentation of the TV industry, it will be increasingly important to have a strong online presence that can help promote awareness of the channel's brand and personality.

▶ It is important to attract new viewers and site users, but as 80% of the current TV viewers are loyal, repeat viewers, they cannot be alienated in favor of attracting new customers.

▶ A site whose content is tailored to the unique interests of each user will ensure targeted content and repeat traffic, and will sustain higher advertising rates.

▶ As a broadcaster, the company's core strength is in packaging and marketing content, not in e-commerce fulfillment and distribution, so specialist partners will be sought to manage this side of the e-business.

▶ As a broadcaster, the opportunities in interactive digital TV are huge, though it is going to be some years before this becomes commercially viable.

▶ The broadcaster's unique selling point (USP) is that it has access to airtime through which it can reach an audience of millions. This is the key weapon in the battle to get eyeballs to the site.

5.3 The Creative Solution

The communications brief, part of the project brief, will contain the information on target audience, design styles and guidelines, technical parameters, brand attributes, competitor activity, and creative likes/dislikes that allow the creative team to work on the creative solution. The Web strategy should be defined, as this is likely to provide further valuable information to the creative team as to the message they need to communicate to the target market.

5.3.1 The Creative Environment

At this stage the art director will be leading the creative process working with the client, the project manager, copywriters, and other design resources (illustrators, animators, and so on) as required. Programmers and commercial consultants are usually happy to work in isolation if need be, but the creative process works best when set in a creative environment embracing as many other creative stimuli as possible.

5.3.2 Brainstorming

It is likely that there will be larger group sessions to stimulate the creative process. One of the most effective ways of developing creative ideas is first to expand hugely on your ideas before contracting to a refined few. Expand by holding a brainstorming session. As many people as possible should attend, having received a brief on what to think about a few days before. Write everything and anything down as people suggest ideas, even if seemingly irrelevant, as it may spark a brilliant idea later. In the cold light of a following day, you should sit down with the core team and revisit the ideas from the brainstorming session to sanity-check them and measure them against the strategy, the limitations of technology, and, to a lesser degree, the likely cost of implementation if it is extravagant.

5.3.3 Brand Development

The amount of creative work that needs to be done will depend on how much work has already been done in defining the brand, name, identity, and look and feel of the site. Sometimes a third-party brand consultant will be brought in at this stage to develop the brand identity for the Web site. This may be an entirely new brand or an extension of the existing company brand.

TIP   **What's in a name?**

At this stage there may be several possible names that are being discussed for the online brand, if different from the offline brand. Check the proprietary status of all names you have come up with (a domain name registering agency such as *www.netnames.com* helps with this). Once a name is registered, it is unlikely you will be able to obtain it unless it clearly breaks your client's trademarks.

If key names are not registered, register them now. Undoubtedly the best way to avoid any problems with domain names is to make sure you register any names you might want to use as soon as you can.

With so much information on the Internet, and many losing faith in the search engines, a large proportion of users will try to find what they are after by guessing the site's URL. They will tend to try both top-level domain (TLD) and country-level domain variants of the name (e.g., .com and .co.uk) before resorting to a search engine or a directory. Any company should register potential domain names, even if they don't intend on having a Web site for the time being.

There has been a lot of talk surrounding new TLDs (such as .shop and .firm) and improved search mechanisms (such as Realnames), but in reality the majority of Internet users are only just putting a handle on the look and format of current URLs without being bombarded with yet more combinations. Go with what people are used to if you can.

Once a name has been settled on, you might also want to register names in the countries in which the client operates. Think also about domain names relating to the client's products, telephone numbers, slogans, and anything else by which the client's customers might know them.

5.3.4   The Look and Feel

As well as developing the online brand identity, the creative team needs to set the brand within a design concept that complements the brand attributes and dictates the overall "look and feel" of the site. Often this is done by mocking up several example pages from the site, in particular the site home page and the key section home pages of the site. If there are any sections of the site that will have a different look and feel (perhaps because they need to stand apart from the rest of the site to promote to a special product or appeal to a particular audience segment), representative pages from these sections should be mocked up as well.

5.3.5   The Tone and Editorial Voice

Thought needs to be given to the tone and editorial style of the copy on the site. Web copy tends to be shorter and more informal, and contain more calls to action, than traditional copy. This is because people do not read large amounts of text on-screen, and the Web is a one-to-one interactive medium. Interface and information design will also be touched on at this stage, although the functional specification and site map, created as part of the project specification, are needed before this can be fully fleshed out.

TIP   **It will look much better than this once it's done, of course …**

It is very costly and time consuming to produce fully programmed and interactive Web pages in order to present a design concept, and most disappointing if the design is then rejected. However, it is also difficult to convey the full excitement of the design without showing any on-screen interactivity. A good halfway measure is to create high-resolution JPGs of the screen mockups and then create basic HTML image maps that walk through a predetermined path demonstrating the site's interactive features. Present the graphics on a laptop. This way you will avoid spending unnecessary time on complicated programming, but it will still look like a Web site and you will benefit from the stronger colors you get on screen versus on paper.

The creative solution presented at this stage is not normally a working prototype or even a fully worked-up set of HTML pages. You might expect to produce color printouts of the identity designs and page mockups that are then presented verbally with a creative rationale. The feedback will then be incorporated into a second iteration of the design.

5.4   The Technical Solution

Much as you might fancy yourself a bit of a strategist or an inspired creative thinker, there are probably many elements of the technical solution you should be prepared to leave to the experts. On the other hand, you will have a fair degree of technical knowledge and will understand the basic concepts, and will probably have a much more in-depth knowledge of the particular systems and software you have incorporated in past projects.

Experience will also teach you that the details of the technical solution—even though you may not understand them at the outset, and even though the client might see them as boring and insignificant—are often one of the biggest causes of problems on a Web project. The devil is indeed in the technical detail. Whereas a design is ultimately a subjective piece of work that elicits subjective and emotive responses, the functionality made possible by the underlying technology is not subjective. If it doesn't work, it doesn't work, however you look at it.

At this stage the technical consultants on your team, who may be the advanced programmers working on the project, need to understand the site requirements and objectives in order to make some high-level technical recommendations. The detailed technical specification comes in the project specification once the recommendations have been reviewed and accepted.

5.4.1   Keeping Abreast of Technical Advances

Technology changes rapidly, and it is the job of technical consultants to keep abreast of change and up to date with the latest software products and developments that might benefit the project delivery teams by making their work faster, more error free, more flexible, and better matched to the evolving needs of the client.

5.4.2   The Responsibilities of the Technical Solution Team

The following are the types of areas you would expect technical consultants to define solutions for at this stage.

▶ A hosting solution: in-house or with an ISP, recommending the most suitable ISP
▶ Server hardware and software
▶ Server load capabilities and capacity planning
▶ Server and systems configuration
▶ Site architecture: front end, middleware, and back end
▶ Technical SLAs
▶ Escalation procedures in the event of a technical problem
▶ Research and development into new technologies; for example, mobile Internet and broadband Web applications
▶ Backup and data recovery procedures
▶ Testing strategy
▶ Definition of the development environment, programming protocols, and coding languages

▶ Recommendation of boxed versus proprietary application development

▶ Networking and connectivity

▶ Knowledge of leading software vendors' products and the ability to recommend

▶ Definition of code documentation standards

▶ Recommendations on how to implement required levels of security

▶ Interoperability; for example, with likely partners (e.g., content) and internal systems

▶ Assessment of specialist programming skills needed

▶ Job descriptions and training needs of technical staff needed to support site

The technical solution will typically be presented as a document or series of documents that include systems drawings, architectural diagrams, network infrastructures, and data-flow diagrams providing pictorial representations of proposed technical recommendations. Often these will mean little to the client if they are not technical. It is vital that a suitably qualified technical person reviews and agrees to the technical recommendations on the client's behalf. You must make absolutely sure the client is clear that these technical specifications are extremely important to the project, and that they must be comfortable having a nominated technical representative take responsibility for approving the specifications.

5.5   The Content Solution

Recognition of the importance of good content on Web sites has been steadily increasing. What used to be acceptable as a content offering is now no longer good enough. Site users expect to see a certain quality of content, and if they cannot find it on your site they will go elsewhere. Hence, you hear the much-used expression "sticky content," which refers to material that keeps users on your site.

You should have defined during the project clarification stages the key content areas to be covered. You should also have an idea about where this content might come from, and how the content should be updated.

5.5.1 Working with an External Content Provider

At this stage you will be looking into the content sources and the content formats in more detail. You might be talking to other Web sites or content providers, who can supply you with content in order to further explore the terms on which they are prepared to offer it. You should be asking yourself how well the content serves your customers' needs, whether or not if fits with your brand and editorial style, what are the costs, how reliable is the content feed, how often it is updated, and how well it integrates with your architecture.

If the site requires a lot of content that necessitates making deals with third parties, you will find this takes up a lot of time and requires contacts, content channel management knowledge, and contractual expertise that are beyond the abilities and expectations of a project manager. You will be working with an editor or commercial manager who will fill this role. You will be responsible, however, for making sure this person is furnished with all data-format and technical details necessary to negotiating appropriate deals. The technical team can inform you of these details if you are not sure.

5.5.2 The Importance of the Format of Content

If the client has referred to content she can provide, you should ask to see some examples of this content and get a precise definition of the format in which the content will be supplied. Often the client will not know what format the content is in, as it is not relevant to what they need to know. They may know only that the company has a customer details database, used at their call center, or that they have a company brochure that needs to be on the Web site.

It speeds up the project enormously if content arrives as expected. It can take a lot of time to convert files from Mac to PC; to scan in text and images; to obtain the correct fonts and pasteboard extensions to see, for example, a Quark file as it should be; to re-request files that were saved in too recent a version of the application for you to read; to create the necessary PDF files; and so on. Even more tricky are databases. It is rare that a database will arrive precisely as you imagined. Usually the most time-consuming part of creating a database-driven Web application is getting the data itself in the specified format and structure and getting it clean.

At this stage you should be very clear about how you should receive the content, and this should be reiterated in the assumptions that accompany the budget and timeline in the project specification. If you request some sample content or examine the database in question or talk to the people who create or work with the proposed content assets, you could be doing yourself and your client a big favor. Not only can you then be sure of what state the content is currently in, but you will get a feel for the likely speed at which the content is going to be supplied to you. This means that you can structure your project much more effectively.

5.5.3   Ensure Content Is Ready for Web Use

Think also about how the content is going to need to be adapted, edited, and abridged for the Web. It is all very well to put the company brochure on the Web, but the content might have been written for print and could seem very dry and formal on the site. Databases may be in the correct format and structure, but they may contain additional data or may not be sufficiently cleansed to use reliably for the Web application you have planned.

5.5.4   Start Content Creation and Preparation Early

Often there is no shortcut to creating or acquiring the content you need, so in some cases you should think about starting work on the content at this early stage. Often this can be done by the client and therefore does not raise questions of costs and contractual commitments between the Web development team and the client. Freelance journalists, researchers, editors, and data entry personnel can also be taken on by the client to begin work on the content.

If the client's business is in publishing, and they do not yet have an editor for the Web site, it is very likely they are going to need one. As with other key appointments the strategy might recommend, starting the recruitment process for any full-time editorial resources as early as possible is certainly advisable, as it is difficult to find good people quickly.

5.5.5   Defining Editorial Procedures and Update Mechanisms

There are many ways a site can be updated: there might be a Webmaster who performs updates directly at a code level; there might be content contributors who use WYSIWYG (what you see is what you get) HTML editors with a configured FTP function for making changes; the content might be stored in a database and updated via a form on a password-protected Web page; or a content management system might control the update process.

During the project clarification stage you will have obtained a good idea of what the client would like to see happening, how often, and by whom, where, and why. You now need to work with your technical team and content contributors (whether people or an automated feed from another system) to make sure a solution is defined that both team and contributors are satisfied will work.

5.6 The Project Management Solution

During this work stage you will be managing people with very different skills and knowledge to ensure they contribute to the project solution to the greatest extent possible. Don't forget, however, that this is also your opportunity to apply your expertise in running a project. This will be conveyed in what you do, but should also be documented in the project specification, albeit as part of an appendix.

Your document will contain the project method you intend to follow in general terms—hopefully not dissimilar to the method presented in this book. There are other steps you can take at this stage to start to put some of the theory into practice. The subsections that follow explore these steps.

5.6.1 Start to Involve the Implementation Team

It may be that the same people who have worked on the first two work stages will continue to the end of the preproduction phase and into the production phase. You should try to make sure that whoever is going to be working on the production team begins to have some involvement at this stage so that they will develop a sense of ownership in the project. If you merely present the solution and ask people to get on with it, they will understandably feel less valued.

5.6.2   Set Up Regular Meetings

You will be having regular meetings during the production phase to keep everyone up to date on the project status. Now is a good time to start to hold regular meetings with the team and client personnel involved in these pre-production work stages. Set a regular meeting time and make sure people commit to attending the meeting. This way they will form a habit, making it easier to assemble people on a regular basis once production has begun.

5.6.3   Team Agreements, Main Points of Contact, Reporting, and Sign-Off

At this stage you are mainly producing documents as your deliverables. They can be changed with relative ease and have less "hard-coded" interdependencies. However, it is good to begin to instill the discipline of signing things off to establish this practice for when it becomes more crucial in the production phase. This will get the client used to recognizing that change does not just happen automatically but has to be accounted for through a combination of time, cost, and quality changes. The client will see that they are going to have to take responsibility and make decisions throughout the project that cannot easily be reversed.

In establishing a sign-off structure and process, it will also become clear who has what authority. You can map out a team reporting structure and agree who the main points of contact should be, as well as who will be performing what functions throughout the project. If you are an external agency, it is usually during this work stage you begin to more clearly understand the internal politics, tensions, and personal agendas that may lie beneath the surface of the client organization. You will have to use your tact and client management skills to tread carefully through the minefields, but you should also be quite clear about what you need from the client team for the project to work.

5.6.4   Set Up Working Environment

Whether you are in-house, at an agency, or assembling a team of freelancers, you will need to define what the working environment for the project team is going to be. You will need to think through questions such as the following:

▶ *Physical location:* Should the entire project team be together? Should the team be on the client site or at the agency?

▶ *Tools and materials:* What does each team member need to do her job? What software, hardware, networking, Internet connectivity, and means of communication with the team do they have?

▶ *Management:* Is it clear who will be performing what role? Does each team member know who will be briefing them, and who they should go to with their work, questions, and problems?

▶ *Development environment:* Is there a production server set up to review work in progress? Is there a staging server and live server? Who has what access to the servers? How is version control being managed? How is work backed up? How are files structured?

TIP   **A project site**

Some project managers advocate the use of a project Web site to control project communications and to centralize the most important documents, files, and other project assets. There are some dangers with having such a site: if you don't keep it up to date or if some team members don't use it, it quickly becomes useless; it can cost a lot of time and money to set up, which the client is unlikely to pay for; if it malfunctions or doesn't look good (quite possible, as you don't want to spend money on its design), this can easily give the client a bad initial impression of the quality of your work; and it can give rise to security concerns, as confidential documents are potentially accessible from the Web server.

That said, if you are coordinating a virtual team that is not physically together, possibly spread across different countries, it can be a very useful tool. To get around the issue of how the site looks or how much time it costs to set up, use one of the free services available on the Web, such as *www.egroups.com*, where all necessary functionality is available and the design standardized.

5.6.5   Terms and Conditions of Work

Although any contract is more likely to be based on the project specification (which defines a set of deliverables) than another vehicle, you are already doing work that needs to be paid for, and you have agreed on a budget and schedule for the preproduction phase. If you have not already signed a contract of any type with the client, it is likely that contractual and payment discussions will now begin, before you have committed a large amount of resource time to the production phase. There will inevitably be negotiations on how payment is to be structured, what the agreed levels of service are, who owns the intellectual property rights to the work, and so on. The project specification should pin down these issues.

5.6.6   Fallback and Recovery Plans

It seems a little negative to be thinking about contingency plans and second options before the production phase has begun, but it is worth trying to look ahead and predict problems toward developing contingency plans to deal with them. For example, you might suspect that you will lose access to a significant amount of your resources at some stage and therefore might want to explore the availability of alternate resources.

5.6.7   Resourcing

If you know that the project is going to involve skills and resources you don't have readily available (particularly specialist programming skills), the sooner you start tracking down the right people the better. Equally you may need specialist illustration, animation, video, research, or copywriting talent. These are not areas you can fudge or try to do yourself, as the lack of quality will be painfully evident. The end result will only be as good as the worst element, so it is important that all elements work together to deliver outstanding quality.

As talented people with specialist skills tend to be in great demand, it is never too early to at least contact them and establish their availability. If you leave this until you actually want them to start, you greatly risk project delays.

5.7   Summary

The following areas are significant points raised in this chapter.

► In a pitch situation, the entire preproduction phase is condensed into a deliverable that seeks to show the client the quality of the work your company is capable of.

▶ A clear Web strategy is extremely important in guiding everything you do in the short term, as well as giving you a context within which to work toward longer-term goals.

▶ To arrive at the best creative solutions, you need people with a wide range of skills, the right working environment, and an understanding of what you are trying to achieve.

▶ Make sure that proposed technical solutions are agreed to with a client representative who understands the proposals and any implications they have.

▶ Content is the biggest cause of delay in Web project development. Make sure you define content formats, sources, delivery schedules, update mechanisms, and consequences of incorrect or late delivery.

▶ Establish your project management working practices at this stage.

So now it's all systems go? You are still not ready to go into production. First, you need to finish the preproduction phase by writing and agreeing on the project specification.

chapter 6

Work Stage 3: Project Specification

Be realistic: Stand back and look at the complete picture—it's easy to get carried away on your own thing.

Stick to your guns: ideas, ideas, ideas. Peoples' brains in this industry move quicker than their plans, so stick to your guns on your project or else you'll get distracted.

Check yourself: What could go wrong here? What can we do about it? Have something in place …
—**Lorraine Eaton, Account Manager, *www.douno.com*, U.K.**

Preproduction			Production			Maintenance	Evaluation
Project clarification	Solution definition	Project specification	Content	Design and construction	Testing, launch, and handover	Maintenance	Review and evaluation

T
he project specification covers in detail all of the things you need to have agreement on and documented before you start building the site. This chapter breaks down and explains what should be in the project specification. An example project specification can be downloaded from *www.e-consultancy.com/book*.

6.1   The Importance of the Project Specification

As far as actually implementing the site and running the Web project are concerned, the project specification is the most important document. Although it can bring together the work of a large team of people, it is ultimately the responsibility of the project manager to produce this document.

As a producer or project manager, it is your "bible," committing you to what you have to deliver, how and with what resources, and by when. As an account director or account manager, or as the client, it is your "bible" because it specifies what the agency or internal Web development team must deliver, by when, and for how much. A good project specification makes for a good project and a good product. If everyone has contributed to, read, understood, and signed off on the project specification, managing the project is infinitely easier. There should be no issues with what was and what wasn't included in the budget, for example.

6.1.1   The Importance to the Team

A good project specification improves team morale and commitment. Everyone can see what he or she has to do and why it is important that they do it well and on time: it is part of a greater whole the team is creating. Make sure you get everyone who is going to work on the project involved in contributing to the specification to enhance this sense of ownership and commitment.

The expertise needed to create the project specification should be held by the senior project manager on the team, with the input of other team members as necessary. If the project specification is well done, it should allow other project managers, producers, and development team members to pick up the project and run with it, as all of the elements are clearly explained and mapped out.

6.1.2   The Work Involved

As you can imagine, creating the project specification is quite a lot of work. For projects of a reasonable scale, it would be difficult to complete the project specification in less than two weeks. It is worth putting in this time up front, however, as it will save a lot more time and avert potential problems once the production phase has begun. Any issues and debates you need to resolve with the client should be gone through at this stage rather than later. You may feel uncomfortable doing this, as you have yet to produce anything tangible and are already raising issues. It is much better to fight any battles at this stage rather than further down the line, where they will be much more costly and ugly.

6.1.3   The Cost Involved

You will have quoted the time and cost in creating the project specification as part of your preproduction budget at the end of the project clarification work stage. The deliverable is the project specification itself, so if you have done one before, you can show it to the client for them to see more tangibly the value and importance of it. The more project specifications you do, the easier they are to do, as you will have a series of templates to work from. This will keep costs down, while maintaining speed and quality.

In our method, we have worked on the basis that the preproduction and production phase budgets are split. This is not always the case. Often clients will want a fixed budget for all work right from the outset. If at all possible, try to avoid this unless you can be absolutely sure of the amount of work involved. Keeping the budgets separate ensures that the development team will be paid for all work it does on the project specification, but it also benefits the client, who will only have committed to a limited initial cost exposure.

At the end of the preproduction phase, the development team and client can then agree on the main production phase budget. This can be fixed, with both sides confident of what will be delivered for the budget. What tends to happen during the preproduction phase is that the client begins to realize just how much work is involved in the project. This means that they will appreciate more easily why the production budget is as it is, or why it is higher than the budget put forward at the bidding stage (if relevant), which was based on a series of assumptions.

You might be concerned that if the preproduction phase is separated from the main production phase, as previously described, the client could take the project specification you create and take it around to other development teams to see who will produce it for the lowest cost. In practice, this is highly unlikely. Clients want to know above all that you can be trusted to do the work, and if you have done a good job so far, who better to implement the plan than those that devised it?

6.1.4 Contracts

Not all Web projects have a contract between the development team and client. The larger the project and bigger the client, the more likely there is to be a contract. The contract may be based on a number of things, but the project specification, with the deliverables it defines, is an obvious candidate. In many ways, it is good if this is the case because there is nothing like a legally binding contract to focus the attention on getting things right and doing them thoroughly!

6.2 The Content of the Project Specification Document

The particular nature of the project will dictate how much detail you need to go into for each section of the project specification, and will even define what sections need to be in the document. The items that follow cover all of the main elements you need to consider. Hopefully you can use this as a form of checklist and guide when putting together your own specifications. So, what should be included in the project specification? A sample specification might include the following:

▶ Version control
▶ Distribution list
▶ Contents
▶ Introduction
▶ Project objectives
▶ Success criteria → predictions in detail
▶ Site map

- ▶ Functional specification
- ▶ Technical specification
- ▶ Content plan
- ▶ Marketing initiatives
- ▶ Testing plan
- ▶ Site updates and maintenance
- ▶ Critical path
- ▶ Budget
- ▶ Appendix
  - · Credentials
  - · Project brief
  - · Project resources
  - · Design concepts
  - · Prototyping
  - · Assumptions
  - · Glossary of terms
  - · Methods
  - · Risk management
  - · Change control
  - · Intellectual property
  - · SLAs
  - · Terms and conditions

Read on to find out in more detail what each of these sections should include.

6.2.1   Version Control

The project specification is a living document. Changes and additions are made, and items are removed from it. As such, it is very important for you to keep a record of who has made what changes, and at what stage. This is particularly important when multiple authors are contributing to and controlling the document. If there is a contract based on the project specification, it is clearly also very important to establish what state the document was in when the contract was signed.

All you need is a version control table showing the document's history. Table 6.1, which follows, is an example of such a table.

Table 6.1 An example document version control table.

Version	Date	Author	Description
1.0	09.17.00	A. Friedlein	First draft version
1.1	09.20.00	A. Nother	Revisions to technical specification, especially hosting solution
1.2	10.04.00	A. Nother	Added e-commerce section to functional specification
1.3	10.14.00	A. Friedlein	Final amends and changes for contract

6.2.2 Distribution List

This simply shows who the project specification is being circulated to, and for what purposes that person is being sent the document. For example, there may be some on the list who are being sent the document for information only, whereas others need to sign off on the document.

A distribution list is important if you are dealing with a large organization, where not everyone working on the project will necessarily know each other. It facilitates internal communication and, for political reasons, helps show the level and importance at which the project is operating. If those contributing can see that there are senior people on the distribution list, you will better get their attention and prompt reply.

6.2.3 Contents

The project specification can become quite a tome. On larger-scale projects, about 80 pages is not an unusual length. In order to help the reader make his or her way around the document, and to facilitate discussion of the document, you should make sure the pages are properly numbered, the sections clearly labeled, and the content arranged and indexed in a sensible manner. The Contents page is the key navigational and orientation tool that aids readers in making the best sense of the document.

You might want to consider numbering sections as you would in a contract, so that you can refer, for example, to section 4.3.1 and everyone would be able to quickly find what you are talking about. Also include a header and footer on the document. The header should contain the name of the document, including the project title, and whether it is private, confidential, for internal use only, and so on. The footer should contain the page numbering, the version, the file name, and the date last edited. Including this header and footer information is important because single pages become separated from the main document. It will be instantly clear where the pages belong and whether or not you should be seeing them.

6.2.4   Introduction

This section serves primarily to outline the purpose and background of the document. It may also give some background to the project, and the parties involved and how they came together. For example, you might include a section such as the following:

> This document is a working document to which commercial, creative, technical, and editorial personnel involved in the project have contributed. It is intended to capture the detailed requirements and to document where appropriate outstanding considerations and questions.
>
> As each of these areas is explored and the project evolves, the document will be updated to reflect the current position. The document has been drawn up through project workshops and individual meetings, with the appropriate experts being consulted throughout.
>
> Subsequent changes to the project scope will need to go through formal change control, and, if approved, will be incorporated into the project specification, so as to provide an up-to-date and complete point of reference for all members of the project team.

6.2.5   Project Objectives

The project objectives will be set very much in the context of the Web strategy. The strategy may go beyond the specifications of the initial project, but the project objectives will be born of the strategic aims. What is this project trying to achieve and why?

You should also note here any dependencies on other projects. If this project forms part of a larger project, is part of a phased implementation, or exists only in relation to other projects, these contexts should be made clear.

Reiterate the key deliverables for the project and the key target release dates, and note any important intervening stages, such as a prototype release date or new system go-live date. Finally, if you would like to make clear what the project inclusions are, and perhaps more importantly what is specifically *excluded* (what you consider "out of scope"), do so here.

6.2.6   Success Criteria

It is important for you to specify as far as possible what the success criteria for the project are. This gives you yardsticks to measure by during the project, and gives you a structure and benchmarks against which you can conduct your project review. It is easier to feel good about the project if you can point to how it has met, or even exceeded, its expectations.

Some of the success criteria may even be tied to the contract; that is, contractually they have to be achieved. The rewards for the team members working on the project, both financial and for career progression, may also be tied to meeting stipulated success criteria.

As the Web is still a relatively new arena for business, it is less easy to define the benchmarks of success. There are fewer case studies to consult, fewer established patterns and trends, and more opportunity for explosive growth and change in the market. Many companies take a leap of faith and then measure the ongoing success of their Web venture relative to itself; that is, how it performs over time against certain metrics. You can break down the more common criteria for measuring the success of a Web project into direct and indirect benefits, as outlined in Table 6.2.

Where you can match numbers to success criteria, you should (e.g., page impressions and e-commerce sales targets). Don't try to be too ambitious, but do give fixed and quantifiable targets to aim for. Having these benchmarks and yardsticks helps your client assess the performance of the site and justify further expenditure where necessary. Don't overcommit to levels of success you can't deliver.

6.2.7   The Site Map

The site map is a visual representation of the content areas of the site, showing the various levels of content and how they relate to one another in the navigational hierarchy. It is a graphic representation of the site as a user would want it depicted to get an overview of where things are and how they relate to one another. You will probably be producing an HTML version of this site map to go on the site itself.

Table 6.2 The direct and indirect benefits of a Web business.

Direct (measurable) success criteria

E-commerce revenue: sales through the site

Leads generation: sales as a result of the Web site (e.g., customers visiting shop and telephoning)

New customers: the increase in the number of new customers provided by the Web site

Market share: the increase in market share attributable to the Web site

Shareholder value: the rise in share price attributable to your Web project

Site performance: uptime, availability, speed, lack of errors, lack of broken links, and so on

Page impressions: number of page impressions the site gets per month

Data capture: the value of data captured on visitors to the site; CRM value of finding out about unique users

Cost savings: streamlined processes; print, distribution, and telecommunications savings; and so on

Indirect (harder to measure) benefits

Building in-house expertise and skills for the developing e-business environment

Building relationships with other online businesses, suppliers, and contractors

Staff retention: your Web projects may be the reason talented staff stay

Extending customer reach to new markets

Seven days, 24-hour availability

PR and marketing value through awards, press coverage, and so on

Improved customer service

Competitor advantage

Improved staff morale: the organization is felt to be progressive, forward thinking

There are various software tools to help you create this site map (e.g., MS Organization charts and Visio), but all it really needs to be is a series of boxes, like a data-flow diagram, linked together at different levels, each with a name to briefly describe the content of that section.

Creating the site map should be done in conjunction with an information designer because in creating the site map you are also creating the navigational architecture designers will then use as the template to create their navigational system and interface. The site map does not attempt to show what the navigation system will look like or how the user will interact with the site. However, it does show how the content will be organized, what levels users would have to go through to get to a particular piece of content, and how many clicks they might then need to get somewhere else on the site. The site map may also influence the directory structure of the site, a detail that will be important to the Webmaster or whoever is going to be maintaining the servers.

To make the site map more informative, mark different content boxes in different styles (dashed lines, patterns, gradient fills, and so on), and create a legend to show what those markings mean. For example, there might be content that belongs to different phases of the project, static versus updated content, database versus flat-file content, third-party content feeds, and so on.

As the site map is easily digestible at a glance, and shows the skeleton of the site itself, you will find it is one of the things the client gets most excited about. Along with the budget and schedules . . .

For an example site map, go to *www.e-consultancy.com/book* and download the example project specification provided. The original was created in PowerPoint before being copied into Word.

6.2.8   The Functional Specification

The functional specification is a description of what the content is from a user's perspective. You might call it the "user experience document." It is not about why the content works or why it is there, but what exactly does it do? If you were a user coming to the site, how would you describe what the Web page does?

It is also a good idea to include some suggestions for future content. This will show you are already thinking ahead, being proactive on behalf of your client, and will begin to sow the seeds of possibility that will hopefully germinate into more work for your development team.

You should try to include the total number of pages for content. It is difficult to be precise at this stage, and "pages" can be misunderstood: is that an HTML page, which might be long and scrolling with internal page links, or a "screen's worth" the user sees without scrolling? The client usually understands the latter as a "page," so it is probably best to use this and approximate.

The reason for giving the number of pages for each piece of content in the functional specification is just to check that you and the client are imagining roughly the same proportional amount of content between the sections.

Some clients think they are getting more for their money if they get more pages. This is a fallacy you need to explain. Creating applications and interfaces is what is expensive, as can be the content itself. Ten pages of HTML text as displayed from a Web-enabled database will cost almost the same as one line from that database. More content doesn't always make for more traffic or a better site. Targeted, quality, functionally rich content does. Padding content is worse than no content at all.

As an example, on the site map for a bank's Web site there may be a box that says "Mortgage Calculator." In the functional specification you might explain this further as follows:

> The mortgage calculator will be a single page with an interactive calculator function that allows the user to calculate their mortgage repayments. The user can choose to configure the calculator using the bank's currently offered interest rate (which will be updated daily by the Webmaster) or they can input their own rate. The user can also choose between different types of mortgage offered by the bank, and alter the repayment period to see how this will affect monthly repayment amounts. There will be direct links to the relevant mortgage products from this page.
>
> At this stage, the calculator will only return monthly repayment amounts and will only give dollar values. It is envisaged that future developments will allow the user to calculate the maximum mortgage available to them, as well as to input other monthly outgoings that can be added to the mortgage repayments to help users balance their personal finances. This will help position the bank as the first point of contact for all personal finance matters and show that the bank recognizes that every person's situation is unique.

The functional specification (which defines content and functionality as born of user requirements) and the site map (which defines the navigational architecture) are the two key documents that form the basis for briefing your technical and creative resources. Most importantly, the functional specification should be detailed enough to allow the members of your team to accurately quote the amount of time they will need to implement what is specified. The better the functional specification, the more accurate the budget.

6.2.9   The Technical Specification

For the project managers, and certainly the programming team, the technical specification is arguably the most important part of the project specification to get right the first time. Whereas many of the other elements can be changed, even at a late stage if absolutely necessary, or are subject to interpretation, the technical specification contains only hard facts. A mistake in the technical specification is quite unequivocally a mistake and can cause havoc in a project.

In many cases the technical specification will mean very little to the client, riddled as it is with abbreviations and terminology. It is *very important* that a suitably qualified technologist representing the client is involved in ratifying the technical specification and that the client understands the importance of this. The following are the elements a technical specification should cover.

▶ Technical architecture
▶ Security
▶ Server specification
▶ User machine specification
▶ Other

The subsections that follow take a look at the items in the previous list in more detail.

Technical Architecture

The technical architecture differs from the site map, as it does not show what the user will see but the technical infrastructure needed to provide the "user experience," as defined in the functional specification. The technical architecture will be defined by your team's site architect in conjunction with any technical consultants and advanced programmers who have been working on the project. In some cases, the entire site might consist only of HTML files sitting on a Web server. In this case, the site architecture is only really the file and directory structure of the site.

As sites gets larger, the architecture will become more of a network diagram showing how the front end will integrate with the middleware and back- end systems, and what connectivity and security is in place. Figure 6.1 shows the technical site architecture for an e-commerce ordering and fulfillment system.

Security

Working with technical consultants, you will define here what is going to be put in place to meet the required levels of security defined in the project

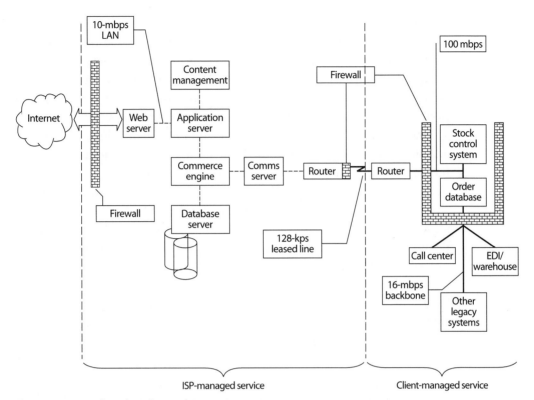

Figure 6.1 Example technical site architecture.

brief. You will need to specify the methods and technology you are using, and the level of security attained (e.g., encryption bit strength).

The goals you are likely to be trying to achieve are data integrity, user authentication, and other forms of validation using SSL, Java, firewalls, PGP, digital certificates, and so on. Standards and methods (e.g., SET and PKI) have been developed, which you can follow here.

Server Specification

In this section your technical team will specify the technical environment for the server, including host, hardware, and software to handle the antici-pated load (in particular, simultaneous user sessions) to a defined level of performance.

The site may be hosted by the client or by an ISP. Most commonly it is the latter. Using an ISP is usually recommended, as it takes the burden of 24-hour hosting and technical support away from the client and places the onus of responsibility on a third party, who should be experts in this field. It is worth paying for quality hosting so that you are guaranteed reliable and fast site performance, good technical support, and scalable solutions.

Choose an ISP that offers an SLA that commits them to levels of support and site uptime. Make sure they perform backups of the server, and that they have a defined escalation procedure to alert the relevant people in case of a problem, plenty of bandwidth that can be allocated as needed to cover traffic spikes, an easily scalable service offering, and a suitably flexible charging structure. In many cases the development team will be asked by the client to recommend an ISP, so you can often choose to work with a company that has proved efficient and reliable in the past.

In addition to choosing an ISP, your technical team will also specify the hardware and software for the server. What operating system (generally a UNIX or NT box)? How many processors? How much memory? How much hard disk storage space? What additional software will need to be on the server? How many servers will there be, how will they be clustered, what load balancing will be used, and so on?

As a rule, the more powerful the server, the more the hosting will cost, as the ISP will be expecting greater bandwidth usage. Extra processors and extra memory deliver the greatest improvements in server performance, as server load can be better balanced and managed.

The biggest jump in cost, and hence biggest decision to be made, is going from sharing disk space with other sites on the same server to having your own dedicated server(s). If the site is fairly small and not too complex functionally, and the budget is not large, shared space will be fine. It does impose quite a few limitations, however, that the client should understand. If they want to boost functionality in the near future, it might be better to go with a dedicated server straight off. With a dedicated server, you can

▶ have total remote control of the machine;

▶ install any software you want on it;

▶ restart the machine;

▶ configure the Web server, FTP, and other servers exactly how you want; and

▶ configure the hard drives, fine-tune elements of the operating system, set up log file analysis reports on the server, and create password-protected areas using the system's security administration features.

You can do all of this without going through the ISP or risking interfering with other companies' sites. Virtual servers give you a fairly high level of control, including some of the elements previously listed, but you still only have virtual control as defined and limited by the ISP.

You should also specify what server-side technologies and interfaces you are, or are not, supporting. This would include ASP, database connectivity standards (JDBC, ODBC, and so on), Java servlets, JavaScript/Jscript, XML, JSP, CGI/Perl, ISAPI/NSAPI, and CORBA.

User Machine Specification

As there are so many configurations of hardware, software, and connectivity users' machines might be coming to your site with, it is very important that you specify minimum user machine requirements. In the same way that all software comes with minimum system requirements, you should make minimum (and recommended) specifications so that you can limit the scope of the testing you will need to do, and can design and code the site to make the most of the capabilities your specified user machine has. The following are user machine capabilities you should consider.

Screen resolution, color depth, and monitor size: Screen resolution is of the most important items to specify. The lowest common denominator is 640×480, so if you wanted to be sure to cater to absolutely anyone, you would need to go for this. However, this resolution does not give you much screen space to play with. It is increasingly rare for anyone to view at this resolution, and the site could appear comparatively small at the most common resolution of 800×600.

All new computers sold within the last few years have graphics cards capable of at least 800×600 display. Most can go higher, but users never realize that the settings can be changed and therefore stick to the default. It would be very unusual at present to design a site specifically for users viewing at 1024×768 or higher. Remember that many users browse without their browser window maximized. As a result, it is standard to optimize the design for 800×600 viewing. Depending on the nature of how the site is constructed, this does not mean it won't work at other resolutions. If the site is based on tables that fill a percentage width of available space, the content will scale accordingly. If, however, your design hinges on fixed width content, make sure you explain to the client what will happen at lower resolutions, which is usually many scrollbars.

Deciding on screen resolutions should be made easy by the Web strategy. If your target audience is the home user and you have an entertainment site, you won't need to worry about slow or old equipment, as home users tend to be up to the eyeballs in the latest whiz-bang technology.

It is worth specifying the minimum monitor size so that you don't get caught by users who have a perfectly good graphics card but an ancient and tiny monitor that adversely affects how they see the site. Also confirm how you intend to use color. Are you only going to use Web-safe colors, or are you going to use thousands, even millions, of colors and allow them to dither where users are viewing at a lower color depth? Again, think of your target audience and decide what the benefits are of upping the minimum spec versus catering to the lowest common denominator.

User operating system (OS): Again, this is very important: you need to define which operating systems the site you develop will work on. Be very wary of just saying it will work on all operating systems or allowing yourself to commit to this. Don't just specify the operating system, make clear whether you are talking about the 16-bit or 32-bit version, and which release. In some cases you may even need to specify a release that has particular service patches or bug fixes with it. For example, you would be unlikely to say that the site will work on all Windows PCs. You should be more precise and say, for example, that you are not supporting the 16-bit Windows 3.x OSs but are supporting Windows 95/98/2000 and NT 3.51 or higher with Service Pack 2.

Typically, Windows and Macintosh OSs are supported to varying degrees. Windows systems account for about 93% of the Internet user market, with Macs at 5% and the other 2% represented by all the rest. For some specialist sites, it might be worth including various flavors of UNIX or other less common user machine OSs. The more operating systems you support, the more testing time you will need. Adding just one build of one release of one other OS could mean going through the entire site another five times on different browsers, even 15 times if you are checking the design integrity at three different screen resolutions.

CPU/RAM: It may not seem relevant at first, but it is worth specifying a minimum CPU/RAM requirement of any user machine. If your site requires a lot of the user machine's processor (e.g., when scaling vector graphics), you will notice that the site that runs wonderfully on your programmer's supercomputer hardly runs at all on an old and slow machine.

Likewise, if your site requires a version 4 (or higher) browser, the browser application alone will require a certain amount of RAM to perform properly, particularly if the user is multitasking with other applications.

Audio: Will the site use sound? If so, what format will the sound be in? WAV, AU, AVI, MOV, embedded into Flash, or streaming audio? Is the use of sound merely for effect, or is it necessary to use of the site? If so, you will need to stipulate that users' computers have a sound card and speakers.

Video: Are you planning to have video clips available on the site? Will they be streamed, provided as downloadable files, or both? What file formats are you planning to use? This will define what plug-ins, software, or hardware the user will need to have to view the content. Connection speeds (discussed later in this chapter) are particularly important when considering the quality of streamed video playback over the Web.

Browsers: Along with operating systems, the browsers you specify for the site make a huge impact on the amount of work you will have to do on the site, particularly at the testing stage. Browser incompatibilities are the bane of the Web developer's life. Working on an intranet (where you can specify a single, up-to-date browser) is a godsend compared to the mire of potential bugs and problems born of the browser wars.

Although there are other browsers (e.g., Opera), the two browsers you will generally want to recommend are those developed by Netscape and Microsoft. You should specify release and build version. It is rare now to specify anything lower than Navigator 2.0 and Internet Explorer 3.0, as both are capable of displaying frames and both support JavaScript, though in slightly different ways. It is more common to talk of a site catering to version 3 browsers, although there are increasingly fewer people still using browsers as old as this.

As the first versions of a new release can be buggy, specify IE 3.02 and Navigator 3.04 as minimum for version 3 browsers. Anything higher and there are usually fewer problems. Increasingly there is a shift, being pushed by developers and software manufacturers, to no longer support version 3 browsers but only versions 4 and higher. Home users will tend to have the latest browsers. It is usually large corporations with reticent and wary IS departments who will be using older browser technologies. Version 4 browsers obviously allow you to do a lot more (using DHTML, for example), and with the advent of XML (which IE 5 first supported) sites will be able to do even more with the right browser.

Be very aware of how frustrating it is for a user if the site you develop does not work in their browser. Although IE is the industry leader, there is nothing more irritating for a Netscape user than to be told that the site is optimized for IE, or, even worse, that the site doesn't work properly or crashes with Netscape. If WebTV users can't order things from your online store due to a JavaScript bug, you will lose customers. Experience will teach you the pitfalls of the various browsers, allowing you to avoid the most common conflicts.

You can, of course, detect the browser a site user has and deliver site content to suit that browser. This is fine, but be aware of the time (and therefore, cost) implications that doing this for all pages across several different browsers could entail.

Plug-ins: Plug-ins can be used both on the user machine and server side to enhance the user's experience of the site in some way. They are almost all freely downloadable, but you will again need to look to your Web strategy, target audience, and browser specification to decide on your policy regarding plug-ins. If you think the vast majority of your site users will have version 4 browsers, there is less of an issue with using plug-ins such as Flash or RealPlayer, as they will usually have been installed with the browser.

JavaScript, Java, frames, cookies, and scrolling: You may or may not intend to use some or all of these elements in the site, but you need to specify whether it is acceptable to do so, and the client needs to understand and agree to what you propose. If you are going for version 3 browser support and higher, you will not have any problems with the browsers not being able to handle any of these technologies, though the extent of each browser's implementation and support for the technology varies. However, there are many other considerations in deciding if and how you are going to use these elements, not least that JavaScript, Java, and cookies won't work at all if the user has them disabled in their browser settings.

What is important for the technical specification is that you cover all possible technical parameters so that you know what you can and cannot do. If the client has agreed to the project specification, including the IS department giving the go-ahead to the technical specification, they cannot come back at a later stage and make you change the entire site from a frame-based site to a table-based one without at least paying you to do so.

TIP   **To use frames or not to use frames? That is the question.**

The browser compatibility argument is increasingly less valid these days, as frames are supported by Navigator 2 and Internet Explorer 3 and up, which themselves are old browsers by any standard. The reasons to use frames usually hinge on ease of navigation and limiting the need for scrolling. These are valid reasons. However, there are reasons not to use frames, which are not always taken into account but can be very important.

- *Bookmarks:* Bookmarking pages is more difficult with frames, as the URL is not page specific. Workarounds are possible but are more complicated.
- *Site speed:* The site can be slightly slower, as more requests for separate HTML pages are being sent to the server to make up a single screen view.
- *Search engines:* Many search engines' robots cannot spider and index frame-based sites. It is more difficult to submit specific pages with targeted keywords and body text (called "portal" or "doorway" pages, often used for promoting a specific product) if the page belongs in a frame set.
- *Links:* Again, because of the URL, it is trickier (though still possible) to give external sites a direct link to a particular page within your site if it needs to be part of a frame set containing multiple pages.
- *Printing:* Browsers will print the frame that has focus by default. This could lead to confusion for some users.
- *Statistical reporting:* The more frames there are, the more difficult it is to accurately track usage across a site and give credible page impression figures.
- *Banner ads:* If you plan to have banner ads on your site, you should think twice before having a frame-laden site. Advertising space is most often sold by CPM (cost per thousand) page impressions. A page impression is registered by the ad server software every time a new banner is loaded. If you have no frames, it is easy, as every link to a new page will refresh the banner ad. If you have a few frames, it is trickier but still quite possible to refresh the banner ad page when

the user goes to each new section. With many frames, however, the frame targeting and page refreshing becomes much more complex and messy, possibly resulting in cross-browser and scripting issues, along with lost revenue due to the banner ad not always properly refreshing.

- *Programming:* The more frames there are, the more difficult it becomes to keep track of all the HTML files and make cross-site changes. File and site management in general becomes less easy.
- *Content management systems:* Large, information-driven sites that use content management systems to dynamically publish content on the Web don't tend to use frames, as they fit poorly with the way the software works.
- *Padlock and key:* If you use frames, be aware that in order for the browser padlock to close or key to become whole, showing users that they are on a secure page, *all* pages within the frame set need to be secure. If the page that takes the credit card details is secure, but others in the frame set are not, the padlock will remain open, giving users the impression that their credit card details are not going to be securely transmitted.

Connection speeds: State what you would expect to be the most common connection speed for a typical site user. Is it likely to be a 56.6-kps dial-up connection, only 28.8 kps, or will it be ISDN or an office LAN connection? If you have specified 33.6 kps, for instance, you can explain why the site seems so slow over a 14.4-kps modem.

Other

There may be additional information worth including, or that is required by the client. If a Webmaster is to be employed by the client to update the site, you might want to include a job description detailing the skills that person will need, along with a specification for the PC and software the Webmaster will need to do the job.

You might include a section describing your code documentation practices and file naming conventions if this is not part of your technical method documentation included in an appendix. You might also want to detail the manufacturers of any specified software, including customer support contact information for each. SLAs for each should be contained in an appendix.

In regard to domain names, we have already discussed how important it is to check the status of all relevant domain names and register any that are available. Here you could document the current status for all relevant names.

6.2.10   The Content Plan

The content plan specifies who will be providing the content described in the functional specification. It should also define what format they should provide the content in, who they should provide the content to, and how often they will update the content and to what deadlines. Some content will be created new, some content will be repackaged for the Web, and other content may be syndicated or taken directly into the site as a content feed from a third-party supplier. These are all issues you should have raised in the first work stage, found a solution for in the second work stage, and are now setting down in this document.

If you are using a content management system or interface for middleware or back-end systems beyond your control, make sure the client understands what you as the development team can and cannot do, what you can be responsible for, and what the third party has control over. In most cases the client will have a separate contract and/or SLA with the third party that defines the nature of that party's service, level of commitment, technical support, and so on. If there is a major bug in the content management software, or if a data feed is suddenly cut off, you can notify the client and help resolve the problem, but as you did not create the software or content you cannot, and certainly should not, try to remedy the problem directly.

6.2.11   Marketing

Increasingly site owners are realizing the importance of marketing their site. Putting up a site and waiting for those millions of online users to arrive doesn't work. With ever more sites competing for user eyeball time, the marketing and promotion of the site is a vital component to its success.

Online and Offline Traffic Generation Techniques

There are all sorts of ways a site can be marketed. Offline you can incorporate the site's URL on all corporate stationery; print it on the side of the company's vehicles (the airline EasyJet famously painted their URL in huge letters on the side of their airplanes); and print it on shopping bags, receipts, or anywhere else customers might see and remember it.

You can hold competitions where the answer is on the Web site, have parties in an Internet Café, and give a prize to the 1000th site visitor. Traditional means such as print, radio, TV, billboards, and direct mail can all form part of an integrated site marketing campaign. Online you can use banner advertising, site sponsorship, mutual site links, Usenet, search engines, and directories (to name but a few of the more common ways) to attract traffic.

The Importance of Marketing Funding

If the site *is* the business and you are relying on the e-commerce revenue created by it, you should count on spending significantly more on marketing the site than creating it. Putting together an integrated marketing campaign to promote your site may require specialist skills (such as online media buying and planning), which larger agencies will have in-house and smaller agencies will obtain by partnering with another company.

TIP   **A tip for the top**

Don't promise you'll get your client's site to appear at the top of every search engine result for a search on their company name or related keyword. It can't be guaranteed. On the major search engines, you can buy the right to have your banner ad appear against a particular word search, but not the right to have your URL appear foremost in search results. For a great site for all things to do with search engines, go to *www.searchenginewatch.com.*

The precise details of the marketing campaign may not be known at the project specification stage, but an outline of likely initiatives should at least be drawn up in order to set aside some budget for it. If there are to be marketing initiatives that build over time—such as a campaign built around a countdown to launch—these will need to be considered and implemented much sooner in the process. Some of the simpler and more common marketing initiatives, such as registering the site with the search engines, should be done as a matter of course, but you still need to account for them in the budget.

6.2.12   QA and Testing

This section details your quality assurance (QA) and testing plan for the site. The testing strategy will largely be put together between the project manager and technical consultants. Where there is a quality assurance manager, clearly they will lead this element.

You will probably test site elements as you develop them. It is often difficult, however, to do the final testing yourself because you have been so intimately involved with the product that you may overlook problems that someone with a fresh pair of eyes will immediately see. Consequently, it is quite common for specialist external testers to come in to do the testing. If so, they will have a testing strategy you can refer to here.

There are many forms of QA and testing you might want to include. These are looked at in more detail in Chapter 9, but in outline they include the following:

▶ User acceptance/usability testing
▶ Scenario testing/load testing
▶ Security/penetration attack testing
▶ Copy proofing
▶ Functional/operational testing

Whatever the level of testing you decide to go for, the following are the two most important things you should try to ensure.

▶ Insist on leaving room in the schedule for testing. Do not be tempted to eat into this time. Try to ensure at least two clear weeks for testing of any project of reasonable size.
▶ Make it clear that the testing phase is used to test for functional and operational problems, not as an opportunity to make further changes to the content or functionality.

6.2.13   Updates and Maintenance

Once you are into the heat of the site production phase, it is difficult to make time to think about what happens after the site has launched. It is acknowledged, however, that if you want site visitors to come back you need to keep the content of the site up to date. Nothing looks less professional than a site whose content is clearly very old. It is better not to have a site at all than create such a negative impression on your would-be customers. You can be sure that site visitors who find old content, or get the impression that the content is never updated, will not return to the site.

As with most business, it is much more costly and time consuming to gain new customers than it is to retain existing ones. After all of the effort of launching and marketing the site, you really don't want to lose all of your hard-earned customers and have to continually rely on new ones to view content that never changes.

What You Need to Cover

The functional specification defines what content will be dynamic and how often it will be updated. The content plan specifies who will provide the content, and how often and in what format. What the content plan does not specifically cover is general site maintenance issues (such as fixing broken links and bugs, making minor text changes, adding the occasional new graphic, and reporting on site traffic) or who will be responsible for implementing entirely *new* sections of content and functionality. Whereas the content plan is for the editorial team, this section is aimed more at defining the responsibilities of you and your development team.

6.2.14   Critical Path

The client will understandably be interested in when they can have their site. As large companies suddenly wake up to the importance of a successful online presence, the delivery date(s) are sometimes of more interest to them than the budget. The sections that follow explore issues related to the critical path.

Controlling Delivery Deadlines

If you work in an agency environment, you will recognize that from the client and account teams' points of view, the sooner the site can be delivered the better. The client wants the site up, and the account team wants the billings. Whereas it is ultimately up to the account director to decide how much the agency charges for the site, it is up to you and your development team to define how long it is going to take to deliver the project. It is important that you keep deadlines realistic, or you will begin to compromise on quality, skip testing, hack together code, and stay up all night and weekend in a desperate bid to cobble together the promised site in time. This will only lead to worse problems later, as bugs surface on the site, a client complains they never had

Heuristics Search, Inc., *www.heur.com.*

time to sign something off and want it changed free of charge, and your talented resources leave to work somewhere less pressurized.

The quality of the planning and the people working on the project are what decide how fast the project can be delivered without sacrificing quality. Throwing extra resources at a project rarely makes it happen any faster or better. As a producer or project manager, you need to fight for your corner, to get the schedules you need to deliver the project, as it will ultimately be you who is first called to account if project schedules begin to slip.

How to Create the Critical Path

The most important thing in putting together a critical path, in addition to the budget and most elements of the project specification, is to consult the people who are actually going to be doing the work. You should brief designers, programmers, and copywriters as precisely as you can on what is required, and ask them to tell you how long they think it will take. It will then be your experience as a Web project manager, as well as your knowledge of whether the individuals tend to under- or overestimate time, that allows you to make a final quote. If the budget and schedules are not a problem, obviously you are always safer if you overestimate quotes. It is sensible practice in any case to give yourself margins in which to maneuver in all aspects of a project. Individuals tend to quote on how long it will take to do the work *their* way, without allowing for the fact that a client may not like what they have done and will require modifications. Often they will fail to build testing time into their quotes. Make sure you do allow for this extra time in your critical path.

Tools That Can Help You with the Critical Path

The best way to develop the critical path is in the form of a Gantt chart. You can do this by using Excel and filling in cells as necessary, but it is far easier to use a dedicated tool such as MS Project to create and maintain the critical path. As long as you can create a list of tasks, assign who is going to do them, know how long they will take, and which tasks are dependent on which other tasks, project management software tools such as MS Project will create the Gantt chart for you. You can then easily maintain and tweak the critical path during the course of the project. You can input how much of a task is complete, which is then visually represented on the chart. There are a lot of other functions MS Project and other project management software tools provide (e.g., budget and meeting management tools), which you may also want to use.

Critical Path as a Visual Aid

What is most important is that you have a visual map of how the project should progress. This will become an extremely important point of reference for the entire team once production begins. You will immediately be able to compare where you are with the project against the critical path, to see how behind or ahead of schedule you are. For the production phase, the critical path is the all-seeing overlord that governs you and your team. The client will be most interested in the key milestones and care less about how things get done on a day-to-day basis. For you as a project manager, however, monitoring how things get done on a daily basis is the lifeblood of your job. If the critical path is clearly thought through and adhered to, the project will be delivered as promised, on time and to budget, and that, as we have seen, is a very large part of what being a project manager is all about.

Milestones, Meetings, Sign-Off, and Hot Spots

Apart from showing task times in the critical path, there are several other elements you should include: key milestones, meetings, and sign-off points. Key milestones give both the agency and the client yardsticks by which they can measure progress. They represent deadlines within the context of the final delivery deadline, and give everyone on the project something to work toward and achieve. It is easier and more motivating to work toward a series of smaller targets than to worry about one large end goal looming sometime in the future. Success by the inch rather than the mile, it has been called.

Meetings should be a part of the critical path so that they are formalized, with everyone aware of them and making sure they set aside time to attend. Sign-off points are in themselves milestones. If they too are formalized in the critical path, it is clear when they need to happen, who needs to perform the sign-off, and what impact it will have on the project if these things don't happen.

One final section to include in the critical path is a "hot spots" list, which represents the highest risks on the project. You will usually be working to tight deadlines, but there will be particular elements you know are critical to the success of the project. It is very important to point these out to the client. For example, you may need a database of information from one of the client's partner businesses, without which you cannot start an entire section. The client has a lot of work to do on their end, and by listing the hot spots you help them prioritize what they need to do to help you out. The hot spots can be maintained and updated as a rolling list of risks with associated controls and actions during the production phase of the project.

6.2.15 Budget

Try as you might, placing the budget near the end of the project specification is unlikely to stop the client from flipping to the back of the document and scanning to find the bottom-line figure. I have yet to see a client who falls off her chair because the total budget is so much lower than she had expected.

Provide as Much Detail as Possible

It is important to provide as much detail in the budget as possible, breaking down the total into component costs to show how the total was arrived at. As well as giving the detailed breakdown, you should also give subtotals, or totals for different phases, to give a broader overview of the costs involved. It is up to you how you charge for materials used in creating the project. Usually material costs will be included in the daily rates, though you would budget separately for hardware and software required specifically for the project. Whether you make a provision for costs such as travel, photocopying, printing, and so on will depend on your relationship with the client. You can either itemize these or include them under a labor cost.

Most agencies charge for their time, and different people will be charged at different hourly or daily rates. Agencies rarely hand out rate cards, as different clients will be charged different rates, depending on what they have negotiated with the account director. For a large amount of business, the daily rate will typically be lowered. There is almost always an internal rate card, however, that project managers, producers, and account managers will work to when creating budgets. This ensures that a project does not lose the agency money. In the budget breakdown you should itemize how much time a particular resource is spending on a particular section, along with a corresponding cost. The cost divided by the time gives the rate per day/hour charged for that resource.

You will find that the greater the detail you give in breaking down the costs, the easier it is to justify the budget. The client will see that you have not just picked a figure out of the air but have carefully costed every element. They will see just how much work is involved and appreciate all of the things you are doing that may not have been explicitly discussed so far in the project.

For example, in the testing and launch phase, you might put in some time for creating a list of meta-tag keywords and a meta-tag description of the site with the client, and then submitting the site to the search engines. This is clearly something the client will appreciate, but it will require some expenditure of time over and above everything else being done. However, it is not likely to be uppermost in their minds, so remember that it would be more difficult for them to swallow a lump sum budget, into which this would have been included, than an itemized budget detailing this as one of the elements.

Structuring the Budget

It is helpful to break down the budget into key areas that reflect the phases and elements of the project, such as the following:

▶ Preproduction
▶ Production
▶ Testing and launch
▶ Site updates and maintenance
▶ Hosting, software, and hardware costs
▶ Other costs (e.g., copyright fees, expenses, legal fees, next phase costs, marketing and advertising funding, cost of management time, opportunity cost, and so on)
▶ Assumptions accompanying the budget
▶ Schedule of payments

You should break down the costs for each of these areas, giving each phase a subtotal. Often clients will want to take a "shopping list" approach, whereby they can see their options costed out and then pick and choose the elements they want based on price and perceived value. This creates more work for the project manager, as several permutations of various options need to be thought through and costed. It is also not always possible to pick and choose content, as some content may depend on other content, some costs may be lower as they assume the functionality has already been developed elsewhere in the site. A fair amount of cost is incurred before any of the site content is delivered in the preproduction phase (and in hosting, software, and hardware).

The "Other costs" section is important to remember, as it could contain considerable sums if, for example, there is to be a large marketing push or sizeable copyright fees are incurred. These other costs arise as a result of activities surrounding the creation and maintenance of the site. Often they will not even be paid to your development team. Hosting costs will usually be paid directly to the ISP, copyright fees to the copyright owner, legal costs to the lawyers, and so on.

Assumptions Accompanying the Budget

The assumptions accompanying the budget are very important and could turn out to be a lifesaver, or rope with which to hang yourself, in the event of any dispute. The assumptions can cover areas such as the following:

▶ Tax
▶ Ownership of intellectual property for the site
▶ Provision of content/formats and deadlines

▶ Penalty clause exceptions
▶ Author's errors and omissions
▶ Payment terms
▶ Expenses
▶ Budget based on project specification as of a particular date
▶ Extent of any prototypes
▶ Levels of client resource commitment

Schedule of Payments

The schedule of payments specifies how the client will be invoiced for the full amount over the life of the project. Whether this is accepted will be a matter for discussion with the client. Not surprisingly, an agency will want to be pre-paid for work, and/or as they are doing it, and the client will want to pay for work once it is done and they are happy with it. There is no answer to how this should work; it will depend on what can be agreed to, and the nature of the relationship between the client and the development team. The longer the relationship, and the greater the trust and goodwill present, the more flexible both sides will be.

Accurate Budgeting Skills

Putting together the budget and the critical path are probably the two most worrying responsibilities for the project manager. This is understandable, as time and money are rather fundamental to any business, any project, and any job. You get them right, and you do well and make a profit. You get them wrong, and you lose your job or go bust. Actually, it's not always quite that harsh; there is some margin for error, particularly if you are learning. The project isn't always a matter of commercial life and death for the client's business.

However, it is generally you personally and the client who have most to lose by getting the budget terribly wrong. Either you will have to swallow huge costs and wipe out any profit margins, or your client will lose face internally, which certainly won't endear you to him or her.

The project specification should, by defining its deliverables, clearly define the level of expectation the client has of the project. How do you ensure the budget fits the cost of achieving these deliverables? Summarized in Table 6.3 are some of the ways you might be able to improve the accuracy of your budgeting.

Table 6.3 Tips on creating accurate budgets.

Budgeting recommendation	Explanation
Give yourself a buffer zone	It's always a good idea to add a little to the time and budget quotes you generate to give yourself room for error. Depending on your relationship with the client, you could hide this buffer zone in the quotes themselves, or you could be more open and include a contingency in your fees. Typically this would be 10 to 15% for a Web project.
Make your budget as detailed as possible	Force yourself to go into as much detail as possible on the budget. This is not just for your client's benefit but for your own, to try to eliminate the risk that you are overlooking anything. Often you will find that when you add up the smaller costs it comes to more than you would originally have estimated for the total cost.
Maintain a catch-all template budget	Keep a template budget that details every cost element possible in a Web project. As you do new projects and come across new cost areas, add to your template so that you build up a Frankenstein monster of a thing that you can use as a checklist for all possible cost areas you need to consider when putting together a project budget.
Talk to the project resources involved	We discussed this in putting together the critical path. Your largest costs will probably be related to time people spend working on the project. To ensure you get an accurate cost, talk to the people who will be doing the work to get their quote; don't guess on their behalf. Then use your discretion and experience to adjust their quote; that is, usually to increase it.
Get the assumptions right	See the previous subsection for more details on assumptions. They really are very important; less so in getting the budget right the first time but more in making sure that, if you have got it wrong, you have escape routes for adjusting it.
Have your budget checked by others	Swallow your pride and make sure that others, ideally more experienced than yourself, look through your budget to check you have covered all necessary areas. This spreads the responsibility for getting the budget right, makes it more likely that mistakes will get picked up, and gives you the chance to learn from others.
Time and materials (T&M)	It is quite unusual that a client will give you free rein to charge time and materials for the entire project, as they feel understandably financially exposed. However, if you feel uncomfortable with accurately budgeting a particular budget element or project work stage, try to negotiate T&M payment at least until you are in a position to provide a fixed price.
Only budget for what you can budget	Sound confusing? What this means is that as far as possible, put together a budget only if you are happy that you are in a position to create it. Sometimes you may be asked to put together costs for something you know nothing about (e.g., you have not been involved in the first two project work stages, or they have not even happened). You should avoid doing this if at all possible. If you do, make sure your assumptions are very tight. If you feel

continued on next page

Table 6.3 (continued)

Budgeting recommendation	Explanation
Only budget for what you can budget (continued)	you are not in a position to budget something (e.g., it is so far in the distance you cannot be sure how technologies may have changed), try to break the work down into discrete chunks you *can* accurately budget. This is exactly the same thinking and process as having a preproduction budget in order to do the production budget as described in this book's project method.
Pay very careful attention to software costings	You need to make sure you fully understand the costs involved when budgeting for a piece of software. It is easy to be caught by licensing costs. Check whether there are additional costs for a Web license (e.g., the SQL server Web connector license). Watch out for ongoing, nonfixed costs: for some software you have to pay more if site traffic goes up. Watch out for licenses costed per processor rather than by server box (e.g., Macromedia's Generator), as a dual processor server will cost you twice as much.
Know your client, team, and industry	These are three key variables that can have a huge impact on how you would budget exactly the same piece of work in different circumstances. The state of the industry and the market will have an effect on what you can charge, and the quality of your team will clearly make a difference, as will the helpfulness and efficiency or otherwise of the client. You will need to be the judge of these factors.

As the last item in the table implies, it is unfortunately a matter of experience that ultimately counts for most in improving your budgeting skills. After awhile, you will have a much better gut feel for how much something will cost, how long it will take, and what implications it might have. When you have done similar projects before, with a similar or the same client, using a similar or the same development team, you will have a much better idea of what to expect and will be able to budget accordingly.

6.2.16   Appendix

The appendix contains any documentation relating to the project. Often the project specification will refer to documents contained in the appendix. There is no fixed format for what the appendix should contain, but the following are some of the things that might typically be included.

▶ Credentials
▶ Project brief

- ▶ Project resources
- ▶ Design concepts
- ▶ Prototyping
- ▶ Assumptions
- ▶ Glossary of terms
- ▶ Methods
- ▶ Risk management
- ▶ Change control
- ▶ Intellectual property
- ▶ SLAs
- ▶ Terms and conditions

Credentials

If you are working for an agency doing work on behalf of an external client, you would probably include a brief company credentials section here. This would include the company's areas of expertise, and previous clients and experience relevant to the project at hand.

Project Brief

The project brief created as the deliverable for the end of the first work stage should be attached here. It will serve as a reminder and reference point for seeing where the project specification has come from.

Project Resources

This should simply be a list and organizational chart of all people working on the project, with their roles and responsibilities, as well as all necessary contact details, in particular phone numbers and email addresses. This is a directory of information on the people involved with the project that can easily be referred to, particularly by new additions to the team. The organizational chart should show how different groups of people are working on the project, and how the groups interact with one another (e.g., how a work group reports to an operational group that reports to a steering committee).

Design Concepts

By this stage, you will probably have done some initial design work, either for the pitch or as part of the creative solution in the second work stage. If you have not done any design concepts yet, or feel that what you have done so far can be improved on, it is worth presenting your design concepts in the project specification, in order to get sign-off and because the client will be glad to see some design work. Together with the site map, a design concept presentation is visual evidence that a site really is about to be born.

TIP   **If it's printing you want …**

If printing out the site is important, beware of frames, as only the last frame to be given focus will print by default (though version 4 browsers and up give more options). Beware also that 800 × 600 screen resolution is wider than A4, so clipping could occur in printing the page. Note also that background colors and images generally don't print. Black-and-white printers will print anything off-white as black, whereas grayscale printers will print a degree of gray corresponding to the darkness of color. As a general rule, if printing out text from the site is important, you should go for a dark-colored text (black, ideally), which means a light-colored background. If it is to be read on-screen only, many people claim that light text on a dark background is easier to read.

For a design concept, you need to convey the overall look and feel, tone, and navigational system. The home page and two subsequent sublayers are usually enough. Where appropriate, it is worth spending some time on example copy to show the tone and length you would imagine using on the site. This section will include the creative solution work that went on in the previous work stage.

Prototyping

If you are going to be creating a prototype before the "real" product, you should define the extent of the prototype here. If you are working on a very large project, the prototype might have its own project specification. It is more likely you will be developing a limited prototype in order to get to a further stage of sign-off, or to aid market research. In this case, you should clearly explain the scope and nature of the prototype. For example, it may only work in one browser version and run locally on a laptop.

Assumptions

You may have made various statements in the project specification that need backing up with facts, figures, sources, and so on. Include them here.

Glossary of Terms

In order to help educate those involved on the project and to ensure that everyone is communicating clearly with one another, you might want to include a glossary of the more important terms that will be used during the project. If a contract is based on the project specification, it might be important to define here the terms used in the wording of the document.

Methods

If you are following a particular project management, technical, software development, testing, or other method, you might want to include an overview of that method here. This has a similar function to the credentials section: it aims to show that you are capable of performing to certain standards.

Risk Management

In this section, you describe how you will be managing risk in the project. Table 6.4, which follows, outlines some of the key areas you might want to include to outline your risk analysis and management method.

For example, Tables 6.5 through 6.7 provide examples of risk overview for several elements of a Web project. Table 6.5 is an example of a risk analysis table. Table 6.6 is an example of a table for rating risk, and Table 6.7 is an example of a table for rating vulnerability to a risk.

Table 6.4 A risk analysis method.

Risk element	Description
Risk description	A description of the risk
Rating	A numerical or descriptive rating of the risk's likely impact on the project
Impact type	A description of the type of impact the risk will have; that is, operational, financial, intangible (e.g., loss of confidence); threats to availability, threats to integrity (e.g., corruption of data); threats to confidentiality (e.g., inadequate control of access privileges); and so on
Impact description	A more detailed description of the impact of the risk on the project
Probability/ vulnerability	A numerical or descriptive rating of the probability the risk will occur; very similar to rating the vulnerability to the risk of the project
Mitigation/control	A description of factors that mitigate the risk or help control the extent of the risk
Risk owner	Who is responsible for managing and monitoring the risk
Date mitigated	A record of when a particular risk was mitigated or closed

Table 6.5 Example risk analysis table for a Web project.

Risk description + rating		Impact type	Impact description + probability		Mitigation/ control	Risk owner	Date mitigated
Site is not accessible for launch date	2	Financial, intangible	Users go to URL but site cannot be seen	4	There is already a holding page in place for users to access.	AF, TH	11.14.00
Script errors on out-of-scope browsers	4	Intangible, operational	User who have older browsers get script errors, which means the site does not perform as expected	1	We have not tested the site in out-of-scope browsers. We estimated only 3% of site users will be using out-of-scope browsers.	IC, AF	11.14.00
Site performs very slowly	3	Operational, intangible	Due to high levels of traffic, the server performs slowly under the load, meaning pages take a long time to load	3	We have specified a server that could perform at normal speed, with double the predicted levels of traffic.	AJ, AS	11.14.00

Change Control

More detail on change control practices is provided in Chapter 8, but if you are proposing to use a change request form to be filled in and approved by the required authorities before you make any change, include an example here. Such a form might include the following elements:

▶ Project name
▶ Date
▶ Change description
▶ Change requested by
▶ Impact of change on other project elements
▶ Requested start and completion dates
▶ Resources required
▶ Approved by

Table 6.6 Example risk rating table.

Rating	Category	Meaning
1	Catastrophic	Business survival threatened
2	Intolerable	Serious damage to business
3	Undesirable	Significant damage
4	Tolerable	Minor damage
5	Inconsequential	Negligible impact

Table 6.7 Example probability rating table.

Rating	Meaning
1	Probable
2	Highly possible
3	Possible
4	Unlikely
5	Impossible

Intellectual Property

Intellectual property (IP) is a complicated subject that deserves its own book to be covered properly. There is not much case law currently to go by. Equally, different jurisdictions will have different IP laws, including copyright and data protection laws. Although you cannot be an expert on the subject matter (hire a specialist, if necessary), it is important that you have a grasp of the underlying principles, as they can have a big impact on project costs and liabilities.

Copyright   Generally, whoever creates a piece of content also then owns the rights to that content. Unless explicitly stated otherwise, all the client is paying for is the right to use the content your team or others have created, not the underlying rights to the content itself. Usually clients will want to know that what you are creating for them is for them alone, and that they will have the right to use that content as they please. In this case, the content creators need to assign all intellectual property rights to the client.

Some content specifically states that it is copyright free and anyone can use it (e.g., promotional blurbs). For other content, you can buy the rights for unlimited use for a flat fee (e.g., image banks, sound libraries, and so on). Otherwise, you pay per use and negotiate a fee.

Although it is beginning to enter the realms of IP legal niceties, the agency can use elements of programming code from one site on another site if the end application is significantly different or is a very common site feature such as a piece of search code. Code is a little like words: you cannot copyright the words themselves, or common phrases, but you can copyright the way they are assembled to create a book.

Data Protection   Laws governing data protection and privacy vary. The United States has no data protection law in the way the United Kingdom does, for example. However, legislation has been proposed in the United States (such as the Children Online Privacy Protection Act) that will require privacy policies to be posted on all sites that collect personal information from children. The Web being a global medium, it is often difficult to know which jurisdiction you are governed by. Usually, the location of the registered offices of the client company and the physical location of the site will have a strong bearing on this.

As a matter of course, you should have a data protection and privacy statement on the site, more for the user's benefit than yours or the client's. However, you do need to be clear with the client who will own and manage the user data the site gathers. This is important, as it defines, in some jurisdictions, legal responsibilities each party involved has. The data owner, usually your client, is bound by regulations you will probably not want to be involved in.

Apart from clearly defining data ownership boundaries, you need to make clear in the project specification who will be liable for paying copyright and other IP costs. Don't let fear of rights infringement or costs curb your creative ideas, but be aware that anything to do with sound (in particular, well-known music tracks) or well-known imagery (particularly images of famous people) could have large copyright usage costs attached to them. More importantly, it will often take a long time to get permission to use the content, if you get it at all.

Service-Level Agreements

It is quite probable that you, your team, and the client's organization will not be the only parties involved in the Web project. If you are working with other third-party suppliers, contractors, software vendors, ISPs, and so on, and are responsible for managing their input to the project, you should include a record of what they are committing to here. This will usually be in the form of an SLA, warranty, guarantee, or other such commitment that defines the product or service they are providing and outlines the level of ongoing support and maintenance they will provide.

Terms and Conditions

If you are not working in-house for the client, it is likely your employer will have a standard terms and conditions document defining the basis upon which the company takes on work. It is important that this be included in the appendix.

6.3   Summary

The following are significant points raised in this chapter.

▶ The project specification is the most important document you will create. Treat it as a deliverable in its own right. Recognize that it will take quite a lot of time and effort to create and maintain.

▶ Use the template project specification downloadable at *www.e-consultancy .com/book* as a starting point for creating your own specifications.

▶ The size of the project will determine the scope of the elements needed in the project specification. At the very least, you will need a functional specification, a technical specification, a critical path, and a budget.

▶ Project specifications often form the basis of a contract between the client and the development team. Ensure issues such as intellectual property rights and service-level commitments are clearly defined.

This just about covers everything you need to include in the preproduction stage. The larger the project, the more work and documentation there will be to do. For smaller projects, you should still include all of the elements presented here, but some of them may only be a brief paragraph or two in length. The more project specifications you do, the faster and more easily you will do them, as you will often be modifying existing templates.

If you can get this phase right, and it is a lot of work, you can sit back and relax, because everything is defined, agreed upon, and ready to go. All you've got to do now is actually build the thing.

7

Work Stage 4: Content

Leadership is all about knowing and expressing the outcome and trusting those who work for you to do the work necessary to get there. Make sure that your team understands what is at stake and that they're working for the customer. Listen to and acknowledge feedback, and let them know why, if you don't accept their position. [...] Communication, communication, communication, organization, patience, insanity ...

—Jay Goldbach, Corporate Webmaster, Harcourt Inc., USA

Preproduction			Production			Maintenance	Evaluation
Project clarification	Solution definition	Project specificatio	Content	Design and construction	Testing, launch, and handover	Maintenance	Review and evaluation

I

If you look back to Chapter 3, The Project Road Map, you will see that as you move from project specification into the content work stage you are entering the production phase of the project. This means that all of your planning and solution defining should be done. It is now time to put your plans into action.

The next three chapters in particular are about putting into practice the project specification you have created. There is much more of a practical focus than a planning and documenting one, though you will need to continue to plan ahead and to document the project's progress. The coming chapters hope to give you some more practical information and guidelines as to how to keep the project on course during the production phase.

If you go into the production phase armed with a good project specification, including a clear critical path and the resources you need, you are well placed to triumph. However, there will still be many hurdles to overcome, and a lot of what the project manager's job becomes during site construction is about troubleshooting to keep the project on track. The most important skill the project manager can bring to bear during this phase is that of good communication.

In briefing programmers and designers, giving the client progress reports, dealing with problems as they arise, keeping team morale going, giving tactful and positive criticism or praise where necessary, chasing people for content and for work that has not been done, the project manager is a linchpin who must know how to communicate well in all sorts of ways: politically, tactfully, firmly, encouragingly. As we have discussed before, communication skills are part learned and part natural. We will be looking at some of the ways you can communicate effectively and manage a team of people toward a common goal.

7.1   Introduction to the Content Work Stage

The work stage we are looking at in this chapter, content, could in many ways be grouped under the design and construction work stage. Whereas the other eight work stages run very much in sequence (apart perhaps from maintenance and evaluation, which can also run in parallel), content is part of the design and construction of the site.

It has been separated into its own work stage because there is a lot of work to be done at these early stages on the content, because it can involve skills that are not necessarily part of the core design/programming/project management site construction team, and because it is an area that is increasingly becoming worthy in importance of an entire book, let alone a work stage.

Earlier we talked about the need for good-quality "sticky" content, and how this is not easy or inexpensive to find or create. We also talked about the need to define an editorial and copy style, as well as guidelines for updating the content of the site. We discussed the need to clearly define content delivery responsibilities, including formats, Web suitability, and deadlines. We will be looking at some of the practical sides to these issues in this chapter.

7.2   Responsibilities of the Project Manager

It is unlikely that it would be part of a Web project manager's job description to have in-depth skills in content sourcing and content creation. It is much more of an editorial or commercial function to define and source the content for a site, or to commission the creation of content. However, it is often the case that the project manager will be called upon to suggest where the necessary content might come from. In some cases, the project manager finds himself or herself writing some of the content, as there is no one else available to do it. Although we have defined written skills as part of the required skill set for a good project manager, this is perhaps taking it a little far.

The project manager is, however, responsible for ensuring that the content management process runs smoothly. Depending on the size of the project and your team, there could be an assistant producer, who can help you with the day-to-day content management once you have defined the processes. As you will spend a lot of your time in meetings and flitting between team members and the client, you do not have as much time as is often required to keep an eye on the content management process. This includes chasing outstanding content, making sure the content is then prepared as needed for the development team, storing and returning the content as required, logging the use of any material that requires copyright fees to be paid, arranging for payment, and so on. As you may be involved with any or all of the roles described, the following sections look into each area in a little more detail.

7.3   Sourcing Content

It will depend on the nature of the content on the site as to how far you will be involved in the sourcing of it. There are many types of content the site might use: free content or functionality provided on the Web (e.g., free news tickers, or search functions), content that is syndicated from a Web content provider (have a look at *www.isyndicate.com* or any large publisher to get an idea), content that is created, content that is repackaged for the Web from existing content, and content that is created using library or stock material.

7.3.1   Content Syndication and Creation

Of these types of content, the two types that require skills that are not part of the project manager's role are content syndication and original content creation. Although the project manager will no doubt be involved to some degree in both, most likely in advising on who to talk to based on previous experience or in defining the technical requirements of any content, these types of content usually cost the most and require separate contracts to be negotiated with the content provider. The project manager needs to understand the processes involved to know how long they are likely to take, so that this can be built into the project schedule from the outset.

7.3.2   Free Content and Functionality

There is any amount of free content and functionality available on the Web. Over time, you will build up a list of bookmarks or favorites from past projects that will constitute a library of possible content sources. Have a look at Part V of this book, where some of these types of resources are listed. There is always a reason content is given away for free, whether it is for spreading another brand in return for reciprocal links or page impressions, or as a pre-sale loss leader for something bigger and better. You will need to weigh these considerations against the budget, ambitions, and schedules of your project.

7.3.3   Content Repurposing

If the client is to be providing the content for the site, you need to think about the extent of repurposing necessary before it is suitable for the Web site. You need to establish the quantity and format of this content to gauge how much work will be involved in this repurposing. Do not take the client's word for the state of the content; ask to see it, and the sooner examples of it are provided, the better. If budgets are tight, or the client is in a better position to do the repurposing (e.g., if they hold the content in a database format they know how to extract but you may not), you could leave this work to them. If you do this, make sure you are very clear what they need to deliver so that you don't end up having to do a further round of content preparation for which you cannot charge. Leave much longer than you think for this process to happen. If the client is happy to pay for the content preparation process, take charge of this yourself, as you have much more control over something that can drastically affect the smooth running of the rest of the project.

7.3.4   Stock and Library Content

You should also have a fair amount of library material available to use. This could include imagery, audio, video, and text. Common in the development of Web projects is the use of stock imagery. Your designers should know their way around your image libraries well, so that they can quite quickly source a particular image they have in mind. The image libraries usually provide their CD-ROMs or access to their Web sites for free, so that you can search for the image you are after before paying for them. Not that long ago the copyright situation regarding the Web, being a worldwide medium, was a little confused, and each deal needed to be negotiated separately. Now, in particular with the image libraries provided online, you should be able to find pretty much anything you want and purchase Web usage rights that are not exorbitantly high.

Rarely does stock imagery cost more than it would to create an image that required a professional photo shoot. However, with it now being so easy to take high-quality digital pictures using digital cameras that are not excessively expensive, consider creating simple images (e.g., product shots, personnel photos, and so on) yourself. With stock imagery or digital images you take yourself, it is usually easy and inexpensive to show the client several alternatives before they commit to a particular one.

Once you have decided which one is to be used, you should make a note of which library it came from and its reference number. If you don't, it is often difficult at the end of the project to remember where all of the images came from, particularly if you have used images in layers or as background images. Another problem is that they can be so heavily stylized that you are not even sure what the original image was. Even if you cannot quite recognize the image, you can be sure those who created it will. You should not rush to pay the fees, however, until the project is complete and has been signed off, as you should be able to negotiate the fees depending on exactly how the image has been used. If, for example, you use the image as a background image in all pages of the site, you do not want to pay per page but per image. If the image is very faded or stylized, you might be able to negotiate a lower fee. Likewise, if the site will only have a very small user base, you might obtain the image at lower cost. For example, the image might be in a protected area of the site, meaning that only 200 people will ever get to see it.

7.4   Managing Content Providers

In the case of a client/agency relationship, what agencies complain about most is their clients supplying them content late, not at all, or in an entirely inappropriate format. This might seem like a fair complaint. However, it is the agency that is being paid for its expertise, so it should be the agency that manages the content collection process by managing their client correctly.

A content plan is the best way to do this. If you have gone through the content solution-definition process and have created the content plan for the project specification, you should already have mapped out what the client needs to give you, in what format, and by when. If the client has agreed to and signed the project specification, they have accepted the content plan you put together. As such, if the content is coming late or in the incorrect format, you can politely chase them, explaining clearly the implications for delayed or incorrectly presented content. Make sure the deadlines you have given are even more generous than you would normally allow. If you assume that the content will be late, this will give you a buffer zone.

You should do everything you can to accommodate the client, as there may be good reasons particular content is late in coming. Usually your main client contact will be as frustrated as you are that certain internal resources are not providing content as agreed. Often you can shuffle work around to get ahead in other areas before coming back to the section once the content has arrived. If this cannot be done and nothing can move forward without the client's content, make sure the relevant senior people on the project are aware of the situation, and keep any communication regarding the matter, often emails.

If the content that is late comes under the terms of a contract that has been signed with a third-party content supplier, clearly you have contractual rights to get the content as agreed. This will not necessarily make you feel much better if it holds up your project, but you might at least be able to claim back some lost money if you were able to negotiate late delivery penalty clauses in the contract.

If you work for an agency, it is largely up to you how far you keep transparent to your client the relationship you have with the resources and content providers you have working on the project. You might not want the client to know you have a team of freelance journalists and copywriters working on the project, as you had made a point during the pitch to win the business of the advantages your firm had in having these resources in-house.

This is a risky game to play, particularly with content providers. If the client assumes you are creating content in-house, it will be less easy for you to explain why content is late if, for example, your content providers fall behind schedule or, worse, quit the project. It is better to be very open about what external resources you intend to use. This is not so that you can blame someone else if things go wrong, but so that the client can see that there are other elements in the project you are trying to control but that you cannot necessarily completely account for.

If the amount or complexity of content reaches a level where you feel it to be critical to the project's success, or if the content is one of the largest costs in the project, try to ensure that the client has the contract direct with the content provider. Manage the provision and integration of content from that provider, but if there are any real problems or contractual issues, it is ultimately up to the client and the provider to resolve them.

Heuristics Search, Inc., *www.heur.com.*

7.5   Content Formats

There are too many file formats to go into great detail on every one in this section. There are numerous Web sites that will give you very good explanations of the ins and outs of every conceivable format. See Appendix A for pointers in the right direction.

Tables 7.1 through 7.4, which follow, summarize the most common file formats you are likely to encounter, as well as giving you an idea of the source format, the Web format, and the issues you might want to consider for each content type.

7.5.1   Considerations for Text

Table 7.1 summarizes source formats and Web format outcomes for text content.

Table 7.1 Source formats for text content.

Content type	Most common source format	Web format it will probably become
Text	Word document, hard copy (paper or fax), Quark file, PDF, or plain text (in email often)	HTML, data in a database, PDF, or sometimes part of an image

The following are considerations to keep in mind when dealing with text content types.

▶ Make sure you exchange documents in a version that both parties can read. RTF is a good format to ensure compatibility between word processing software packages. For Quark and the like, it is less easy so make sure you know what version of Quark the content provider is using.

▶ Specify that you must receive text content digitally, it takes ages to retype. If the text exists only in hard copy, see if you can use optical character recognition (OCR) software to scan the text into a digitally editable format.

▶ If you want text to be entered into a database correctly, consider creating a Web form that can use validation to help with quality control.

▶ Creating PDFs is in theory easy, but can take longer than you think. Be aware that the version of Adobe Acrobat you use will affect which Reader version the user will need to see the document.

▶ Note that Macs and PCs have different fonts available to them, so text won't necessarily be rendered the same on each of the operating systems.

▶ Remember HTML can only mark up text using fonts that exist on the user's machine, so you are effectively limited to the fonts you can use. (Typically, fonts such as Times New Roman, Arial, Verdana, and Helvetica are used with default font families defined; for example, sans serif.)

▶ You can export the text out of a Quark document. However, make sure you are sent the fonts and pasteboard extensions used in the Quark document, as well as the .qxd file itself.

7.5.2   Considerations for Imagery

Table 7.2 summarizes content formats for image content.

Table 7.2 Content formats for image content.

Content type	Most common source format	Web format it will probably become
Imagery	Hard copy (photos, brochures, and printed material), JPEG, Photoshop document (PSD), TIFF, BMP, Adobe Illustrator (AI), Encapsulated Post-Script (EPS), PICT, and Targa (TGA)	JPEG, GIF, Flash, or Shockwave

The following are considerations to keep in mind when dealing with image content types.

▶ As a rule of thumb, you want to have as high a resolution for images as possible to start with. This allows you to better control the final image quality.

▶ Many designers use Macs for creating graphics. If you are using a PC and are to receive Mac files, ask the designers to add the PC file extension to the Mac file names, or to at least let you know what format the files are in. Otherwise, you will spend a while guessing the file format.

▶ If you receive a Quark document, make sure you ask for the high-resolution images the document will refer to separately, as well as the thumbnails the .qxd file contains.

▶ Monitors display images at 72 dpi (dots per inch). Source imagery can be at a much higher resolution (e.g., 300), but should ultimately be saved down to 72 dpi.

▶ Use your Print Screen function to capture screen images (e.g., another site's home page) before pasting them into a document or graphics editor. If the image is then shrunk or used as part of a background, the quality is just about good enough to get away with.

▶ If you are in any doubt that the client can supply the images digitally, it is often easier to do all the scanning and so on yourself from hard copies, though you will need to allow for this work in the budget.

▶ Often you will be working with a client's print design agency, who may not be eager to cooperate: they may not be paid for their work or they may feel that they should be doing the work in the first place. Make sure the client gets you the authority to obtain what you need.

▶ Try and get logos as vector graphics (e.g., as an Adobe Illustrator file) rather than as bitmaps. This means that you can scale the logo as you wish, without losing quality. Any line art should also be delivered in vector format.

▶ If you are going to be using a vector format such as Flash, try to make sure the graphics that form the Flash movie are vector graphics. Flash can work with bitmap images, but the quality will drop when the image is made larger, and the file size will be significantly larger.

▶ If the image has larger areas of flat color, the GIF format is the best compression method to use. For photographs or other images with wide gradients of tone or color, use the JPEG format.

▶ GIFs support transparency, JPEGs don't. GIFs are only 8-bit images (256 colors); JPEGs are 24-bit (up to 16 million colors); with JPEGs you can specify the level of compression, with GIFs you cannot. GIFs can be indexed against a particular color palette.

7.5.3 Considerations for Audio

Table 7.3 summarizes content formats for audio content.

The following are considerations to keep in mind when dealing with audio content types.

▶ As with imagery, go for the highest level of source quality you can.

▶ Ask for a source format you have playback and encoding facilities for. Otherwise, you can spend much time and money converting between formats.

▶ Be aware that audio is often provided bundled with accompanying video (e.g., AVI or on a videotape). This means you will have to record the audio separately; and it means the source file sizes, if they include video, will be very large.

Table 7.3 Content formats for audio content.

Content type	Most common source format	Web format it will probably become
Audio	Cassette, CD, DAT, mini disc, videotape (Digital Betacam, SVHS, VHS, Hi-8, Secam, DVCAM, DVCPro, and so on), AVI, MPEG, MP3, WAV, AU, MOV, and QuickTime	MP3, WAV, QuickTIme, RealAudio, NetShow, and embedded in Flash/Shockwave

▶ Make sure you are entirely clear as to whether you will be doing any audio editing or only audio encoding/conversion to a Web format. Doing the encoding is one thing, and fairly simple, whereas editing the original source material is quite another skill, and usually requires much more sophisticated audio postproduction equipment. Doing a fade-in or fade-out for a single clip of sound is relatively simple, but editing out the bird singing in the background is not so easy.

▶ You will need to decide whether you are going for a streaming audio format (plays as it downloads) or whether the user will need to download the audio file before they can play it. Refer to your Web strategy, target audience, and technical specification to see what plug-ins and connection speeds the users are likely to have. They will need the appropriate plug-ins to play streamed audio (RealAudio, NetShow, QuickTime, and so on), and the quality will depend on how you have encoded the audio and the user's Internet connection speed. If the file is downloaded, you can control the quality more easily but the download could take a while.

▶ If you are going to stream audio, make sure you have fully looked into server- and client-side technical requirements, hosting and bandwidth issues, pricing models, user experience, and content availability. Microsoft's NetShow, for example, is free, whereas the more advanced server-side software provided by RealNetworks can be very expensive, especially on a highly trafficked site.

▶ Adding rollover sounds to buttons may sound good and bring the site to life, but be aware that this will significantly add to download times. Audio files are generally much larger than graphics files.

▶ Try keeping audio file sizes small by looping an audio sample.

▶ If you are providing downloadable audio files that rely on system software or hardware for playback, make sure you provide the file in the appropriate formats to suit the user's OS (e.g., Mac vs. PC).

▶ Clients might want to use a famous piece of music on their site. If you are not using library material, or specially composed music, or music that is out of copyright, you will find it takes a long time and costs a lot of money to get permission to use the music. There are many levels of permission needed. If the client is insistent on using a particular piece of popular music, see if you can shift the responsibility for getting permission to them.

▶ There are many shareware or even freeware audio editing tools available on the Web. Look in Appendix A for guidance.

7.5.4   Considerations for Video

Table 7.4 summarizes content formats for video content.

The following are considerations to keep in mind when dealing with video content types.

▶ As with audio and imagery, if you put bad quality in, you will get bad quality out, so try to obtain good-quality video source material.
▶ Many of the considerations for video are the same as those for audio. See Section 7.5.3 for streaming, copyrights, playback software, and hardware.
▶ Video is even more expensive to create and edit than audio. The file sizes are vastly larger, making it, on the surface, not ideal for Web delivery.
▶ Because of current typical Internet connection speeds, video is less reliable in quality of playback when streaming over the Web than is audio.
▶ Broadband Internet will mean video becomes a much more important and integral part of the Web experience, so learn about it now if you can.
▶ Be aware of the different video standards across the world. The United Kingdom and the United States use VHS and Betacam as fairly standard video formats, but the United Kingdom uses PAL, whereas the United States has NTSC, each with a different frame rate. France and other European countries use Secam. This means that your machines may not be able to properly play back video content that comes from abroad or that exists only in another standard.
▶ You can digitize video in order to take screen captures for use as imagery on the site. Try to digitize the source material at as high a rate as possible (though it really eats up hard disk space) so that screen captures will be as

Table 7.4 Content formats for video content.

Content type	Most common source format	Web format it will probably become
Video	Videotape (Digital Betacam, SVHS, VHS, Hi-8, Secam, DVCAM, DVCPro, and so on), AVI, MPEG, MOV, and QuickTime	RealVideo, NetShow, AVI, MOV, and QuickTime

good as they can be for further editing. The resolution of TV images is lower than for a computer monitor. For example, PAL is 768 × 576, compared to a typical 800 × 600 for a computer screen. The scan rate for the lines that make up a TV picture is also considerably lower than for a monitor. The quality of a video screen capture will not be that good. It will, however, be sufficient if the image is not primary in the design.

▶ There is not enough space here to go into the details of Webcasting (broadcasting video and audio over the Net), but you will need specialist skills to do this. These include a knowledge of AV capture, editing, encoding, and transmission, with expertise in the serving of Webcast material, including server-side software options, pricing models, bandwidth, and accessibility issues.

7.6   Content Delivery

As well as considering the format you would like the content to arrive in, and how you will then need to treat the content to prepare it for the Web, you should also define the best way for the content providers to actually deliver the content. The sections that follow discuss content delivery parameters.

7.6.1   Mail and Email

There are many ways that this can be done: through the post, by courier or special delivery, by email, ISDN, HTTP, or FTP. Most clients and nontechnical content providers will feel most at home using a delivery mechanism they feel comfortable with, usually mail or email. Whether you choose ordinary mail, special delivery, recorded delivery, and so on will obviously depend on how time critical the content delivery is, how sensitive the content is, and even how fragile the content is. Email works well for the exchange of textual content, and even for some images, at least for preview purposes. However, notwithstanding security concerns that some clients will have over emailing sensitive content (these can be allayed by encrypting the email content using PGP, for example), most image, and certainly audiovisual, content is too large in file size to be emailed. You will not be popular with your client, or certainly the people responsible for the mail servers and bandwidth usage at each end, if you are continually trying to send emails with file attachments in excess of 2 Mb.

7.6.2   ISDN

ISDN is a good alternative to email. It is a bit like a high-power email in this context, where you can send much larger files through. However, both you and your client need to have compatible ISDN software for the connection to work (not usually a problem). More of a problem is that the content provider himself or herself will probably not know much about the ISDN service the company has, and will therefore have to rely on others to send and receive content. Introducing further obstacles and other resources not directly related to the project is always to be avoided if possible.

7.6.3   HTTP and FTP

HTTP and FTP are effective ways of transferring digital content. If you have an available Web server or FTP server, you can upload content to it that you or the client, or anyone granted access, can then download. The great thing about this is that the content then becomes one-to-many; that is, one version of it is available for anyone to access. It is also good because you are less limited to file size (though very large files should be broken down into smaller files or, if particularly large, such as 30 Mb+, best sent on a disk), and you can include HTML text by way of explanation or comment for each piece of content. This method works particularly well if you are using a project site to help run your project. Even if you aren't using a full-blown project site, as soon as the production server or live server is available, you can use a protected part on it for storing, transferring, and exchanging digital content files. This has the added advantages that it gets the content contributors used to the FTP process, and the client will appreciate seeing the unborn Web site actually beginning to take life, albeit only for content transfer purposes.

7.6.4   Zipping and Stuffing

Don't forget that zipping (stuffing for a Mac) content can also make it easier to transfer, not just because the total file size will be smaller but because you can more easily manage multiple file attachments (attaching 1 file is easier than attaching 17), and you can then extract the content into a desired file structure (e.g., an entire Web site with links intact).

7.7   Asset Tracking and Management

Making sure that the correct content is coming in and that it is then stored, prepared, named, and passed on as necessary takes up a lot of time. If there isn't a huge amount of content or the project team is quite small, it may well be you who will perform this role. If at all possible, you should have someone else on the team who can be responsible for this. You might have a dedicated "content master," or you might have an assistant producer who can perform this role. Whoever it is will need to be very aware of the content plan, and know how to work with the production unit and the designers and programmers to ensure the correct content is going to them to continue to fuel their work. There are software tools designed to help with asset tracking and management, not dissimilar to version control software, and there are proprietary systems that some teams or project managers work with (e.g., content databases built in-house), but it is still important for a *person* to take responsibility for managing the content.

7.7.1   File Structures

Whether you are using a project site's Web server or a file server, one of the simplest and most effective ways of managing content is to create a file structure that mirrors the site map, and then store content assets according to where they belong in the site. Within each content area you might want to create subfolders that describe the status of the content (e.g., source photos from client, Photoshop screen mockups, GIFs/JPGs, images signed off, and so on). You will probably find that designers will keep their own copies of the content as they need it, you will have a copy of the source content, and the programmers will have content only as required for the actual Web site. There may well be replication of content going on here, which is not a very efficient use of disk space but is better than relying only on one master copy of the content. This also caters to the different ways each individual chooses to work with their content. Disk space is not very expensive in any case.

7.7.2   Databases

For large projects involving a lot of content, perhaps multiple-language versions, it might be worth developing a database that stores and helps manage the content. This could be the natural evolution of your content plan or a spreadsheet you have been using to track and manage content. Similar to a test database, a content database is useful for

▶ more advanced indexing and categorizing of content,
▶ searching content,
▶ providing content input controls and access privileges,
▶ providing advanced sorting and querying features,
▶ better enabling multiple content controllers to work together efficiently on the same project, and
▶ providing printed reports that quickly summarize the situation.

7.7.3   Content Tracking

You should use your content plan and the site map to check to see what content you are still awaiting, and cross off content as you receive it. Acknowledge receipts of content by email, and copy yourself on the email so that you have a record of what you have received. Be careful with emailed file attachments to save the attachment to a disk drive as soon as you open the email. Otherwise, it is very easy to delete the email, forgetting that there is a file containing content attached to it. If the email itself is the content, copy the email into a Word document and save it as a file with a suitable name. It is otherwise easy to forget about content contained in the text of an email. If you are using a project site, you should use it to show an updated version of the content plan, highlighting what has been received and what is outstanding. This way, the content providers can see for themselves where they are falling behind without you having to pester them quite so much.

7.7.4   Viruses

Viruses are clearly something you should be wary of when dealing with multiple sources and types of content. Make sure you have good antivirus software, updated with all of the latest DAT files, installed on your machine. Do not open file attachments, particularly executable files, if you don't know where they have come from, and scan any file attachment before opening it. If you have just one piece of content that turns out to be infected, you should scan all other content to make sure the virus has not spread. If you do receive a piece of content that contains a virus, make sure you inform the sender so that they can eradicate it on their end and send you clean content in the future.

It is easy to forget about viruses, until the day you manage either to send your client a virus-infected piece of example content, which then goes on to severely contaminate their internal systems, or you receive a virus that causes weeks worth of damage to your project. You won't take viruses so lightly thereafter.

7.7.5   Back Up

Following hot on the heels of viruses, and even more important, is backing up your content—not just the content, but everything to do with the project. Backing your work up properly, dull as it may seem, isn't an option; it's an absolute necessity you ignore at your own peril. Six months of time and $200,000 of work on a Web site can fit on a floppy disk. It can be erased in a few seconds. Think about it. One unfortunate search-and-replace and you can be set back months. A virus can wreak hurricane-like havoc. Back up, and back up regularly, with clear version documenting. Trust me, it can reduce a grown man to tears: "Oh yeah, that folder was deleted because there was no room on the drive and I needed to save something. Was it important . . . ?"

7.8   Managing Copywriters

In earlier chapters, we looked at how copywriting for the Web was a different skill than writing for print. We looked at some of the differences between good Web copy and more traditional print copy. However, we did not talk about how to manage Web copywriters effectively.

7.8.1   The Challenges the Copywriter Faces

It can be difficult for the Web copywriter if, as is often the case, the content and presentation elements of the Web site are not brought together until late in the process. If they are to create copy that makes the most of the interactivity made possible with hypermedia, it is very difficult to do so until they can see the context and environment of the copy once the presentation and content elements are brought together. Furthermore, it can be difficult if copywriters are working in isolation, where changes and requirements are not communicated to them until they have already done a lot of work going down a different path.

7.8.2   How to Help the Copywriter

If at all possible, try to make sure the copywriter comes along to team meetings, even if they prefer to write alone, to make them part of the team and to ensure they stay abreast of any new developments. Make sure the copywriters and designers meet and talk regularly to ensure the presentation and content layers will fuse as planned. Both designers and copywriters should be working to the communication brief put together as part of the project brief and included in the project specification. The designer and copywriter should work together to make sure the desired message is communicated through the words and images as effectively as possible. The design style and style of the copy should complement each other to convey the message to the user.

The communication brief will help the copywriter picture the person she needs to write for by describing a typical person from the site's target market. However, you might want to add a description of the "tone and voice" the text should have. This will come out of the brand's attributes. If you can, you should provide an example of the type of copy you think hits the mark. Give examples of other sites or advertising campaigns that get across the right feel through the style of the copy.

The copywriter will also need to know the length of copy she is expected to produce. Depending on the site, this might be the number of words per article or may be more about the number of words required to fill a certain space on the page. If the site is template and database driven, and the text content is largely independent of the graphics, the brief to the copywriter should be fairly straightforward. The navigational structure, and the way content interrelates, will be more rigidly set in stone, lengths of textual pieces will be clearly defined, and screen space will usually be a window left for text that scrolls as necessary.

If, however, you have a highly designed interface, the relationship between the words and the images is much more complex. The words themselves may need to be rendered as an image to ensure correct positioning and required fonts. The length of the text may be critical, as it has to fit between images or be short enough to ensure ugly scrollbars don't appear. In these cases, the copywriter clearly needs to work more closely with the designers to make sure what she is producing fits with the overall page design, and that what the designers are producing leaves enough room for the copywriter to get her message across.

One way to facilitate this is to create dummy text, whether nonsensical "Latin" text (e.g., *laudatus est in horto per sequitur eunt canis et perpetuum*), or text that conveys the basic message but without the required final finesse or style. This way, the designers have text elements they can use on the page and the copywriters know roughly how much space they have to play with and what it is that needs to be said. Creating this dummy content is one of those "not in anyone's job description" tasks that tends to end up falling into the project manager's or producer's lap. Arguably, this forms part of storyboarding (see Section 7.9), which is a skill project managers and producers can benefit from mastering.

7.8.3   Presenting Copy Work to the Client

Before the copywriters get carried away and write reams of text, you should create a page that includes some of their content, set within the design if possible, to run it past the client for their feedback. Like the design, the style of the copy will get a subjective reaction. Every individual will react differently, and there are no definitive rights or wrongs. Make sure you give a rationale for the copy style, as you would for the design. Point out how it fits with any style guides or editorial guidelines set down. Show examples of how it complements the brand attributes. Ask the client not to rely purely on their own gut reactions but to allow other people to comment, ideally members of the target audience, before making any final decisions or judgments.

7.8.4   Constructive Criticism

Try to remember that writing copy, particularly if it is meant to be funny or have a certain "attitude," requires the writer to lay a little of their soul on the line. There is a personal statement in there, just as a designer will put some of herself into a design. To get the most out of either, you need to be sensitive to these issues and tread carefully with criticism. Different people are best handled in different ways, of course, but imagine your partner has dressed up for a particular occasion and you really don't like what they are wearing. Think how you might get the message across without causing so much offense that they would never get dressed up again. Designers and copywriters are professionals who should be used to criticism, but you will still get the best work out of them if you can respect what they are trying to do. If you can gain their respect, they will want to do good work for you.

7.9   Storyboarding

The purpose of creating storyboards is threefold. First, they are useful in presentations to the client as an outline of the design approach. Second, they are useful to the development team, in particular the designers at this stage, in defining the elements that need to go on the page. Third, they are useful to the team in showing the navigational architecture and information flow; that is, how the pages are to work together to provide the user's interactive experience.

7.9.1   What Storyboards Should Contain

To create effective storyboards, you do not have to be particularly good at graphic design. In fact, it might be a hindrance, because you would spend too long trying to get the design just right. You need to know what the elements required on the page are. This you should be able to find out from the functional specification. You also need to know how the pages fit into the grander architecture and navigation of the site, not from a technical point of view but from a functional, user point of view. This again you can establish from the functional specification and the site map. As the project manager, you are probably the person with the best understanding of the project specification, as you put it together. You are also very aware of how all of the elements (content, design, programming, and so on) are progressing, and how they will work together to produce the final result. You are the person who needs to brief them on what it is that needs doing. For all these reasons, it is beneficial if the project manager can be closely involved in creating storyboards, whether alone, or, ideally, working with an information architect and designer.

7.9.2   Methods of Storyboarding

You will no doubt develop a preferred method of storyboarding. You might like to produce pencil sketches on paper, you might like to use a graphics package such as Photoshop or Illustrator, or you might draw and annotate the pages using Word. It isn't necessary to go as far as creating images, or even using color. In fact, it would be preempting the design to do so, and you risk upsetting the designers if you, as a project manager, were beginning to create your own designs. The storyboards need only be black and white, the fonts are irrelevant, the copy usually only dummy text, and the images only representative (clip art, for example).

My preferred tool for doing storyboards is PowerPoint. It is easy to use, easily creates templates you can reuse (e.g., the master slide might contain the core navigation), creates grouped elements for things such as drop-down boxes, and contains enough basic shapes and functions (e.g., graphs and charts) to cover pretty much any page you might want to storyboard. Furthermore, because it is clearly not a design tool, you can show all elements of a page without risking imposing any design. You do not therefore offend the designer, and the client will not be disappointed, as they can clearly see it is not the design. This is not to say that you cannot convey the design concept. One of the advantages of storyboards is precisely to get the design concept across to the client. The senior designers will hatch the design concept, often with input from you as the project manager. For example, your design concept for an interface to a soccer site might be to use the grid-shaped pattern of holes of a goal's net to represent various sections of the site. This would be quite easy to knock together in PowerPoint, with a few lines to create a storyboard, but it would by no means be the design itself.

7.10 Content Management Systems

You may decide to use a content management system (CMS) to help manage large amounts of content, and in particular to help mange the Web publishing workflow. Publishers (whether in books, magazines, or newspapers) will follow an editorial process that represents a workflow from inception through commission, creation, review, revision, editing, integration, and publication. There may be several iterations at each stage, and various people with various skills involved in managing and shaping the content through the publishing workflow. Content management systems aim to create a similar environment, suited to Web publishing.

7.10.1 Separation of Content and Presentation

CMS applications are middleware that sits between the Web front end (the Web server) and back office systems and processes. Content and presentation are much more separated than usual when using a CMS. If you are used to database-driven sites, you will recognize how pages are created "on the fly" by code that is sensitive to the context of the user or the request and that pulls together the correct design template and content to then serve the page back to the user. CMSs use databases and special applications to manage content and to create dynamic pages with real-time integration of content with presentation.

7.10.2 Customer Relationship Management

However, most CMSs have gone beyond pure content management. There are advanced content management features such as version control, go-live times, editorial sign-off and access procedures, rollback capabilities, and flexible template designs. In addition to these features, the CMS can use its database-driven infrastructure to offer a suite of tools and applications that aim to provide enhanced customer relationship management (CRM) opportunities to the site owner. These services might include the following:

▶ Personalization and customization services through the customer life cycle
▶ User profiling databases for use in one-to-one marketing applications

▶ Dynamic content versioning according to user or context of site
▶ Navigation that is context sensitive and adapts itself to suit the user
▶ Advanced reporting tools to see how the site is being used (e.g., buying trends, paths through the site, and so on) to aid commercial decision support

As you can see, the CMS manages users, profiles, and site data, as well as content assets. Furthermore, some of the CMSs will allow content exchange with other systems, which could be important if content syndication forms an important part of the site's business plan.

7.10.3   Considerations Surrounding CMS

With all of these advantages, you might wonder why every site doesn't use a CMS. Probably the single largest factor is cost. To buy the software licenses and pay the necessary development team to implement the CMS, you will be spending in excess of $100,000, and possibly a whole lot more. Unless you have a large number of content contributors, a large amount of content, and a big budget, this is often not worth the investment when you could develop a more rudimentary database-driven application yourself (in less time and for less money) and retain control of the software. Table 7.5, which follows, summarizes some of the areas you need to be aware of as a project manager when considering or implementing a CMS.

Table 7.5 Considerations for content management systems.

Issue	Considerations
Cost	CMSs are expensive. You have to consider not just the software licensing costs, which are usually ongoing and can depend on the levels of site usage so are not even controllable, but also the cost for consultants to implement the system, any additional technical infrastructure costs that arise as a result of the CMS, and support/upgrade and other ongoing costs.
Interoperability	Think of the long term. You may not yet be tying the CMS that closely into back office systems, but you probably will be soon. Is the software based on open standards so that systems integration isn't a total nightmare?

continued on next page

Table 7.5 (continued)

Issue	Considerations
Control	If you use someone else's software application as a mission-critical tool, be aware that you are then tied to them and reliant on their specialist skills, their response times, and their technical support. How confident are you that they will perform as you hope? Might they go bankrupt or be bought, which could severely affect your position?
Reliability	Internet software development is an incredibly competitive market, and users often complain that the products are released before being properly tested. Try to make sure you can distinguish the hype from the truth. Talk to other users if possible. Trial-run demo versions. How cutting edge is the technology?
Support and training	Make sure the levels of technical and implementation support are adequate. If not, suggest creating a contract that specifies the levels you require. This can be particularly important if the software company is based abroad and can only provide support when it is the middle of the night your time. What training do they provide? Can your team be trained to take on responsibility for supporting and developing the system? Does the CMS vendor have a partner program or approved implementation partners?
Design freedom	Some people say that all CMS sites look the same and consequently dull and unappealing. In worrying about workflow and content management, it is easy to lose site of the users who only see the front end. Because of the dynamic, real-time integration of content and presentation, designing for a CMS is restricted to templates and is less flexible than when creating individual static pages. You can use frames and rich media, but it quickly becomes complex to the point of unmanageable or at least prohibitively expensive in the size of team you need to maintain the site.
Performance	Adding layers of middleware and relying on dynamic content generation can have a negative effect on site performance, particularly speed. Be aware that by introducing a CMS you may need to revisit your technical specifications to provide enough bandwidth and processing power to keep speed levels acceptable. Adding large software applications, particularly if you did not code them, means fixing bugs becomes more complicated. Who should fix the bug? What element of the site is responsible for the bug?

7.11 **Summary**

The following are significant points raised in this chapter.

▶ Good content is expensive. The more important the content is to the project, the more likely you will need someone who specializes in sourcing, creating, or brokering content.

▶ Make sure you specify the content format, and how it will be delivered, stored, backed up, and updated.

▶ Storyboarding is an effective method of helping you and the client begin to visualize how the content and navigation elements will work together on the page.

▶ Asset tracking systems and content management systems offer enormous benefits in efficiently handling and updating large amounts of content. However, they are expensive, and necessarily impose templates and structures that might limit what you want to do.

With content coming in, you have the building blocks to start assembling the site's pages and applications. It is time to begin the design and construction work stage in earnest.

Work Stage 5: Design and Construction

The sign of an experienced professional is, more than anything else, the ability to set (and enforce) limits on a client's expectations.

—Mike Stone, Web Consultant, YAWP

Preproduction			Production			Maintenance	Evaluation
Project clarification	Solution definition	Project specification	Content	Design and construction	Testing, launch, and handover	Maintenance	Review and evaluation

Although the preproduction phase is the most important phase in the development of any commercial Web site, there is no doubt that as a project manager it isn't until the production phase gets under way, and you are managing the design and construction of a site, that it feels like your job really kicks in. You are responsible for marshalling the troops, steering the ship, grasping the ring, seizing the bull by the horns, and no doubt many other guidance and leadership clichés as the project rolls toward that final milestone.

You will already have been using many of the skills necessary in this phase during earlier parts of the project: communication, planning, management of expectations, and coordination of a team effort. If you have been building a prototype (see Section 8.10 for more details) or working on large elements of design or content, you will already have started the design and construction in earnest.

This work stage represents the point in the project where the largest team will be working together. You will have less input from the consultants and strategists, and considerably more from the design and programming teams, and, for the first time perhaps, they will be working alongside one another to integrate content and functionality with presentation to produce a fully designed and working product.

The sections in this chapter run through a series of skills, tasks, and work areas you will be involved in during this work stage. There are practical suggestions and tips that should help you approach these responsibilities with more confidence.

8.1 Forward Planning

Before you go diving into the day-to-day management of a Web project, religiously following your project specification and critical path, you should take a moment to think through what things you need to be doing now to facilitate work later in the project. There will be some elements of the project that are beyond your control, and however hard you work, however much money you spend or number of people you employ, they will not happen significantly faster. It is very important to place priority on these elements over day-to-day issues and concentrate your energies in making sure they are covered. Once done, you can relax in the knowledge that something big and nasty isn't about to creep up and spoil your otherwise perfect project.

TIP   **Do the most difficult stuff first**

Try to tackle the most complex work first. At this stage, the team is still fresh and relishing the challenge. It also gives more leeway if there prove to be unforeseen problems. If you leave the tough stuff until last, it risks delaying the delivery date. If you can crack the more difficult parts, the team will feel confident about tackling the rest of the project.

8.1.1   Things to Prioritize in Forward Planning

The following are some of the more common elements that require forward planning.

▶ *Applications:* For example, for a merchant or Internet merchant ID to be allowed to conduct online credit card transactions. This can take up to six weeks, depending on the bank and the company's status.

▶ *Server setup*: If you are having a dedicated facility-managed server, it can take up to 20 days for some ISPs to set up and configure the server for use.

▶ *Copyright negotiations:* If certain content that needs special copyright clearance is fundamental to the site, you should prioritize getting authorization to use the content, as this can take a long time.

▶ *Legal or contractual matters:* This is very wide ranging, but if elements of the site cannot progress without prior contractual or other legal agreements in place, you should expect them to take a while to push through.

▶ *Recruitment:* It is difficult to find good people fast, and it is foolish just to take the first people that come along. Recruitment is very important and takes up a lot of time.

▶ *Software and hardware purchases:* If you need a particular piece of software or hardware, on the whole you can get it quite quickly. However, do not assume this. You might find that the version you need has a waiting time or needs to be specially ordered from overseas. Don't take the chance. Once you know what software and hardware you will need, start the purchase procedures.

▶ *Content:* As discussed in the previous chapter, some content takes a long time to assemble, and there are few shortcuts, so you should take the necessary steps as soon as possible on this front.

8.1.2   Setting Up the Server

Try to get access to the actual server the site will be hosted on as soon as possible, and install any software you will need on it as a priority. Make sure your traffic analysis software is on the server and is definitely working well before launch. The first question clients will ask once the site has gone live is "What's the traffic like?" You need to be able to tell them, and you want them to be able to see the results through their browser so that you do not spend a lot of time downloading and analyzing log files, printing reports, mailing materials to the client, and so on.

There is a temptation to leave setting up the live server as late as possible to save on hosting costs. You may think you can replicate the server environment exactly locally, and so the transfer to live will be entirely seamless. It *may* be, but it is highly unlikely. By using the live server with a password-protected area to review work in progress, you are effectively conducting testing as you go, which will help speed up the final testing, avoid any last-minute delays, and mitigate against nasty surprises.

TIP   **Just checking …**

As you go through the production phase, you will be periodically checking the work as a form of iterative testing. Double-check up front that fundamental errors have not been made. This might include programmers coding functionality in Perl when it should have been in ASP. It might be designers using a design template to create a fixed-width site for a particular resolution that turns out to be the incorrect width: it only needs to be a few pixels out, and the entire site could need redesigning and programming.

8.2   Meetings

You spend a good proportion of your time in meetings of one sort or another during the production phase. There are different types of meetings (e.g., status report meetings, crisis meetings, kick-off meetings, and team meetings), and each will have a different atmosphere and need to be managed slightly differently. However, there are certain elements and techniques, outlined in the material that follows, that should help ensure you run meetings effectively.

It isn't always the project manager who is responsible for organizing and leading meetings. You might be going to a meeting called by another party involved with the client, such as an advertising agency or media buyer, or you might be going to a meeting that is a presentation on a particular technology product or market research that relates to the project. However, in the majority of cases it is the project manager who will instigate and run meetings. It is a fundamental part of the job, and is one of the primary means of maintaining that all-important communication.

8.2.1 Importance of Meetings

We have already discussed the enormous importance of good communication in determining the success of the project. Along with email, meetings represent the most important communication tool at your disposal. Conducted well, meetings can be extremely effective. Used poorly, meetings can be very damaging. Unlike email, meetings are face-to-face, so interpersonal skills are vital. Table 8.1, which follows, considers some of the other reasons meetings are so important.

Given that meetings are so important, you should make sure they are held regularly and that the necessary people commit to attending. Make sure meetings are focused, so that they are productive; with many people gathered in a room, the total cost in man-hours for every meeting is very high.

TIP   **The power of food**

It is pretty obvious, really, but providing refreshments at a meeting is a great way of ensuring people attend. Be careful not to provide too lavish a spread, however, as people tend in this case to concentrate more on the food than the task at hand. Let them know when the food will be coming, or don't let them have the food until the meeting is over.

Table 8.1 Reasons for the importance of meetings.

Reason for importance	Explanation
Contact with project sponsors	Often meetings are one of the rare occasions you can expect to get the involvement of more senior management and project sponsors. This is valuable time and can be used to cover a lot of ground.
Resolving issues	There is only so much you can do over the phone or by email. Sometimes you need to have a meeting in which everyone gets together to resolve an issue.
Bigger-picture awareness	Meetings give team members the chance to catch up on what other members in the team have been doing. Without meetings to bring people together, there is a danger they will work in an insular fashion and become unaware of changes and developments that affect what they should be doing.
Forces you into action	If you have regular meetings set up, you have to prepare for them, as you will be confronting issues, reporting on progress, and making decisions. They act as mini milestones the team can focus around and pin deliverables to.
Peer pressure	If someone commits to something during a meeting, or a decision is made, it is more likely to happen, and more accountable, because it was made before a group of people who can bear witness to it.
Team spirit	Getting together with others working on the project is good for building team spirit. It gives you a chance to catch up with people informally before or after the meeting, albeit briefly.

8.2.2   A Format for Effective Meetings

Table 8.2, which follows, provides a format to follow, which breaks the meeting down into before, during, and after stages.

The following are some of the items that might normally be on the agenda.

▶ A review of last week's meeting; in particular, checking on the status of action points still outstanding

▶ An update on particular areas of project progress

▶ Hot spots; risk evaluations and controls, flagging issues you think could become a problem and need attention

▶ Longer-term issues; looking ahead and forward planning

Table 8.2 A breakdown of steps taken before, during, and after meetings.

Before the meeting

The following should be clear:

▶ Who is chairing and guiding the meeting (including timekeeping)

▶ Who is taking minutes at the meeting

▶ Who is attending the meeting

▶ When the meeting is

▶ Where the meeting is

▶ What the purpose of the meeting is

You should also ensure the following:

▶ A copy of the agenda is distributed to all attendees prior to the meeting.

▶ Any important/relevant material is circulated in advance of the meeting. Not too far in advance; otherwise it will be ignored. About a day or two is usually right.

During the meeting

▶ The appointed person should chair the meeting and guide it

▶ The points on the agenda should be worked through systematically

▶ Questions, issues, and other comments not on the agenda should be raised at the end

▶ There should be a roundup at the end summarizing what was agreed, next steps, and action points with owners

▶ The next meeting should be scheduled, with times and availability confirmed

▶ Set roles and agenda for next meeting

▶ The meeting should be closed

After the meeting

A progress report should be circulated, reiterating the meeting details (as specified in the "Before the meeting" section). The contact report details the *actual* circumstances of the meeting, as opposed to the proposed circumstances before the meeting (e.g., absentees will be noted). It should detail what was discussed, who proposed what, any decisions made, next steps, action points with owners, and the details of the next meeting.

TIP   **My big red pen**

During the production phase, mount the project's critical path on a big board so that everyone can plainly see what needs to be done. At team meetings, take a red pen and draw a big line across the critical path at that day's date. This gives a useful visual representation of where the project should be and how much is left to go. Team members can then see how their hard work has paid off, as well as if you are ahead of schedule, on schedule, or have caught up. If you are behind schedule, they can appreciate where you need to be and what will happen if you don't catch up.

Progress reports are among the most important documents created during the production phase, as they create a paper trail of decisions. This can be an invaluable recourse in case of any dispute. If your client is replaced by someone else, you have on paper the decisions accepted by your former client.

You need to make it clear to the client that the progress report captures decisions made, and as such is very important to the project. They should check the progress report to make sure they agree with all that is documented. If they do not agree, they should say so as soon as possible, so that the progress report can be amended and redistributed. In some cases, you may feel that the client should acknowledge and accept the progress report in writing.

8.2.3   Kick-Off Meetings

Kick-off meetings are governed by many of the same criteria as any other meeting, but they are particularly important for setting off on the right path, setting the tone, and as a symbolic gesture to say "This project team is now officially inaugurated and ready to go!"

You will already have spent a good deal of time meeting with the client and talking to the people who are going to work on the project. However, you should still hold kick-off meetings with both.

For the development team kick-off meeting you should get together everyone who is working on the project. Give a recap of what the project is all about, who the client is, and what you want to achieve. Remind everyone of where you currently are in the process and, if they are interested, give them a copy of the project specification for a little bedtime reading. You should then talk through the critical path, hot spots, and key milestones before going into a little more detail on the short-term goals for the coming days. Explain when you will be having meetings as a team, and when with the client, so that everyone knows when and where to turn up if needed. These meeting times should be kept sacrosanct and attended, even if it is only for 10 minutes. Also explain how the success of the site is going to be measured, so that everyone knows there are real targets to aim for.

If you've got any carrots you can dangle to urge people on, do so to help people feel good about the project. It's amazing what even free client merchandise or products can do, especially if you are working for a brewer. The kick-off meeting should inspire confidence, motivation, and excitement about being part of a really good team that is going to have fun doing a really good piece of work.

The kick-off meeting with the client is really more of a milestone to say "After all that thinking and planning, we're now all systems go!" You should use the meeting to gently remind the client of the content plan and their commitments, confirm any regular meetings you are expecting to have with them, and explain how you will report project progress to them and how they will be able to review work in progress. Finally, if you've already got any hot spots flagged, bring them up now. You are sure to need to repeat them, but it's good to start early!

8.3   Briefing Your Team

For much of the production phase, the project manager's time will be taken up making sure that everyone is briefed on what they are doing, and has the right content and tools to do the job. The sections that follow explore these issues.

8.3.1   When to Prepare Briefs

While the team is busy working away, you need to be checking the work that has just been done, and presenting it to the client, as well as preparing briefs for work to follow. If you have a team of eight working on a project, you can imagine the cost to the business if the project manager hasn't briefed the team and they spend just one day twiddling their thumbs wondering what they should be doing.

To maximize efficiency and speed of development, your briefs need to be created so that they are always ahead of where the work is at the moment. As soon as a piece of work is finished, you have the brief for the next section of work ready. This means that just when everyone else in the team is working hardest to do the work set out in your brief, you might actually find that you have the most time and the most freedom. However, it also means that you can find yourself working before the rest of the team starts, in order to prepare briefs for them, and after they have finished, as you assess how far they have progressed and outline briefs for the coming days.

On a big project during the production phase, you might have a meeting with the other project managers and producers half an hour before the day begins, and half an hour after the day ends. This is to ensure that all are still thinking along the same lines, and that you have your briefs ready for the coming days.

8.3.2   Briefing Meetings

Sometimes it will make sense to get the entire team together at the beginning of each day for a briefing session, in which you run through general issues before briefing each member individually. If you have the time and not too large a team, this can be positive, as everyone hears what others are doing. Sometimes you won't have the time for this, or it seems better to leave people alone to get on with a task requiring a couple of days. If there are several of you on the project management team, it is often effective to assign the tasks that need managing to different people, so that work can run in parallel, ensuring maximum development speed.

8.3.3   Scope of the Brief

You and your team will have a fairly high level of documentation and specificity to work to from the project specification. However, the team members will tend to think more in terms of what they need to do over the next few days rather than about the project as a whole. It is important for them to be able to focus at the micro levels of implementation and leave the macro project issues to you. You should not set tasks that stretch much beyond a few days or a week, or your briefs will begin to lose focus and there will be too much for the designer, programmer, or other team member to try to take in at once.

8.3.4   Content of the Brief

You can give a brief verbally, and often this is all you have time to do, but as far as possible you should create a written brief. It does not need to be very long or stylish, but it does need to convey some key points about the tasks. A written brief is invaluable if you are called away to a meeting or fall ill and someone else has to take your place and do the briefing. If the brief only exists in your head, this will be difficult for them to do. Table 8.3, which follows, outlines the key elements to be included in a brief.

Table 8.3 Elements that should be included in a written brief.

Brief element	Description
Description of task	This is a description of what needs doing (e.g., doing the HTML for the "About this site" pages).
Deadlines	When must the task be finished (e.g., close of day tomorrow)?
Technical specifications	Reiterate any important technical parameters (e.g., it must work in version 3 browsers, must not be created using a particular HTML editor, and so on).
Client/job number/ reference	Can be important if you or your team members are working on multiple projects and you need to track who has spent time on what.
Location of digital assets	Very important. Where is the content? What is it called? What format is it in?
Accompanying (paper) work	Nondigital assets or support documents (e.g., black-and-white printout of the design marked up to show how the Photoshop document should be cut up for programming purposes).
Contacts	Who are the other people that the person you are briefing needs to know about and might need to contact (e.g., who was the designer that worked on this)? Who is the copywriter? How can they be contacted? Where are you going to be in case of questions? How are you contactable? If you aren't available, who should be contacted?
Other tasks	If the person you have briefed cannot continue with the tasks, or they finish your tasks quicker than expected, what other work is there to be done? How could they be getting ahead or catching up on other work?

8.3.5   Briefing on Changes

One thing that can annoy members of your development team is continually pestering them and hanging over them to make minor changes or bug fixes the moment they appear. If they are working on complex code or trying to get design inspiration, the last thing they need is a petty change to break their concentration.

Conversely, the client, if they have access to the work in progress, will pounce on any tiny inaccuracy, such as a text amendment, and consider it important that it get done quickly. You will have to strike a balance between being seen to be responsive to the client and respecting the working practices of your development team.

For the team's benefit, it is much better to save up a list of minor changes and set aside time in the development schedule for the development team to do all of these changes in one go. If you have all of the changes listed, a designer or programmer can very quickly go through them all. Ideally, you want to do this no more often than every couple of days, but if you feel it needs doing every day, perhaps you should make it clear to the team that the last half hour of every day will be spent making minor changes. For more on how to manage the client's expectations and requests for changes, see Section 8.8.

8.4   Working Environment

If you look back to Chapter 5, Section 5.7, you will see that you should already have considered and defined what type of working environment you and your team require to do their jobs to the best of their ability. This included variables such as physical location, tools and materials, management and reporting structures, the development environment, and the possibility of using a project site. The subsections that follow contain suggestions on these and other factors that affect the team's working environment.

8.4.1   Location of the Team

If you can, get the project team as physically near one another as possible for projects that have a dedicated team. This will create a team spirit and facilitate more immediate and effective communication. Try to create an environment that reflects the project, whether it is having posters up that relate to the project for design inspiration; client merchandise such as calendars, pens, and notepads to reinforce a sense of project ownership; or even the team's own coffee machine, coatrack, or supply of cookies to enhance team spirit.

Typically, programmers and copywriters may need more peace and quiet and work more in isolation than designers, who get a lot of their inspiration from other designers by talking ideas through and seeing what others are working on. Bear this in mind. Talk to the team and the individuals about where they would prefer to be located.

8.4.2   Tools and Materials

This quite simply means helping ensure each team member has the software, hardware, and other tools and materials needed to do their job. Sometimes team members would rather suffer in silence than fight for the tools and materials they really need. As a result, their work might be inferior to their capability or might, at the very least, greatly slow down.

When you compare what most of these tools and materials cost to the amount of time that could be wasted or saved in resource costs, it just doesn't make sense not to give people the tools they need to do their jobs properly. Often it is the unfortunate lot of the project manager to fight these battles on behalf of his or her team members.

8.4.3   Management and Reporting Structures

This is much less about trying to create hierarchies in the team than it is about ensuring team members are clear about their role within the team, who they will be working with (and how), who they are responsible for managing, and who they should go to in the case of problems. Once this is clear (and in teams who have worked together before it is clear from the outset), communication is much more fluid and informal, and boundaries are instinctively understood.

It is important that the senior members in the team meet to talk through and agree on the management and reporting structures within a project team. Usually the project team will be assembled from disparate sources and may not have worked together before, or not in this particular configuration. Although the project manager may be guiding and leading the work of the team, this does not necessarily mean that he line-manages anyone on the team or that he is at a higher level of authority to everyone on the team. This is rarely the case.

Senior managers may want to ensure that particular people are given particular opportunities, or are required to report to someone other than usual on the project. As team members are promoted, they are going to want to perform a slightly different role on the project to the one they performed the last time you may have worked together. As long as the senior managers on the project are clear on all of these issues from the outset, there should be no problems.

8.4.4   The Development Environment

Assuming team members have the correct tools and materials, it is also important to set up the best possible development environment if you are to optimize speed and quality of delivery. The subsections that follow discuss some of the key elements to consider.

Servers

Clearly there will at some point have to be a server on which the live site is hosted. By live, I mean the server on which the site that is accessible to the target end users is hosted. As discussed previously, the earlier this can be set up, the better.

It is highly likely you will also want a production server you can use internally to host and review work in progress. Having a local server makes it much easier to configure, and much quicker to save work to (rather than having to upload it), and page load times are much faster, as you are connecting to the server over the LAN rather than the Internet. As far as possible, this production server should mirror exactly the final live server so that you can do iterative development testing on the production server and be confident that you will get the same results on the live server. However, you should not assume this will be the case.

You should also set up a "staging" server, or at least a staging area, on the live server. A staging server is an exact replica of the live server, and should be physically as close to the live server as possible. Having an extra server will clearly add to the cost, but it is very useful for reviewing work in progress, and for testing scenarios, and it can act as a backup if the live server goes down. A staging server or area allows you to "rehearse" the real thing before the big opening night, when your site will be performing for its intended audience.

If you cannot justify a separate staging server, you can create a replica of the site in a password-protected directory on the live server. This allows you and the client to see and test the site before you transfer files from the staging area of the server into the live directory. Here you can be sure that the server environment is exactly the same, as it is the same server, though you still need to be careful about relative and absolute path names when moving directories (or you could end up with broken links). If there is a problem with the server, however, this type of staging area does not provide you with any type of backup.

As already discussed, email is a very important tool. Think about how you can use your mail server effectively. You could set up a project directory on the mail server that only the project team has access to. Create an email group for the project so that you can easily email everyone on the team. Both of these measures help people find things more quickly, ease communication, and foster a feeling of belonging to a group. If you are going to be doing a lot of content transfer by email, you may also want to check to see what file size limits you have on your inbound and outbound emails, and what limits your client is working to. You could then change your settings to reflect the client's to avoid emails not going through.

Version Control and Backups

Both version control and backing up data are important elements of a successful development environment, for obvious reasons. Make sure version control practices, or software, are being used as necessary, particularly if many people are working on the same project elements. This tends to occur most often in programming.

Be careful when editing files on the live site. Sometimes files are edited on the live site, usually either because the programmer is in a rush or a problem needs fixing immediately. If this must happen, make sure the newly edited file gets transferred or downloaded to the production and staging servers. There's nothing quite as frustrating or embarrassing as another programmer taking over and unwittingly uploading the original buggy file over the live, corrected one, requiring that an old problem that resurfaces be fixed a second time.

Backing up and archiving files has to be done, and done regularly—ideally, every night. Hopefully your company has a policy for doing backups and archiving files that may include storing data offsite. If you do need to retrieve backed-up data, find out in advance how long a process this is and what it involves. If you assume it is straightforward, free, and that anyone can do it, you may be in for a nasty surprise.

Conventions

The senior members in the team for each of the skill areas should define any conventions his or her team members should adhere to when doing their work. This might include file naming conventions, coding standards, code commenting practices, directory structuring conventions, and archiving and backup practices.

Connectivity

It may sound obvious, considering we are talking about Internet development, but trying to make sure the development team has access to a high-speed and reliable Internet connection is very important. As they will be needing to do many uploads and downloads, a fast and reliable connection will save a lot of time and avoid important transfers cutting out at vital points. Typically, the team members are also likely to use the Internet for other personal and professional reasons, making good Internet connectivity a welcome and much appreciated luxury. Unfortunately, once you've had it good once, you expect it to be at least that good all of the time.

8.5   Team Management

You are not capable of producing the site on your own. You don't have the skills or the time. This means you have to rely on a team effort to get the work done. Ultimately, the success of a Web site, as with most things, depends on the experience and talent of the people who work on it, and on how successfully they work together. How well you manage the team, employing all of your skills as a project manager, is critical to the project's success. The following subsections explore some areas and suggestions important to effective team management.

8.5.1   Tell Them About You

You can spend a lot of your time trying to make other peoples' lives easier, trying to sort out their problems while staying calm under pressure. It might seem like you are totally in control, can handle anything, and perhaps even enjoy being under extreme pressure. Although you do need to act as if this were the case, for the sake of the client and the sake of the team, your team should also understand and appreciate that under your cool facade you too may be suffering, that you are doing your best, and that you are trying your hardest to help them out.

Explain the challenges you face as a project manager. The team may not appreciate how well you are brokering the demands of a client with the wishes of the development team. They need to see that you are not just inventing the deadlines you give them. A lot of thought and work has gone into the scheduling and documentation. There is a calculated reason for everything.

8.5.2   Understand Their Jobs

Just as you want your team to appreciate what you are doing, so too should you make an effort to understand what they do. The better you understand what they do, the better you will be able to communicate with them. We all appreciate it if someone shows a genuine interest in our work.

You will improve your team management skills to no end if you can understand the different ways the team's members work and think, the different challenges they face, and the things that make their jobs easier or more difficult. You should also take some reward in learning, picking up new skills and knowledge.

Sometimes you find that you can even cross-fertilize skills and knowledge through teams. For example, if one designer who worked with you had a particularly good tool for optimizing files, you might be able to suggest it to other designers you work with. If you know that one programmer has already developed a piece of code to do what you want, you can pass this on to another programmer. Learning, understanding, and then sharing knowledge and expertise is vital in the creation of really outstanding development teams.

If you can understand the tasks your team members perform, you are in a better position to defend and explain their actions, which can be very important when communicating with the client. You can understand and explain why it isn't that easy to change something. You will understand, for example, that it isn't always as straightforward as uploading new content; there may be, for example, a complicated search-and-replace process (to ensure file paths are correct on the new server) that first needs to take place, and files may need to be zipped to decrease file size, speed upload, and maintain their directory structure. The more you understand the jobs of your team members, the greater trust they will have in you and the greater respect they will have for you.

8.5.3   Involvement in Client Meetings

Sometimes I wish I could swap jobs with some of the resources I work with just so they could see what it is I have to do and how much work is put in on their behalf. It can feel like you have the hard lot and they the easier one.

However, in order to help others see over your particular Web project management fence, it is useful to take them along to client meetings. In many cases this is necessary anyway, but sometimes it is worth taking members of the team along who may not normally need to attend. Not only will this make them feel more in touch with the project but they will also be able to appreciate what it is like to deal with the client. The next time you tell them that X has asked for Y, they will appreciate what X is like and understand the importance that Y gets done. In addition, other members of the team will feel more comfortable speaking to the client in your absence.

8.5.4   Workflow

Managing and facilitating the workflow through a team is clearly important in your effort to maximize speed of production without compromising quality. We have already looked at issues such as communication, management, and reporting structures; briefing skills; and the development environment. These all contribute to the efficient flow of work through the team.

Another consideration is that different team members will be used to working in different ways. Perhaps they are new to the team and bring with them working practices from another company. An example that comes to mind is the handover and transfer of work between designers and programmers. In some cases, designers will only create Photoshop documents and expect the programmers to partition the graphics and optimize the file sizes. Some programmers prefer it this way, as they can be sure to get the graphics as they need them for programming. Other programmers would see cutting up graphics and file optimization as something designers should do.

You might want to investigate team members' understanding of internal sign-off procedures, including at what point the programming team will make work available for you to see on the production server, and then on the staging and live servers. If you do not smooth out these workflow issues, you can run into some bottlenecks and misunderstandings on the project. Usually it will be fairly easy to resolve such issues, but it is worth thinking through such workflow issues for any given project team at the beginning of the production phase.

TIP   **I can't think that far ahead**

Conventional project management wisdom says that in order to keep a team focused and motivated, no project should be longer than three months. If it is, create a separate project. No task, with a set of deliverables, should take longer than two weeks. In fact, for Web projects, three or four days is the usual maximum task time you should work to.

8.5.5   Resolving Issues

Any problems within a team should be overcome through good communication. In fact, if the communication is good, you rarely come across problems. However, there may be times personal problems or particular working relationships cause a breakdown that is affecting the success of the project.

As a project manager your responsibilities are limited to the project itself. Often you will be working with team members who are more senior. Discipline is a line management responsibility rather than a project management responsibility. If a team member is causing problems, you can have a word with them. If this has no effect, you should talk to that person's line manager, whether or not they are on the project, rather than try to discipline that person in any way yourself. This would only sour your relationship with that person and further threaten the project.

If someone in the team has a real problem with you, hopefully they feel comfortable coming to you to talk about it. If the problem remains, they should take it up with their manager, who will discuss it with you. In some cases, often for perfectly harmless reasons, it is better to move someone off the project than risk continued conflict or pain.

8.5.6   Staying in Touch

You should try to make sure you have as much contact with your team during the production phase as possible. You will see them in team meetings and when you are briefing them, but you should also make an effort to drop by from time to time to see how they are getting on.

You might find that they do not always communicate issues as quickly as you would hope, so you can find out what is going wrong sooner if you go to them rather than leaving it up to them to come to you. You will also learn a lot about what they do by chatting with them as they work.

However, you need to balance staying in touch with your team members with being too overbearing. Just like you, they need quality time to think, time to themselves. If you give the impression you do not trust them and are looking over their shoulder to check up on their work, they will object to you coming around. If they feel you are genuinely interested in what they are doing, this should not be an issue.

Recognize that sometimes people do not want to be disturbed in their work. If a programmer or designer is in the midst of thought, you are probably best off leaving them alone. Agree on a good time for you to come and see them, or email them to see if it is all right to come and talk to them.

8.6   Work in Progress

Due to the evolutionary nature of a Web site and the comparative ease with which most changes and additions can be made, you could consider a site never finished: it is always work in progress (WIP). And because a Web site is in one place but can be seen anywhere in the world, the opportunities for seeing WIP during the development period would seem to be excellent.

Clearly this notion that the final product can be viewed at all stages of its development is attractive to the client, because they can make sure they are getting what they want. From the development team's point of view, it should be good news too, as they are in less danger of creating something the client then refuses to accept. The next few subsections look at some of the methods of reporting and showing WIP, and some of the issues these methods raise.

8.6.1   Reporting on WIP

We have already covered the two major ways of reporting on WIP: project status meetings and the resulting progress report. These represent the chance to report, discuss, and review WIP before documenting it and moving on.

However, you will be using other methods to report on WIP. These will include any emails, letters, faxes, and phone calls you make to the client to keep them up to date with what is going on; asking questions; and arranging meetings. You don't want to continually pester your client, but as a rule the more up to date with the project's status they feel, the better. The level of detail into which you go when reporting on WIP will depend on who you are reporting to. The main client may only be interested in hearing about progress at a general level, whereas other contacts you have at the client organization may want much more detail.

As you may be communicating with many different client contacts on the phone, by email, and so on, not everyone will hear everything you say. Your reports risk ending up in small pieces that somehow get put together to form a different picture at the client's end than the picture you had on your end. To avoid this, it is worth doing a project status report, including a summary of WIP, which you email out to all parties concerned, perhaps once a week.

8.6.2   Showing WIP

There is a danger that by showing clients WIP you open yourself up to continual change requests. When the client looks at the work, they cannot help but react to it. They are also not in full possession of the facts, as you are. For example, you may know that a particular function does not yet work, but they may think it is supposed to work. So, although it is good that clients can see WIP and react to it, you need to make sure you control their eagerness to comment and make changes and unfair assumptions. This is discussed in more detail in Section 8.6.3.

TIP   **Be seen in the best light**

Try to make sure that any clients have the necessary browser, operating system, screen resolutions, plug-ins, and so on to see the site at its best during the production phase. On the whole, the client is not interested in cross-browser issues per se, but is interested if what they are looking at is giving error messages or looks all wrong. Make sure they are properly set up before they ever look at any work in progress. If you only configure their setup as a result of "bugs" in what they look at, they will

- lose confidence in your coding abilities,
- think you are upgrading their machine as an excuse,
- worry that all site users will have to go through this upgrade process, and
- not believe that the "bugs" were going to be ironed out at the testing phase.

It's much better to do a subtle check early on and have a small word in the ear of the IS department about upgrades and configuration.

It is clearly very important to find a way to show clients WIP. You need to have their sign-off in order to continue. You also want them to be part of the project, as they will have a much better understanding of their business, their brand, and their customers than you do. To create a really great site, you need a strong partnership between client and development team, where each respects the other's knowledge and expertise and the two complement each other's strengths.

Table 8.4, which follows, looks at some of the vehicles for showing work in progress, and the advantages and disadvantages of each. The order in which they appear in the table reflects the order in which they typically occur in a project.

Table 8.4 Methods of showing WIP.

Method and description of showing work in progress	Advantages	Disadvantages
Storyboards: Black-and-white sketches or outlines of the Web pages	Quick and easy to do; can be done by project manager.	Don't look impressive, risk underselling the finished article, and no design or interactivity.
On-screen talk-through: You talk the client through a design on-screen	You can explain the rationale behind the design, you can try out alternatives as you go, and you get the client's full attention.	You still don't have the motion, audio, and interactivity, so the client can be "underwhelmed." The client makes changes just because they can.
JPGs by email: Create JPGs of the Web pages and email them to the client for review	It is quick, cheap, and easy. It allows for easy dialog. It leaves the client with a copy of the design to show internally.	Still no interaction. Client might think "this is very slow to load." The JPG may get sent to people it shouldn't, and the client might not explain any of the design rationale when passing on the JPG.
Color printouts: Full-color printouts of the Web pages	You can present them with explanatory words and text. These can look very impressive if well bound and mounted. You can include your company's branding in the presentation if you wish.	Costly to produce. Costly and slower to mail over. Not easily changed. Colors when printed out can look different and have less impact than on-screen.
CD-ROM/disk: A copy of the Web pages on a CD-ROM or disk	You can show the site as it will really be, with interactivity and functionality; it will be very fast, as it is running locally; and you do not get caching, firewall, or proxy server problems.	Time consuming to do (see previous tip), risk in client perceiving this as the finished product before testing, and danger that you are then committed to continual disk updates.
Staging server: A version of the site to see on a staging server or in a staging area of the live server	You see the real thing in situ. You are effectively testing the site as you go. The client gets a true impression of how the site performs. The ISP will be backing up your work.	You can spend a lot of valuable time uploading files. The client may allow others access to the site who are using out-of-date technology (e.g., old browsers), bringing up issues that wouldn't otherwise have arisen; you become liable to explaining problems that are outside your control (e.g., the Internet itself, ISP downtime, and outages).

TIP   **Local running version of the site**

A client may want a CD-ROM version of the site to show in development or to show on a laptop to their customers. This is not as straightforward as it sounds. Unless the site is only flat HTML files (which few sites are), a Web server will be needed with the correct operating system, scripting engines, and other software. Path names, .ini files, database registrations, and so on may need to be modified for it to work. Check with your programmers before committing to a schedule. Build this work into your budget and critical path if you know it will be required.

8.7 Sign-Off

Sign-off means that the client has seen the work you have done and approved it. It depends on the nature of the relationship with the client as to how formal this needs to be. A verbal "yes" might suffice, or you may need the actual signature(s) of the client(s), to be sure. Sign-off is very important, as it allows you to progress without being concerned that the client will change their mind. If they do change their mind, you can alter things, but this would have an impact on the budget and the deadlines.

8.7.1 The Dangers in Omitting Sign-Off

Imagine that you have created the entire site and have all along assumed from the client's lack of comment that everything is okay. A week before launch, the client wants the design completely changed. They never liked it in the first place, and have never approved it. What can you do? Not much. Equally, you might be getting verbal OKs from your main client contact, and that person then leaves the company for another job. The new client contact does not like the work you have done and wants it changed. As there is no written evidence of prior approvals, it is more difficult to show why you will need additional time and money to make the changes.

8.7.2 Approaches to Getting Sign-Off

A good middle ground between verbal sign-off and written sign-off is to write progress reports after each meeting that document what was discussed and what was taken as being signed off. This is something we looked at when discussing effective meeting management. If the client does not agree with the progress report, they can document why not. The progress reports are archived by date so that you have the entire history of decisions to fall back on if necessary.

It is important for there to be a point of contact at the client organization who is senior enough to have decision-making and sign-off powers on the majority of decisions concerning the Web project, be they legal, technical, creative, personnel, or commercial. Clearly your client contact will refer to specialists within his company in order to make the decisions. Often sign-off meetings will need to take place, with representatives of the client's IS or legal departments present. Your client contact should still be present at these meetings, so that she understands the issues involved and can make any decisions required.

8.8 Change Control

The way you manage change through the project will depend on the nature of your relationship with the client and the size and nature of the project. Generally, the larger and more complex the project, and the more rigid the specifications, the more tightly you will have to manage change.

8.8.1 Recognizing When a Change Matters

As we have already discussed, change is fundamental to the nature of the Web. One of the things the Internet is sold on is the ease with which you can change your site. For many changes, this is true; it is certainly a lot easier, faster, and cheaper to edit a word in HTML on your site than it is to reprint your entire corporate brochure because of a typing mistake in the print. You and your development team will know the difference between what constitutes a major change that will impact on the project and what is only a very minor change that can be absorbed within the project's schedules and budgets. Your client, however, may not initially understand why one thing is difficult to change and another is simple. Over time, the client will become better educated as to what changes are straightforward and what will have larger implications.

DILBERT reprinted by permission of United Feature Syndicate, Inc.

The project specification exists in part to protect you against having to implement change without gaining extra time or money for doing so. If the change takes you beyond what is detailed in the project specification, which may also mean it is outside the terms of your contracted work, you are entitled to go back to the client to seek further time and payment. In practice, you would seek to build up a trust with your client such that there was some mutually understood give-and-take along these lines throughout the project.

8.8.2   Change Request Forms

If you are concerned that change needs to be more formally controlled, you could borrow from more traditional software project management methods and require that a change request form be filled in and approved by the required authorities before you will make any change. Such a form might include the following elements:

- ▶ Project name
- ▶ Date
- ▶ Change description
- ▶ Change requested by
- ▶ Impact of change on other project elements
- ▶ Requested start and completion dates
- ▶ Resources required
- ▶ Approved by

8.8.3 Managing the Client's Expectations

You should try to educate the client as to the nature of change in the context of the working practices of your team and the nature of the Web. Explain that you can make the change now, but to do so would set back the development schedule and interrupt the workflow of the team. It may be that the client has had experience with print projects in which it is more important to make sure changes are done, and are *seen* to be done, so that a mistake does not slip through and go to press. Assure the client that the changes will be done. Tell them when they will be done and when they will be able to see the changes made. Make a note of every change requested, and add it to an action list you can then discuss and review at your project status meetings with the client. Once they feel comfortable that you do note all of their requested changes, and that they do happen, they will become less insistent that changes happen instantly.

In some cases, you may feel that the requested change is, in any case, not sensible or not feasible within the development schedule. Rather than saying you cannot do it right away, which sounds very defensive and negative, note it down and make it one of the discussion points on your agenda for the next client meeting. You could propose that the changes be incorporated as part of a phase 2 implementation. Sometimes you find that what the client found very important one day does not concern them the next, or that they have completely changed their minds. Giving a little breathing and thinking space immediately after a change is requested, then bringing it up for discussion and confirmation at a meeting, is a good way of weeding out the necessary changes from the impulsive ones.

If you have several clients you are working with on a single project, you can find that one will request a change without consulting the others. You make the change and then the others ask why the change was made, and can it be put back to how it was. To avoid the frustration of this happening, you should again note down the requested change and bring it up for review at your next meeting, where all of the relevant client contacts will be present. Once again, you can then be sure that you only make changes that all are agreed on. It will also then ensure that the several client contacts do not ask for changes without first considering how they will then justify those changes to colleagues and, indeed, to superiors.

8.9 Documentation

After the documentation frenzy of the preproduction phase, which culminates in the project specification grand finale, you may be glad that the production phase requires a lot less in the way of formal documentation. What you need to be doing in this phase is documenting all project communication (in particular, emails, progress reports, and anything in writing) for creating a written project history and paper trails of decisions. This is for reference purposes if need be, or to benefit anyone coming into the project new, particularly on the project management front.

TIP   **Get yourself noticed**

How important is an email? Although the tone of emails is usually informal, and the immediacy of communication less formal than a letter, emails still exist in writing and can be stored away as evidence. If you want to make sure that particular emails you send get noticed rather than deleted without being read, there are several things you can try.

- Set the priority level higher so that the message is flagged.
- Dream up an attention-grabbing subject line.
- Most effective of all is whom you copy the email to. If the receiver sees that the email has gone to important people, they will treat it as important. If they see you have copied it to yourself, they will probably understand you are covering yourself and be intrigued to find out why.

8.10 Prototyping

As part of the preproduction phase, or as part of an elongated pitch process in some cases, you may have created a prototype to demonstrate your abilities and to try to solidify some of the creative and functional ideas and solutions you were proposing. The sections that follow discuss various aspects of prototyping.

8.10.1   Market Research

A prototype can serve a very useful "proof of concept" purpose, and it can be used to conduct usability tests, market research, and focus groups to get feedback before you go on to create the main product. If you are investing a large amount of money in a site and want to be convinced that what you are creating will appeal to your target market, creating a prototype can be very effective.

8.10.2   Approaches to Prototyping

There are two ways of looking at a prototype. You might see the prototype as being the actual site-to-be in its early stages: a version of the site that will then evolve into the final product. Or, you might see a prototype as a "test bed" entity to be developed along different lines to serve a specific purpose. Once that purpose is served, it can then be dropped in order to start from the ground up on the main site, incorporating lessons learned from the prototype. This is often called a "throwaway" prototype.

Although the second option might not seem to capitalize on valuable work already done (in the same way that the first does), it is a better option for Web projects. Why?

The prototype should serve a purpose. With development lead times needing to be compressed as much as possible in a race to get to market, there seems to be little point spending too much time and effort on the prototype, as long as it can do its job. For a prototype, you can dispense with testing, not worry about image sizes, download times, cross-browser functionality, code documentation, server environments, scalability, and all of the other things you will need to do for the actual site. The prototype needs to be developed as quickly and cost effectively as possible.

As long as the target market and client can see and use the site the same way they will finally use it, it matters less if the code is hacked together, the pages are really just giant image maps, the "site" only runs in one browser and only on one particular server, or even if it is a multimedia application disguised as a Web site. Using this approach, you are able to give the users a fuller experience of what the final site will be, even though it may be a "mocked-up" experience. You should do just enough for the prototype to serve its purpose.

There is a large caveat that goes with this approach to prototypes, and that is the need to manage the client's expectations. You need to be clear about the prototype's limitations and give your reasons why it has been done as it has. Most importantly, you need to explain that just because the prototype has been put together in record time does not mean the main site will follow a similar development path. If the client likes the prototype, there is a danger they will feel the site is almost done. You will know that it is only held together by gum and bits of string. If you do create a prototype of this sort, you must make sure the client understands the processes you will still need to go through once an accepted prototype has been created.

If you want to be sure the prototype you create can also then grow to become the actual site, you need to ensure you build it on the firm foundations necessary for the finished product. This will include hosting the site on the actual servers, making sure your files are named and structured correctly, writing cross-browser compatible code, and so on. Every element you add to a prototype of this sort should aim to be what will finally be there. This inevitably means that creating a prototype of this sort takes longer, and you will probably only be able to give users a more limited experience of what the final site will be early on in the development process.

If you try to tread a path between these two prototyping approaches, you risk rushing to create something that then gets changed, is not properly thought through and sufficiently robust, and yet that has to form the foundation of your final site. You will find you are constantly patching up problems, and though your final site may work, it will be a painful process creating and maintaining it. You will live in fear that the house of cards that supports the site may one day come tumbling down.

8.10.3   Forms of Prototyping

As mentioned previously, whatever type of prototype you decide to go for, it is very important to make sure the client has the correct expectations of the extent and nature of the prototype and the purpose it is serving. The nature of the prototype will include defining how you intend to present the prototype. You may not think it is worth doing the prototype as an actual Web site. Consider creating a PowerPoint slide presentation instead, which walks the user through typical paths the site might contain. You can include hot spots, motion, sound, and some degree of interactivity. If there is one particular application on the site that is very important, you might want to show this as a multimedia application if this is quicker and simpler than creating the entire Web application.

For the extent of the prototype, you need to make clear how much of the site you are intending to show. The client will want to see as much of the site as possible, but you need to limit what you do to what is necessary for the purpose. It is generally accepted that you have to show the home page. It represents the first and most important impression a first-time user will get of the site, and it sets the tone and standard for the rest of the site. It is often a good idea not to even start on any of the other pages until you have a home page the client and you are comfortable with. As it defines so much of what else is on the site, you need to get this right first.

Once you have the home page, you have the spine of the site around which you can then begin to build the skeleton, and perhaps flesh out a few areas of interest. You might want to take a horizontal approach, in which you take the top layer of the site map and create the home pages for all main sections of the site. You might decide to take a vertical approach, in which you drill down, following one particular navigational path through all layers of one section of the site.

Perhaps the best approach is to do a combination. This can be called a "T" prototype. The shape of the T, if you imagine it placed on a site map, shows how you will be representing the breadth and depth of the site, enabling the user to picture what the rest of the site might be like. You show what the look and feel for each section will be by creating the top-level section home pages. You show how the navigation and interaction would work by following an example path down through the site.

8.11   Troubleshooting

It would be unrealistic not to have a section on troubleshooting, wouldn't it? Despite the best-laid plans, things can and do go wrong. Talking about the roles and responsibilities of the Web project manager in an earlier chapter, I suggested that if things didn't go wrong, perhaps you weren't pushing yourself or the project hard enough and that actually mistakes and problems are one of the best ways to learn. That said, there will be enough to troubleshoot without you actively creating problems. So, what methods of prevention and cure can you use?

8.11.1 Catch Problems Before They Become Problems

As we know, prevention is better than cure. Don't, whatever you do, hide from a problem you see coming. Address it as soon as possible, even if it is difficult to tell the client. It will always surface later, and be much uglier if you leave it. The severity of a problem increases logarithmically in proportion to the time you don't address it. Flag it early, and you can solve it before it gets to be a big problem. The more experience you have, the more you can feel a problem brewing in your bones, like a tremor out at sea that starts the imperceptible ripple that becomes the tidal wave.

8.11.2 Turn a Problem to Your Favor

Trust is the most important thing you can build with your client. This is difficult to win at first, and can be easy to lose. With trust, the working relationship is much more enjoyable and efficient, and produces better quality.

Ironically perhaps, one of the best ways to win a client's trust is to flag a potential problem, say how you are working to resolve it, and report back to them when you have resolved it. If you do this, when you have a problem you cannot do anything about (e.g., some software bugs), the client will trust you that it really is a problem that is out of your hands rather than an excuse on your part.

The client realizes as well as you do that there are bound to be problems. If you can be seen to tackle them positively and proactively, the client will have increased faith in you. You should always have a solution to the problem, even if it isn't the ideal solution. If possible, don't bring up a problem until you have a solution. Try not to look panicked to the client, even if you are, as it will unsettle them and they will then chase you for a resolution, meaning that you are less likely to get it done.

If there is a problem the client knows they have created, you will do particularly well to solve it for them. If you can put yourself out to help them, you are sure to reap the rewards at another point in the project.

8.11.3   Share the Problem

A problem shared is a problem halved—sometimes, even solved. If you face a problem you don't feel confident about resolving, ask for help. Share and spread the load of the problem to higher-level management. They would rather try to resolve it early than have you come to them when it has become a disaster and it is too late to redeem. Make sure any serious issues are documented, and that your requests for assistance are made in writing and filed.

Although spreading the responsibility of problem solving can be very effective, throwing more people at a problem rarely gets it resolved faster. Throwing people at a problem usually makes it worse, as you confuse the issue and raise levels of concern.

TIP   **Honesty is the best policy**

Be honest with yourself. Do you really think it looks good? Do you really think it will work? Does every instinct tell you that this is going to become an issue? You're often right, and it will all come out in the wash if you don't do something about it early on. Don't hide from problems in the hope they will go away. You will only have yourself to blame if you suffer for it later on.

8.11.4   Why Is the Client Having a Problem That You Are Not?

A typical problem—particularly during the production phase, during which the client is trying to view and comment on work in progress—is that they seem to be having problems you are not. This can be frustrating for all involved, and you can spend a lot of time trying to mend something that perhaps wasn't broken in the first place. The following are some of the more common questions you should ask yourself or your client when trying to work out the problem.

▶ Are they looking at a previous version cached either by their browser or a proxy server?
▶ What is their browser's font size set to?
▶ Is it a Mac/PC issue (e.g., a Mac rendering and sizing of a PC font)?

- ▶ In their browser settings, do they have Java, cookies, JavaScript, or any other options disabled that might be causing the problem?
- ▶ Could it be something to do with settings administered at an organizational level rather than at an individual level? For example, are FTP downloads, cookies, Java, or email file attachments disallowed?
- ▶ Does the corporate firewall prevent content entering through certain server ports you might be using?
- ▶ Is a script or ASP being cached by the Web server for some reason?
- ▶ Have you sent content in too high a software version for the client to open; for example, Word 2000 instead of Word 95?
- ▶ Have you tried to email files that are too big for the client to receive?
- ▶ Are they using a cookies-based function but sitting at a different machine than usual?
- ▶ What build version of what browser are they using?
- ▶ Are they looking at the right site? For example, it is easy to look at the live site and think you are looking at the development site, and vice versa.
- ▶ Do they have Caps Lock on, meaning that they cannot enter a password-protected area?
- ▶ What is their screen resolution and color depth set to?
- ▶ Is there a problem with their Internet connection?
- ▶ Is there a problem with the Internet itself?

If it is none of the previous reasons, check that you are not making any of these "mistakes" at your end. You too might be looking at an older version than the client is seeing. If you have checked at your end and talked things through with your client and still can't work out what is wrong, try overwriting or re-uploading the files and actually going to the client to see for yourself what does or doesn't happen.

8.12 Summary

The following are significant points raised in this chapter.

- ▶ You will need to think both at a macro level (long-term planning, overall objectives, and so on) and a micro level (day-to-day implementation, troubleshooting, and so on) during this work stage. Set aside time to plan, think, recap, and double-check that you are not missing anything important.

▶ Focused meetings and good team management are vital to ensure this work stage is as efficient and productive as possible. The potential for wasting resources is greatest during this phase of the project.

▶ Establish a way to show the client work in progress and keep them regularly updated.

▶ Establish a production "rhythm" that all feel comfortable with. This might include regular meetings, progress reports, deliverables, checklists, sign-off points, change control, and so on.

▶ Make sure you store a "paper trail" of all decisions made. Someone not involved in the project should be able to audit the progress and process of the project from your documentation.

▶ You should be clear about what function the prototype is serving and build it accordingly. Carefully manage the client's expectations of how far the prototype and final site might differ.

The design and construction work stage is often the most gratifying, as it is the point in the project when the largest team is working together and you can build up a good spirit. After the initial documentation and planning, and before the testing, it is also great to see content and applications coming to life. It is often the period in which you encounter the greatest highs and lows of the project, the biggest client problems, as well as the greatest project successes. Every day presents challenges to resolve and decisions that need to be made. To make sure that all of the work you do in the design and construction work stage is not undermined, you need to get the next work stage, "testing, launch, and handover," correct as well.

9

Work Stage 6: Testing, Launch, and Handover

Team motivation is incredibly important. People are motivated when they feel they're on a pathway to success and completion. I once worked in the Interactive Division of a large media company. There was another team there that had been working on "Project X" for over two years that had never gone past the project and budget approval stage. It was Prototype City. Months went by as they watched other teams churning out CD-ROMs and having wrap parties. The difference in morale between the Project X team and the other teams was mind boggling.

—**Janet Kirker, Vice President, Project Development, Global New Media, USA**

Preproduction			Production			Maintenance	Evaluation
Project clarification	Solution definition	Project specification	Content	Design and constructio	Testing, launch, and handover	Maintenance	Review and evaluation

As the project builds toward launch, you and your team will probably be feeling quite tired, and your head will be full of details concerning the project. You may even be dreaming about it. You are buoyed along by the big buildup to the launch, which represents your end goal, and by a chance to have a little bit of a breather and, hopefully, to celebrate the fruits of your labor.

As you move toward the launch, it is easy to become caught up in the marketing and PR that may be going on, or to begin to slack a little, so that you don't properly plan and thoroughly carry through some of the more mundane details of your testing or launch preparations. However, you must make sure these areas are properly covered, or you risk destroying all of the good work you have done. The client will quickly forget how well you handled the production phase if the launch goes horribly wrong and they lose face with their customers.

Earlier I suggested you might want to use an external testing agency to do the rigorous final testing of the site prelaunch. If you have a large site and a budget that will stretch to paying for specialist testers, this is a good way of ensuring the testing does get done as thoroughly and objectively as necessary. You will still need to understand what they are proposing to do in order to brief them correctly and to work with them efficiently to iron out any issues the testing uncovers. In many cases, you and your team may be doing some, if not all, of the testing yourselves.

The section that follows goes through some of the testing methods you might expect to employ, either with your own team or through an external team. Section 9.2, on the launch, reminds you of what things you should be considering and how you should prepare for launch. Section 9.3, Handover, talks about the process and constituent parts of handing over a Web project.

9.1   Testing

Proper time for testing should have been built into the critical path and budgeted for. You should not compromise on the amount of time needed to properly test the site before launch. You should also set a milestone in the critical path after which no new content or changes will be accepted, so that you can concentrate on testing what you do have. The testing phase is to test for functional and operational problems, not as an opportunity to make changes to the content or functionality.

The testing covered in the following sections is largely the testing carried out just prior to product launch following the completion of production. Some of the testing (e.g., focus groups) is also relevant to the preproduction phase. One area of testing not specifically covered is what might be termed "developmental" or "iterative development" testing. Essentially, this means the testing and bug fixing you do as you go. Because you will be viewing the site as work in progress in its final environment, there is a lot you can do to reduce the amount of testing in the final stages. However, this testing is not formalized, it is more a matter of noting down bugs as they arise and then fitting them into the schedule as appropriate, usually along with other small changes. It is not worth spending too much time on developmental testing, as the site may change or you may only create new bugs that then also have to be rectified.

The role of the project manager during the testing phase is largely to ensure that it is done and that it is done to the project specification. This is little different, then, from the project manager's role during the rest of the design and construction phase. What is different, however, is that you will need a different knowledge base to understand and manage the process of testing effectively. On smaller projects, this is often much more "hands on" than during the rest of the design and construction phase. It is not unusual for the project manager to actually *be* one of the testers, as well as coordinating the process.

9.1.1 Selling the Importance of Testing

The client will not always appreciate the need and cost of the testing phase. It works on their browser fine, so isn't it ready to go live? Why does it need to be tested—surely you have been testing as you go, and you wouldn't create something that had something wrong with it in the first place? Why should I pay for bug fixes? These are all understandable comments. You need to explain to the client why the testing phase is so important. An aircraft is not built with the expectation that faults will be found in it, but you would still expect it to be thoroughly tested under all conditions it might be exposed to before you would fly in it. Those conditions are difficult to predict, so the aircraft should be tested to extremes you wouldn't normally encounter. Likewise, you want to make sure the site is not going to disappoint and lose users by underperforming in certain environments. This will include various browsers, operating systems, screen resolutions, and so on, according to the parameters you set in the technical specification. If security is of great importance, you might have recommended further security testing as part of your QA/testing plan included in the project specification.

In order to gain the client's commitment, you might want to charge a reduced rate for the test phase. You might also want to call it something different, such as "quality assurance," but it is very important that you give yourself this buffer zone before the site goes live. At least a two-week testing period for a commercial Web site is recommended.

9.1.2   Types of Testing

In Chapter 6, some of the types of testing you might be carrying out on your site were outlined as follows:

▶ User acceptance/usability testing
▶ Functional testing
▶ Operational testing
▶ Scenario testing/load testing
▶ Security/penetration attack testing
▶ Copy proofing

These varying methods will give you both quantitative and qualitative results, and objective and subjective opinions. The method by which you employ each, or combination of the techniques, will depend on the requirements of the project, in particular the nature of the site's use and the type of end user.

The subsections that follow look at each of these forms of testing in detail. This should help you see which forms of testing are going to be most suitable to your project. You should draw up a testing plan, often in conjunction with your technical consultants or programmers, which should be included in the project specification. By the time you actually reach this stage in the project, you should already know what type of testing you are going to be performing.

User Acceptance Testing

This is sometimes called usability testing, but in the good tradition of Web TLAs (three-letter acronyms), at least "user acceptance testing" gives us the opportunity to refer to it as UAT.

Strictly speaking, acceptance testing is a more accurate description of testing performed to prove that an application meets specified requirements. In the software development world, where specifications are a lot more detailed and more firmly controlled, acceptance testing allows the client to "accept" that the product meets the predefined specification. In the Web world, and with the addition of *user* to *acceptance*, it has come to mean whether the product "works" for the user.

UAT is about trying out your ideas with selected users, usually taken from the target end user group. You have your ideas as to what will work, but UAT provides the opportunity to see your ideas in action; to road test them with the people that count (namely, the prospective customers).

There are a number of methods typically used for UAT, including observation techniques (e.g., accompanied browsing and observing users interacting with the site), moderated email groups, heuristic analysis, card sorting, focus groups, and peer reviews.

There are two points in the development cycle at which you might consider UAT. If you have the time and budget, and particularly if you are creating a prototype, at the end of the preproduction phase (when you have defined a solution), you could use UAT to test run your solution. Any results could then be fed back into the production phase, ensuring the minimum amount of reworking necessary.

You might also conduct UAT during the final testing phase of the project, just before launch. However, this does not give you much room to maneuver. If there turns out to be a major design flaw, it might set the launch date back. However, if you are fairly confident the site is almost right (perhaps you did UAT at the end of the preproduction phase), you could use UAT here to add the finishing touches: users might be able to suggest small changes that dramatically improve the user experience.

Functional Testing

This is perhaps the most obvious and common form of testing you will carry out. You have to go through the entire site to make sure that everything functions as you expect it to, without causing error messages, crashes, or behavior that is totally unexpected. This includes elements such as navigation, not from a subjective point of view as you might get in UAT (e.g., "I don't like the way it does this"), but from an objective, factual point of view (e.g., "This links to the wrong place," or "I can't get to where I want to go").

For Web projects, one large element of this functional testing is to check for cross-browser compatibility. You need to make sure the site operates correctly in all browsers you specified in your technical specification. Similarly, you have to check the sites using the client operating systems you defined.

Finally, you will need to check the design integrity at the various screen resolutions you have specified. If you had specified a total of five operating systems, six different browser versions and configurations, and two different screen resolutions, you would have to go through the entire site 60 times, as indicated in the following formula.

5 operating systems $\times$ 6 browsers $\times$ 2 screen resolutions = 60 site tests

As you can see, with a large site, or even a smaller one, you can very quickly be spending a lot of time on testing. The following are some of the other areas you will be checking as part of functional tests.

- ▶ *Links:* Are there any broken links? Are there incorrect links?
- ▶ *Downloads:* Do all downloads happen as expected?
- ▶ *Online forms:* Can you fill these in and successfully send them?
- ▶ *Load times:* Are there any pages that take too long to load?
- ▶ *Navigation:* Can you get where you want to go?
- ▶ *Design:* Are there elements you can't see or read?
- ▶ *Publishing:* Do all content update and publishing mechanisms work?
- ▶ *Push:* Do list servers, automatic notification features, and so on function properly?
- ▶ *Personalization:* Do the customization and personalization features work?
- ▶ *Printing:* Can you print out Web content where necessary?

When performing functional testing, it is a good idea to start with the lowest common denominator, or the configuration that is likely to cause the most problems. Then test the site using the configuration you think the majority of users will have when accessing the site. If you can make the site work for these two cases, it is likely that it will also work for the other configurations. Once you have made all changes, perform a final test using the setup you think most site users will have, just to check that you haven't created any new problems. This type of test is called a "regression test," where you go back over old ground to make sure nothing unexpected has cropped up to destabilize what was fully functional before.

TIP **Test with Netscape first**

Things may change, but so far Netscape browsers have tended to be slightly more fussy than Internet Explorer about the quality of the code they accept without giving a script error. If you can get the site to work error free in Netscape, it is also likely to work in Internet Explorer.

You should push the boundaries of what might be considered normal site usage when performing the functional testing. For example, when testing a Web form, you should try entering unusual characters. Try entering commas, quotation marks, apostrophes, line breaks, angle brackets, percentage signs, and so on, sometimes all at once, to see if this causes a script error.

There are plenty of software tools available, many that are free, to help you with elements of the functional testing—in particular, for checking for broken links and checking file sizes across the site. See Appendix A, where some of these resources are detailed.

Error Management

As you carry out your testing, you will need to make sure you have an established process for logging and resolving the errors and bugs uncovered. This will involve ensuring that as testers find an error they have a system for logging it. It is recommended that they log all necessary details about the error, pass this information on to the appropriate person for resolution, and finally the resolver logs when the error is resolved. To play it safe, you may want the tester to then try to re-create the error after it has been fixed. If you are conducting regression testing, you may even come back to the error further down the line and try once again to re-create it.

You will develop a preferred method for logging errors and comments during the testing phase. You might feel comfortable controlling the process using a simple Word document, with tables to add the errors to. You might find that Excel is a better tool, in that you can use its sorting functions to good effect (e.g., to rank errors by priority). For smaller projects, where there are only one or two testers, an Excel spreadsheet works quite well. However, because it is a file, it becomes limiting when you have multiple testers working on the same project. You cannot have multiple people inputting to the same Excel file at once, and trying to collate many files into a single master file can become quite tricky, increasing the margin for error.

For a project in which multiple testers are involved, a database is ideal for logging, tracking, and managing errors. Many people can contribute to the database at the same time, and yet there are access and validation controls that make the process more efficient and reliable. The structured nature of a database also forces the defined process to be adhered to. Table 9.1, which

Table 9.1 Elements to include in an error management system.

Error log element	Description
Reference number	If you give every error a unique reference number, it is easier to quickly refer to a particular problem without confusion.
Date logged	The date the error was logged.
Logged by	The tester who logged the error.
Priority	You can assign a level of importance to the error, which might then have an attached turnaround time (see Table 9.2).
Category	For categorizing errors as various types (e.g., links, load time, navigation, and so on).
Description	A detailed description of the error. This should include any error messages generated, as well as a description of exactly how you created the error.
Date error opened	The date the error was first looked at to be resolved.
Error owner	The person responsible for resolving the error.
Comments	Comments of the error owner once he or she has had a chance to look at the error.
Status	The current status of the error (e.g., outstanding, closed, and so on).
Date closed	Date the error is closed.

follows, describes the elements you might want to include in your error logging and management system.

You can assign a priority level to your errors using a numbering system and/or description of the severity of the problem. You should also indicate how quickly the error needs to be addressed. Table 9.2, which follows, is an example of an error prioritization log.

Operational Testing

There is increasingly a need to test the "back-end" operational element of a Web site, particularly if e-commerce is important. Whereas errors seen at the user interface (UI) level are picked up in functional testing, operational testing involves everything that happens after you have left the site, or as a result of your interaction with the site. You need to check, for example, that if you buy a product on the site then it does actually get delivered to you.

These types of operational elements, including stock management and logistics, form a large part of any e-business and contribute enormously to the site's success, as they form a large part of the overall experience for the customer. The following are some of the operational elements you might want to test.

▶ *Delivery times:* Is the product delivered on time?

▶ *Shipping accuracy:* Are you sent the correct product?

▶ *Customer service:* Does the customer service center work? Are there people there to answer your queries? Do they respond within stated periods, and so on?

▶ *Data integrity:* Is data captured by the site properly stored and managed?

Table 9.2 Error prioritization.

Priority	Description	Turnaround time
1	Fatal. Crash or freezing of system, Web site, or application.	4 hours
2	Serious. Incorrect functionality, misconnection between the parts of system/application. It works, but not the way it should.	1 day
3	Significant. Errors that are easier to correct but interfere with the user experience (e.g., JavaScript errors, broken links, and so on).	2 days
4	Minor. Errors that can easily be corrected (e.g., typos, HTML font, color changes, and so on).	At end of test phase

You could also test these elements under various circumstances. How are these elements affected under greater load or volume, for example? This is very important to know if your site is a retail e-business going into the Christmas season. You could test to see how "errors" are handled in an operational context; for example, what happens if you are sent the wrong product? What is the return policy? Who do you contact with complaints?

Defining the limits of your operational testing will depend very much on the scope of the site. In many cases, resolving problems uncovered as a result of this testing will not be something that is the Web development team's responsibility, but the client's or another third party's. However, system integration issues, which might lie at the heart of such problems, may need involvement from both you and the client/third party to finally resolve.

Load Testing

The purpose of load testing is to simulate expected real-life scenarios on a Web site, normally by using automated scripts rather than real-life users. Load testing involves stress testing both the programming technologies used on the site and the hardware capacity of the system.

Using load testing, it is possible to trial run your capacity management provisions. This will show you what you need to cope with spikes in site traffic and allow for future expansion in the server systems based on predicted usage models.

In order to load test the functions of a site, you can simulate usage by emulating GET and POST calls and then checking the server response to make sure the expected message is received. You can benchmark download times, average page response times, and data retrieval times, as well as check for error handling and recovery as you go through various load scenarios.

One of the best ways of testing these scenarios is to use the Perl scripting language and its built-in HTTP socket library. Perl can be used to emulate multiple simultaneous user sessions from a single computer, and thus stress test the Web server and system as if multiple users were interacting with the site. You can gradually increase the simulated volume of simultaneous users, as well as monitor the system's performance over a period of time. When you overload the system, it can crash. You must try to ensure that the Web site knows what to do when the system is becoming overloaded.

There are various software tools and scripts available that can help you perform load testing. See Appendix A, Resources, for some sites to help you get started.

Security Testing

Rigorously testing the security measures on your site may not be necessary. However, if you do have a site where security is extremely important, clearly you should check whether your system is vulnerable.

There are many ways hackers can get into your systems, and it is very difficult (some say impossible) to make something 100% secure. In the preproduction phase, you may have taken recommendations from technical security consultants on measures such as packet filtering using firewalls, encryption, and intrusion detection software. Now is the time to test those recommendations by carrying out controlled penetration attacks. This is a specialist skill that will probably require the help of an external company.

Without going to the extremes of deliberately trying to break into your system, you might want to check more basic features of the site that might compromise security. This could include checking how user names and passwords are controlled, who gives them out, where they are stored, whether they are alphanumeric combinations, and how often they are changed. Check that necessary emails or data really is being encrypted as planned, and that emails are being sent to the correct addresses and not going astray. You could check that there aren't any security breaches made possible by information contained in the source code viewable through the browser. Finally, ensure that you have any necessary security statements available on the site for users to see to what your policies are.

Copy Proofing

Proofing copy may seem like an obvious quality assurance check, and usually it gets done as a matter of course, but the process should be formalized. As the words are there for anyone to see, proofing the copy is often something the client will be eager to do themselves. As you have developed the site, you will probably already have picked up on many typos, missing words, and grammatical errors. It is very easy for these to creep in, particularly where text needs to be rekeyed as part of the programming. With the programmers concentrating on ensuring the code functions as expected, they have less time to be checking for the sense and correctness of the copy itself.

Although you can check for obvious errors and omissions, it is much more difficult for you to know whether all addresses, phone numbers, email addresses, and other contact details are correct. If you are working in-house, you will have a better idea of what these should be. If you are contracted, you have to rely on what the client tells you for correctness. You might, however, have taken details from a brochure that is out of date. Check with the client so that they can confirm all such details. Try phone numbers and send an email to the given addresses just to check that they go through.

9.2 Launch

The big day is coming. Whether it is a completely new site, or a new section of a site, there is a finite point in time when the service will become available to end users. There are several ways you might want to launch your site. You might be launching with much fanfare—with press, marketing, and advertising campaigns to support the launch—or you might decide to set the site live without making any fuss, to see how well it is received and develop it accordingly before you make the big marketing push. With more mature sites, where you might have been asking existing site users to test and respond to new site developments as you go, it is less a case of launching and more a case of adding, evolving, and improving. However, you would still expect to promote the new content on the site and to drive site traffic to your new sections.

These two main approaches to launching a site can be called "soft" launch and "hard" launch. With a soft launch, you are much more understated and subtle about releasing your product. There are many reasons you might want to do this: you may still be developing the full product offering and want to save your marketing budget until it is all ready, you may want to get user feedback before any serious marketing effort, or you may be afraid that a big marketing splash would topple your technical infrastructure. The hard launch can follow on from the soft launch once you are confident that everything is in place, working, and performing as best it can. There is a grave danger that if you hard launch without a soft launch period, even if only a few days, you risk generating a lot of negative press and disappointed customers. It is easy to see why people want the hard launch as soon as possible—to gain market share, to not "miss the boat," and to raise their profile as much as they can—but at least a short soft launch period is advisable. Make sure you have taken all necessary launch precautions to help protect yourself against unwanted problems.

Table 9.3 outlines some of the precautions you should take before launch. Some of these precautions need to be instigated quite a while before the launch date, so make sure you are aware of them at the outset of the project.

Immediately following launch, you should do another brief test just to reassure yourself that everything works as planned in situ. You will probably be asked, and want to know yourself, what the traffic is like at launch and in the coming weeks, to see if there is any spike in activity, reflecting marketing efforts. This also reveals how traffic levels then hold up or dip down before leveling out. If you have your statistics software in place, you should be able to monitor this activity fairly easily. Many ISPs now provide detailed statistical analysis of your server log files.

The other thing you should think about postlaunch is some type of celebration. After all the hard work that has gone in, and before the development and project team is dissolved, you should all get together to celebrate the project. I tend to wait about two weeks after launch. This is to give people some time to recover from the intense work up to launch, and time for verifying that the site continues to perform properly over a period of use, but is not too long that people will be into something else.

9.3   Handover

Earlier in the book, we talked about the evolving nature of a Web site and the fact that the work only really begins once the site is launched. If it always all ended at the handover, the next two chapters of this book wouldn't really be necessary. It is increasingly rare that the handover will represent the final contact between you and your client.

What is most important about the handover is that it usually represents the end of a project, or at least a major shift in the project, where the next stage is likely to have a very different structure, quite possibly a very different set of people working on it. This is the end of the production phase of the project. Often it will be the final milestone in your critical path, with the maintenance and evaluation stages simply bars that can stretch ad infinitum. Although handover is not necessarily a formal sign-off process, it does represent the point at which you and your client agree that the specified preproduction and production work has been completed to both parties' satisfaction. Hopefully you will have an established schedule of payments, whereby your development team was being paid during the project, but the handover marks, if nothing else, the point at which you can invoice the client for the outstanding balance.

Table 9.3 Preparations for site launch.

Preparation	Description	How long before launch
Search engines	Make sure you have registered the site with the major search engines, so that when the client or client's customers look for the site, they can find it.	Some search engines can take up to six weeks to register a site, so you should try to register at least a holding page well in advance of launch.
DNS entries	Ensure that the domain name you are going to use points to the server you are hosting the site on.	Get this done as soon as possible in the project. In theory, most ISPs should be able to do this for you in a couple of days. However, as it is out of your control, do not take chances. Point the URL at a holding page until the site is ready.
Meta-tags	Make sure that all key pages contain the relevant meta-tags in their code for search engines.	Allow six weeks for the pages(s) you register with the search engines. The other pages you can do a day or two before launch.
Legal/ compliance	Make sure that a legal representative of the client signs off on the site, so that you cannot be held responsible for any legal issues.	Allow at least a week before launch. You can make text changes quickly, but image changes could be less quick.
Marketing/PR	Make sure that marketing and PR initiatives are properly coordinated with launch (e.g., press releases have been sent out).	This depends on whether you are soft or hard launching. The marketing and PR is usually planned well before launch, but the big drive might start two weeks after an initial soft launch for final tests, to get feedback, check systems, and so on.
Training	Ensure that any staff who will be maintaining the site postlaunch are trained as necessary.	This will depend on the site, but you will probably need at least three weeks.
Stats software	Make sure any traffic analysis software you are going to be using is up and running, as the client will want to know the stats immediately upon launch.	Plan on at least two weeks in advance.
Warn ISP	Tell the ISP that you are launching the site and whether you are expecting large amounts of traffic. They can keep an eye on the server and allocate more bandwidth if necessary.	Advise the ISP about a week in advance of launch. Email the server support teams to try to get the names of whoever will be around on the launch day, should you need them.
File sizes	Scan the site to make sure all graphics files have been properly optimized.	Take care of this three days before launch.

Table 9.3 (continued)

Preparation	Description	How long before launch
Page names, ALT tags, graphic dimensions	These are all small things you can fine-tune if you have time. Make sure that all HTML pages have an appropriate title, and that ALT tags are given for all images, as well as dimensions in the HTML, so that formatting is preserved during loading.	Handle three days before launch.
Final test	Run through the site one last time, looking closely at areas that have caused problems during testing.	Check two days before launch.
Final sign-off	The client gives you express permission to set the site live.	Obtain the day before launch.
Early launch	Launch the site before the given time, in order to do a final fully live check. Do not specify a specific time for launch, to avoid too large a traffic spike.	Do this the evening before the launch day.

The launch is rarely the handover point. During the launch, everyone's focus is on the launch, not wrapping up the project and any loose ends. There is usually some type of fallout from the launch, as well as traffic analysis and so on, which means it is more likely that handover will happen a week or two after launch. Table 9.4 summarizes some of the other elements that typically occur as part of handover.

9.4 Summary

The following are significant points raised in this chapter.

▶ Testing is very important. It may be clear to you, but it is not necessarily so to the client. Explain the process and benefits of testing to the client where necessary.

▶ There are numerous types of testing you can do. Functional and cross-browser testing will always be necessary, but you should also consider usability testing, load testing, and security testing.

Table 9.4 Description of tasks during handover phase.

Handover element	Description
Training	Although you may have done training prelaunch, there will probably be a need for some follow-up training.
Handover brief	You may or may not need this in written form. If there are details of site maintenance, procedures, or practices (that could form part of the training), help contact numbers, maintenance team details, and so on, they can be included in a handover brief.
Project documentation	A copy of the project specification and any other documents and correspondence relating to the project should be handed over to the client and maintenance team for reference.
Design guide/data architecture	You may have been asked to provide a design guide or final data architecture for the site, to aid the maintenance team. This is often something you only have time to do after site launch, as part of the handover.
Archiving	During handover you should store, return, and archive assets relating to the project as necessary. This may involve returning a lot of printed or digital material to the client.

▶ Do not allow testing time to be compromised. Allow at least 10 working days for functional and cross-browser testing. Reduce the scope of the deliverable rather than reduce the testing time.

▶ Be wary of committing to a "hard" launch, in which the site must go live at a specific time and is accompanied with a high level of promotion. It is safer to "soft" launch the site first, to check that everything is working as expected, before committing to large-scale traffic-generating efforts.

▶ Make sure the maintenance team and client are suitably equipped and trained to take over the site after launch. Clear documentation and a thorough handover briefing will be necessary.

You might want a slight break after the site's launch, but soon it is time to start thinking about maintenance and evaluation.

chapter

Work Stage 7: Maintenance

Read up on as much nontechnical development lifecycle, enterprise architecture, and analysis literature as possible—especially if you don't come from a development background—so you get a good understanding of the factors that can affect the optimization and long-term maintainability of a site.

—Julian Everett, Lead Developer, USWebCKS, USA/U.K.

Preproduction			Production			Maintenance	Evaluation
Project clarification	Solution definition	Project specification	Content	Design and construction	Testing, launch, and handover	Maintenance	Review and evaluation

217

L ooking at the various stages of a Web site's evolution earlier in the book, we saw that it is only relatively recently that sites have begun to become more integral to a company, with an important part to play in the business strategy and involvement of staff throughout the company. The larger and more complex sites now appearing demand a much higher level of maintenance than the earlier brochure-ware sites. As some companies have only just launched such larger sites, they are only now beginning to realize the issues and importance of the maintenance phase of any Web project.

I described the ideal Web development cycle as a "virtuous spiral," wherein a phase of preproduction leads into a phase of production, which leads into a phase of maintenance and evaluation, which all feeds back into the next, renewed and enlarged, preproduction phase. We will talk further about the evaluation phase in the next chapter, but you can see how important both maintenance and evaluation are in ensuring that the Web site continues to go from strength to strength. Again, as discussed earlier, the importance of updating and evolving a site to retain and grow a customer base cannot be overestimated.

10.1   The Project Manager's Input

The role of the Web project manager during the maintenance phase is much more fluid and less well defined than it is in the preproduction and production phases. As maintenance is ongoing, it is difficult to think of it as a project with parameters, deliverables, and a critical path with a defined beginning and end. You define the role you play. You need to decide for yourself how your time is best spent, depending on the project, and allocate your time and members of the development team's time as necessary.

Typically, the project manager will follow through on the handover of the site, including any training and documentation requirements outstanding. He or she will then be the first point of contact for the client for any site servicing and updates, as defined in the SLA. Any new site developments will also make their way to the project manager, so that they can be scoped and costed as part of a new project. You will probably also play a small consultancy role, whereby you attend the occasional planning meeting with the client or help by answering the odd question and helping out over the phone. With Web sites developing so fast, it is unusual for you not to become involved in new projects for the same client, with one often following directly from the last. If you are working in-house, this will be the case. If you work for an agency, it will depend more on your commitment to other projects.

10.2   Who Should Form the Maintenance Team

Just as you worked with a team that had been specially put together for the preproduction and production phases, so too should there be a clearly defined team for the maintenance of a site. The team may not all be full-time (i.e., some team members may only exist as points of contact), but nonetheless, lines of responsibility and roles need to be clear.

The building blocks and much of the work in defining this maintenance team will already have been done. As part of the solution-definition phase, you defined teams, content sources, editorial procedures, and update mechanisms. These were then fleshed out and finalized in the project specification through the content plan, and the project resources and updates and maintenance sections. In reality, you may find that some of the circumstances have changed, requiring you to revisit some of these documents, but most of the thinking, planning, and definition of who is responsible for updates and maintenance should already be there.

The number of client-side versus agency-side resources required to maintain the site will depend on the nature of the site; the types of resources the client has, or intends to employ; and the capabilities of any content update mechanisms. Some clients are very eager to take control of the site themselves, whereas others would rather outsource as much of the work as possible. As a general rule, it makes sense for the client to update existing content, monitor the site's performance for management decision support, manage the marketing and promotion of the site, and handle all of the customer service and client interaction elements (e.g., replying to emails, providing telephone support, and so on). The Web development team should concentrate on fixing any bugs that might arise, planning and implementing new projects, and upgrading the technical infrastructure. This seems to be the most common model for maintenance, using the strengths of the client and the development team most appropriately and cost effectively.

You will remember from the team structure diagram in Chapter 1 that there is a Webmaster. It is during the maintenance phase that the Webmaster becomes really important, though ideally she will have been involved in the production phase as well. Just to remind you, the following is the role description for the Webmaster.

> Webmaster as a job description is used to cover a wide range of tasks and skills. She may work on the client or the agency side. The Webmaster's role really comes into play after the main development effort, when the site needs maintenance, administration, monitoring, and updating. The Webmaster is often more of a generalist than the other roles described here, and will have basic skills in design, programming, content, and project management. The Webmaster is usually responsible for ensuring the correct functioning and uptime of the site once it is running. She is often the first line of support regarding user interaction and issues with the site.

The Webmaster will have the necessary skills to collate, format, and upload content as required. Channeling the content updates through a single person limits the margins for error that can occur if several people have access to the site server, and will ensure consistency of quality and a higher degree of security. The larger the site, the more likely you are to have a content management system, back-end system integration, content syndication, and other dynamic data publishing mechanisms. See Chapter 7 for more on content management.

Once the site is up, apart from the Webmaster and other site support staff, including perhaps a designer updating graphics and journalists updating content, the people who will continue to be heavily involved are the marketing department and customer service staff. The site will market the company and its service or product offering, but it will also need marketing itself. As customers interact with the site and generate sales, enquiries, and complaints, you will need increasing numbers of staff dedicated to managing these customers. People expect a much quicker response online than they do offline, and it is often easy to overlook the extra demands a Web site can put on your customer service resources. Make sure they are properly trained to deal with online customers' enquiries.

10.3   How the Site Should Be Maintained

Once again, you should be able to refer to your content plan and updates and maintenance documents, both part of the project specification, for details on how the site is going to be maintained. These plans will break down the tools and methods by which the maintenance team will control the site, whether it is to update existing content, create site reports, fix bugs, or create entirely new sections. You are likely to be using a combination of code-level corrections, WYSIWYG HTML editors with built-in FTP and site management tools, Web front ends to site databases, content management systems, and site performance and analysis tools.

It is a good idea to continue to have meetings with the client, albeit less frequently, to make sure the site is still performing well, to review capacity projections and requirements, and to develop ideas for new projects. There may be more recent versions of software, service packs, patches, or hardware upgrades that should be implemented to improve the performance of the system. The Y2K compliance issue was a good example of how big a process this could be. You should be careful to define the limits of your responsibilities in this area with the client. It is much better if you and your team manage any software or hardware upgrades, as you know the system better than anyone else, but you need to be careful about committing yourself to work the client does not expect to pay for. The SLA should make this suitably clear to both parties.

10.4   Service-Level Agreements

We looked briefly at SLAs as included in the appendix to the project specification. This was to include any SLAs you had at that stage in the project. This is most likely to have been SLAs as provided by third parties providing a very specific service to the project. The most obvious example of this is the ISP hosting the site. You might have SLAs from other technology or content partners, but what about your SLA with the client?

You will have developed the content plan and updates and maintenance sections for the project specification. These effectively act as prototypes for the SLA you are now in a much better position to draft, for agreement with the client on all work you will commit to as part of your postproject continued services. In the same way the project specification is designed to make it very clear to all parties concerned what is being delivered, and by whom and for how much, the SLA defines the level of service the client can expect you to provide them on an ongoing basis, and what the costs involved are likely to be. It does not replace the commercial or contractual agreement you have made with the client. It is bound by the same general agreements, such as terms and conditions of work, if the contract is still in force.

10.4.1   Content of the SLA

What might you expect to include in an SLA? The extent and complexity of the SLA you will need to draw up with your client will depend on the relationship you have with the client and the size of the project. Sometimes you might not need an SLA at all. If you are working in-house, it may just be built into what you do as part of your daily job. However, it would still be useful to draw up a document that outlines what you and your team are capable of without needing additional resources. The following are some of the areas a typical SLA might include.

- Tasks of client's internal update team
- Ongoing tasks of Web development team
- Commitments to meetings
- Site access control
- Termination notice periods
- Training and development
- Response times/error handling/resolution procedures
- Data storage and site recovery
- Data ownership and use
- Project documentation
- Performance monitoring/management reporting
- Liaison with third parties
- Software and hardware upgrades
- Maintenance team
- Costs

The sections that follow provide detail on the items of the previous list.

10.4.2   Tasks for Client's Internal Update Team

These first two sections of the SLA are about clarifying who is going to be doing what tasks on an ongoing basis. The client may have appointed a Webmaster, Internet coordinator, or other person (or team) to manage the Web site and update content. In order to help that team, and to define the limits of your continued involvement, you should draw up as precise a brief as possible, detailing what this person or team will be doing each day.

You should be able to break down the work into specific tasks and general areas of responsibility. There will be parts of the site you know need updating every Wednesday (e.g., sports results) or every quarter (e.g., company results), and more general areas of responsibility, such as forging partnerships with other online businesses, ongoing documentation, and marketing. The following are the most likely areas of responsibility for an internal Web maintenance team.

▶ Updating content
▶ Sourcing and managing content from within the company
▶ Building relationships with other online or offline providers
▶ Ongoing testing and quality assurance
▶ Statistical and performance monitoring and reporting
▶ Marketing, including search engine submissions
▶ Ongoing documentation
▶ Training and development, especially disseminating skills internally
▶ Customer service support
▶ Interacting with site customers (e.g., participating in forums, replying to emails, and so on)

10.4.3   Ongoing Tasks for Web Development Team

The areas of responsibility for you and your development team are more likely to cover the following areas:

▶ Developing new content and functionality
▶ Ongoing consultancy (e.g., advising client on industry, best practice, opportunities, and so on)
▶ Fixing bugs
▶ Software and hardware updates

10.4.4   Commitments to Meetings

During the production phase, you will have had a lot of meetings with the client. You and the client will probably be quite used to seeing each other and may even have a fixed time every week when you are accustomed to meeting.

It would be a shame to break this rhythm if there is still enough outstanding or new work to be discussed. Although you don't want to lose the opportunity to have access to the client on a regular basis, you also have to try to make sure that if you are an external contractor you limit the use of your time to what you are going to be paid for, or what you think you can reasonably justify as new business development time. There is a danger the client will continue to assume that the meetings go ahead and you can be used as a sounding board and give advice in the capacity of a consultant without being paid for it. The SLA is not only a client-driven document, it is your chance to make sure the boundaries are clear and your services are paid for where necessary.

10.4.5   Site Access Control

Clearly, during the production phase, you and your team will have had full access to the site, and probably the entire technical infrastructure behind the site. In conjunction with the client, you will have controlled access to the servers and networks. Postlaunch and at handover, you will need to decide how site access control is to be managed. The maintenance team will obviously need some form of access to update and manage the site. If the team is technically proficient, they may take over full management of the systems. If the client is very security conscious, they may even decide that all user names, passwords, and access controls be changed so that only they can access the site and you no longer can. This is unlikely to be because they don't trust you, but more to maintain security and control.

You need to know as part of the SLA where you stand with site access. Are you still going to be administering access to the site? In this case, you need to budget for this time as part of your SLA. Are you going to have access control taken away from you? If this is the case, you need to bear in mind the implications this might have on the speed with which you can fix bugs, add new content, and upgrade software or hardware.

10.4.6   Termination Notice Periods

It is likely that notice periods for termination of service will be included in the contractual commercial agreement, and need not be reiterated in the SLA. However, if termination notice periods have not been defined, it would be good to do so here. It may be that the client wants to try to extend or shorten the period originally agreed in the project specification now that the project has gone into a different phase. The client may feel very reliant on you, in which case they might want to tie you in as far as possible. As long as you are comfortable with the SLA, this should be a good thing, as you can predict and plan for the steady work that will come out of it. At the same time, you might want to be careful about committing too wholeheartedly to a particular client, which can mean missing out on a fabulous opportunity for work you can't take on because of a conflict of interest with your existing client.

10.4.7 Training and Development

There is no doubt that in such a fast-moving and evolving industry there is going to be a need for training and development. This is true of you and your team, as well as the client's maintenance team and Web support staff. Increasingly, the client's Web presence is likely to pervade all aspects of the organization, and as its tentacles spread wider within the organization, the need for training in the new e-business paradigms will become apparent.

You need to think carefully about what you, your team, and your company are good at. Obviously you should be good at Web development. But are you good at training? As we all know, the best teachers aren't necessarily the top academics. Unless part of your business specializes in training, the extent of your job is to train the key personnel in the client's internal team to the point they can then take over responsibility for continued training and development within their organization.

You can provide a certain level of training in teaching the maintenance team how the systems and functions work. You can provide a guidance manual on how to update content, and how to publish to certain areas of the site. You might have produced a style and design guide, a technical architecture, and a coding practices guide, and you might have extensively annotated the code. All of these things you can now run through with the maintenance team until they are confident of taking over the management and upkeep of the site. If there are training requirements that extend beyond the confines of the project, you could recommend training organizations to your client that might be of help. For example, the Webmaster might need to learn how to use a particular development tool. Someone in your team is likely to be an expert in using this tool, but is not necessarily an excellent tutor in how to use the tool. A specialist training company is better placed than you are to take on this type of work.

Look at the SLA as an opportunity to make clear what you understand to be your commitments in terms of training and development. You want to try to make sure that you don't become a help desk for anyone at the client's organization to contact, unless that is explicitly part of your SLA.

10.4.8   Response Times, Error Handling, and Resolution Procedures

This is likely to be the area of the SLA most important to the client. During the production phase, everyone was working closely together and the entire project team was on hand at all times. As you move into the maintenance phase, those resources often disperse. The client, understandably, wants to know that they will still be able to get support from you and your team when they need it. Equally, you need to be comfortable in defining response times you feel you can commit to, knowing your resource situation.

Table 10.1 outlines the type of document you might want to draw up to show the client your response times. Don't forget to include what your working hours are if they are not specified in the commercial agreement.

In addition to this type of response-time table, you might want to include details on how the error or issue should be noted and approached. That is, define what needs to be reported to you, and who should be contacted. You

Table 10.1 Response times for resolving site problems.

Description	Maximum response time for defining the solution and quoting the work	Maximum response time to starting work after notification
Stops external users from accessing vital areas of the site	Two working hours	Four working hours
Vital administration functions are not usable	Two working hours	Four working hours
Server issues at the ISP that prevent the site from functioning correctly	Two working hours	Four working hours
Stops external users from accessing nonvital areas of the site	Five working hours	Nine working hours
Nonfunctioning of uploading or amending applications to nonvital areas of the site	Five working hours	Nine working hours
Affects solely the site's aesthetic qualities	Ten working hours	Twenty-four working hours
Talk through any issue on the phone	Immediate	Immediately
Attending a meeting	As soon as possible, usually within two working days	As soon as possible, usually within two working days

might choose to use an error-handling tool or process similar to the bug-tracking device you used during testing in the production phase. See Chapter 9 for further guidelines on this.

10.4.9   Data Storage and Site Recovery

You need to make it clear whose responsibility it is to perform backups of the site and store data the site generates (e.g., emails, log files, and discussion forum messages). Usually the ISP will perform site backups, and will be able to restore the site if there is a serious problem. You need to check how long it will take them to perform the site recovery, how recent a version of the site it will be, and whether additional costs will be incurred. This should be defined in the ISP's SLA with you or the client.

If you are managing the site for the client and performing all of the maintenance functions, you are the de facto guardians of data generated by the site. You should not underestimate the time and effort required in servicing and maintaining site data. If you have databases on the site, you will occasionally need the skills of a database administrator to perform data backups, and perhaps to clean out and store old data, upgrade drivers, maintain proper licensing, and so on. Think carefully about data such as emails that might go directly to the client. Is it your or their responsibility to ensure that these are stored and logged as required? In some businesses, it is a legal requirement for the company to store all customer enquiries for a certain length of time, in the case of any dispute arising, so don't underestimate the importance of this.

10.4.10   Data Ownership and Use

Following on from data management issues, you and the client should also be clear about who owns the data the site generates, and on how it is going to be used. Once again, this should be clear from the contractual agreement you signed on the basis of the project specification, which will have covered data ownership and other intellectual property issues.

Aside from the legal and commercial issues involved with ownership and use of data, you should think through the work that might be required in using the data. For example, you might have set up a mechanism whereby all emails from the site get stored in a database. The client might then want to use this database to send a mass mailing to all its customers. This would require you to extract the email address data from the database. This is not necessarily very difficult, but again you need to make sure the client does not assume that this work is part of the original budget.

You should also be clear on whether you expect to supply source files to the client. If you have assigned the intellectual property rights, it is likely the client will want copies of the source files. However, the client may in any case want these files for updating the site themselves. This is particularly evident in the case of graphical elements related to the site (e.g., Photoshop, Illustrator, or Flash files). If you don't have the source Flash file (.fla), you would need to re-create it in Flash in order to output the final Flash movie (.swf). Some development teams are very protective of their source files, as they feel that if these are given away they have lost all control of the project. Intellectual property rights aside, you should at least consider the time and cost involved in naming, categorizing, and delivering all source files to the client. This is likely not only to involve burning CD-ROMs, but also further time spent talking through the files and how they relate to the site.

10.4.11   Project Documentation

As the maintenance team updates the site it will, of course, change. How scrupulous the team wants to be in updating the site documentation is up to them, but you need to make sure it is clear in your SLA whether the client expects you to be involved in continuing to create and update site-related documentation. This could become important if a new third party, such as a content provider, or perhaps an investor in the site, wants to see copies of the latest site documentation or requests that new documents be created. For example, a new systems supplier would want to see a copy of the technical architecture of the site. If this has not been kept up to date, there will be some work involved in updating it. Is this type of project documentation something you will be doing as part of your SLA or something that becomes the sole responsibility of the client maintenance team?

10.4.12   Performance Monitoring/Management Reporting

Much earlier on in the project you will have defined its objectives and the success criteria. The next chapter looks in more detail at how you can review how well you have met these targets. Depending on the levels of performance monitoring and management reporting you want to do, there can be a lot of work involved. This is not just in gathering the necessary data in the first place, but the subsequent analysis and interpretation of that data.

Once again, you need to be clear what work is going to be done and who is responsible for doing it. Typically, you will be responsible for setting up the required systems, functions, and applications, and will then train the client maintenance team in how to use them so that they can then take over and do the analysis and reporting internally.

10.4.13   Liaison with Third Parties

This is often omitted but can be very important. How far are you prepared to work with and help other third parties the client might bring in to work on the project? In the extreme case, where the client decides to replace you as its Web development team, how far will you aid the newly appointed team? Will you spend a lot of time explaining what you have created, how it works, providing source code, and so on, all so that someone else can do your work? Hopefully this will not be the case, but it is a lot more common for the client to appoint, for example, a marketing agency, who might want to spend time with you going through the site, or a new content provider who needs to work with you to ensure a smooth technical integration. You can spend considerable time working with such third parties, so you need to be clear about the extent of the services you are planning to provide and how you intend to charge for them.

10.4.14   Software and Hardware Upgrades

Over time, software upgrades, service packs, and patches will become available that are relevant to the site you built for the client. There may also be hardware upgrades that the ISP, for example, is offering for free or very little charge. Both software and hardware is improving in features and performance at a great pace. Unless your client's site takes advantage of these upgrades, it risks underperforming, not making the most of the initial hardware and software expenditure, or not exploiting the full potential of the latest technologies to bring benefits to the client and the site users.

In the SLA you need to stipulate who will be responsible primarily for monitoring and recommending upgrades, and secondarily for actually carrying out the upgrade. Obviously you should try to avoid or at least minimize site downtime while carrying out upgrades. You should also perform the upgrades and test them on the staging and production sites first, so that you can be confident that the live site will then continue to function with the upgrade.

10.4.15   Maintenance Team

Just as you defined the production phase team in the project specification, now you should define the maintenance team as part of the SLA. This should include all points of contact for both the client and the development team having roles and responsibilities, including phone, email, and other contact details. In the event of a problem, it should be clear who should be contacted and in what order.

10.4.16   Costs

It is not easy to budget for an SLA. The costs in creating it will probably be contained within the service-level costs themselves. When creating your project budget for the production phase, you are costing out clearly defined deliverables. With the SLA, it is much less defined and therefore more difficult to put a fixed cost to.

Some Internet agencies are trying to move toward more of a retainer model, as used in the advertising world, in which a client pays a fixed sum of money to "retain" the agency with an SLA. This retainer would cover all of the minor site corrections the client cannot do themselves, and pays the agency to provide the client ongoing consultancy, perhaps through a monthly meeting, or reporting on the latest market trends, technical innovations, competitor activity, and so on. A retainer can also guarantee the client agency response times and resource availability. If the client does not want to pay a retainer, work can be costed and paid for ad hoc, though this is more time consuming to manage.

A compromise between the retainer and ad hoc methods to plan for site updates and maintenance costs is for the client to pay a fixed amount into a pool of money each month. If changes are made, the costs are taken out of this pool. If the money is not spent, it rolls over into the next month. The client benefits, as they only pay for what is actually done, and the agency benefits because there is a preapproved sum of money available, which reduces the time required to go through the budgeting, approval, and payment process, thereby requiring less resource time and improving cash flow.

DILBERT reprinted by permission of United Feature Syndicate, Inc.

If the site uses a third-party content management system, or interfaces with middleware or back-end systems to provide content, you should detail who is responsible for maintaining, servicing, and providing support for these systems with relevant costings, response times, resolution procedures, and so on. If this is a third party, as is often the case, they may well provide their own SLA, or even have a separate contract with the client.

In most cases, you should be able to break the costs down into fixed and variable costs. You can usually tell what elements are most likely to need the input of the Web development team. These you can then give a cost for. Any ad hoc or unspecifiable developments will need to be costed separately. You should give daily rates for the resources that would be involved. You may also choose to include a payment schedule for the SLA if it is structured in a different way from the original pre- and production budgets.

10.5   Summary

The following are significant points raised in this chapter.

▶ A Service-Level Agreement (SLA) should be drawn up between the development team and the client. This document defines the ongoing commitments of all parties concerned with the project.

▶ You should be clear about what levels of support and training you are able, or prepared, to provide the client.

▶ The update methods you define will depend on the skills of the maintenance team, the size and nature of the site, and the budget for the project. The higher the degree of ease and automation of update, the more costly the project will be in the short term and the longer it will take to develop. However, these systems can save money in the long term.

▶ Make sure you have a process in place that defines how you respond to future client requests in relation to the site. Who should the client contact, how fast can you react, and how will it be paid for?

▶ Intellectual property: it should be clear who owns the rights to the content of the site. It should also be clear who is responsible for data generated by the site.

▶ Define who is responsible for monitoring the performance of the site, reporting on server uptime, and dealing with outages and connectivity issues. This may involve a separate SLA with an Internet service provider.

▶ Be aware that management reporting on site usage and users, if done well, is a skilled and time-consuming job.

The maintenance work stage is often difficult to get right at first. During the design and construction work stage, you have an entire team at your disposal and everyone is 100% committed to the job. As you go into the maintenance phase, it is often less clear who is expected to do what. Although the client may have said they will do the site maintenance, you may find that you are being asked to do more than you thought, with the client not having been able to recruit and train a maintenance team in time or the maintenance team creating problems you have to fix. Your development team is also likely to be less enthusiastic about maintenance than they were about creating the initial site.

However, once the maintenance team has settled in and update processes are working smoothly, you can finally begin to relax in the knowledge that your job has largely been done. You have created the site and it has "learned how to look after itself." It is now time to look both backward, in a review of the project, and forward, by evaluating the site's performance and planning new projects to help it grow.

Work Stage 8: Review and Evaluation

Anticipating client needs, delivering on schedule, or having a very good reason why not. […] Keep in touch—don't have the client chasing you for anything. —**Annabel King, Media Project Manager, National Art Collections Fund, U.K.**

Preproduction			Production			Maintenance	Evaluation
Project clarification	Solution definition	Project specification	Content	Design and construction	Testing, launch, and handover	Maintenance	Review and evaluation

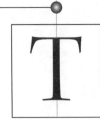

The majority of Web sites are not just Web sites anymore, they are e-businesses doing e-commerce in a fast-evolving and increasingly "wired" e-world. As the Web becomes an ever more integral part of the way we live and do business, the "e" will probably drop away. As with any more traditional business, Web sites will have to justify their existence commercially. If they are not paying their way or performing to stated targets, they will have to evolve or die.

Currently, in the era of the Internet gold rush, there is less of a focus on review and evaluation and more emphasis on building and growing, in an effort to seize a slice of the lucrative digital pie. There will be upturns and downturns, but the Internet has been an incredible growth industry with vast amounts of money made and huge sums still going into backing new Internet ventures, whether established companies or venture capital backed start-ups. As most people feel confident about the Web's future and the importance of it to their businesses, Web budgets have increasingly been easier to obtain and need less justification. Usually, cost control and managing the downside are more of an issue than worrying too much about the exact details of the upside.

However, with increasing competition, a more saturated marketplace, and many Internet companies hoping to float, be bought up, or face the prospect of actually being profitable, the importance of being able to review, evaluate, and measure the success of a Web site is becoming hugely important.

The review and evaluation phase is the final phase in the project method put forward in this book. If you think back to Chapter 3, The Project Road Map, you will recall the "virtuous" spiral of Web development. This final phase enables you to evaluate the success of what you have done, and paves the way to the next new project. The evaluation phase will uncover challenges and opportunities that feed into a new project brief, requiring a solution definition, further development, evaluation, and so on. It is important that you conduct a proper review and evaluation to make sure that this chain isn't broken.

11.1   How the Project Manager Contributes

So you have done the preproduction and production, and have even been involved in the maintenance of the site. Is there really still more to do? If you are working in an ongoing relationship with your client, and you certainly are if you work in-house, then yes, there is a lot to be done in terms of review and evaluation.

This phase of the project runs parallel with the maintenance phase. As soon as the site is launched, you will begin to evaluate its performance. You should also review the success of the project itself. As with previous project phases, your main role in the evaluation phase is to know enough about the specialist tasks in hand to be able to define, plan, budget, schedule, and manage the necessary resources to ensure that objectives are met and that any deliverable meets required standards.

The following sections look first at the project review, and then move on to examine in more detail the value of the evaluation phase to a Web project, and the metrics and analysis, both quantitative and qualitative, you can use for evaluation purposes.

11.2   The Project Review

Once the dust has settled after launch, and at about the same time as the handover, you should conduct a project review. As the Web site is an ever-evolving creature, you could easily indefinitely postpone the project review, feeling that the project hadn't really quite ended. However, you should try to make the project review a milestone, or at least a checkpoint, in the ongoing work, to allow you to look back over the project to learn from its successes and failures. In the following sections of this chapter, we look at ways of assessing the performance of the site itself. The project review is more about assessing the performance of the project and the way it ran. In this sense, it is very relevant to you as a project manager, and will be the period in which you can get the most feedback on how well the client thinks you have done your job.

A project review works in a similar way to a formal appraisal from your manager. It is a recognized chance for both parties to say how they feel things have been going, what has worked well, what could be improved upon, what objectives were met, what new goals need to be set, what was motivating and enjoyable, what was frustrating, and so on. Not all of these topics are subjects you probably discuss with your client or team on a daily basis. To do so would be a little over the top. However, to conduct a project review in which these issues can be aired is a cathartic and positive experience that all parties should learn from. If you can be open with the client and allow them to say what they liked and disliked about the way you worked with them, that client is more likely to continue to want to work with you. Why should they go through the team-building process again with someone else if you are prepared to meet, even exceed, their expectations? Likewise, it is a chance for you to convey to the client how you think they might have worked differently to have achieved even better results, in addition to a really great working relationship. The following are the types of issues you are likely to be discussing in the project review.

► *Efficiency:* Are there ways that work could be done more efficiently?
► *Communication:* Was everyone adequately informed? Did meetings, sign-offs, and reviews of WIP run smoothly and effectively?
► *Response times:* Was the client happy with the responsiveness of the development team?
► *Content provision:* Did content sourcing, preparation, and provision create any problems that could be overcome in the future?
► *Quality:* Was quality sufficiently maintained?
► *Major mistakes:* Were there any major mistakes to be learned from (e.g., a damaging press leak that could have been avoided)?
► *Third parties:* Were they adequately managed on the project? Any lessons to learn?
► *Working environment:* Was it conducive to high quality and efficient output?

The project review is probably best done as a meeting, like any other meeting, with the points on the agenda being discussed in an open and informal manner. You should make sure you have a project review meeting with your development team prior to the meeting with the client, to get feedback on how they felt the project had gone, as this may well bring up points that need to be discussed with the client. Make sure that even if the discussion is quite informal and open ended that you still come up with some action points or learning points that can be used to help improve the next project, or the ongoing work you have with the client.

Don't forget that the project review is of most benefit to you, the project manager. It is unlikely that you will be able to charge for the time spent on the project review, so it can be easy to let it fall by the wayside. It needs to be you that drives the project review and ensures that it happens. You will learn a lot from it, so it is worth pushing to make it happen.

11.3   The Value of Evaluation

Clients are increasingly demanding that their Web sites demonstrate real return on investment (ROI). The site must perform a commercial role as well as a branding and marketing function in order to justify continued investment in the site and the large budgets often necessary. If commercial benefit can be demonstrated, it is much easier to get the funding. Clearly, evaluation of site performance is something of great value to you, as well as your client, if it means that further development work is justified.

11.3.1   Measuring ROI

Proper evaluation means that you can begin to properly measure ROI. It would seem to be very foolish to spend time and money on the planning and preproduction phases (in which you set goals and targets and define strategies and solutions) if you are not to actually then assess how well you performed against these objectives. Equally, your evaluation phase might teach you that your initial objectives were far too optimistic, too conservative, or simply wrong. Part of the value of this project phase is in making sure you get the most out of the money spent earlier in the project, and making sure that continued expenditures are considered, targeted, and as cost-effective as possible.

11.3.2   Increasing ROI

To make the evaluation phase really effective, you should see it not just as an opportunity to measure ROI but to actually increase it. There is an opportunity for the evaluation phase to pay for itself, something that then makes it a no-brainer from the client's point of view. If, for example, you are able to track and capture quantitative and qualitative data about your site users, this can be translated directly into a monetary value. Many Internet companies are valued by their number of users and estimated lifetime value. If you can accurately quantify the number of users you have, and know how they are likely to perform for your site through their customer life cycle, your site's valuation is likely to be that much higher. If you have large amounts of customer data, in many countries you can sell this valuable information to other parties for marketing purposes. If advertising is one of the site's revenue streams, you can negotiate higher CPM rates if you can provide more demographic, geographic, and other user data. You can create greater shareholder value if you find out more about your customers in order to build closer relationships with them and maximize their value by upselling and cross-selling.

11.3.3   Decision Support

The information you glean from evaluating the site also has a huge value in aiding decision making. The client can make decisions based on hard fact rather than supposition or guesswork. This is useful in informing the future direction of the Web site, and might also be important to the longer-term strategy of the client's company. It might be clear that the client's customers want more of the client's offering to move online, or it might be evident that an Internet-only company needs to develop a real-world presence they hadn't anticipated.

From the development team's point of view, proper evaluation will show the client how seriously you take your work and how much importance you place on getting good results. This should encourage the client to stick with you. It also means that you have something concrete to show potential clients: not only can you show them work you have done before but a detailed evaluation of the ROI you create for your clients. If you want to expand the type of work you do beyond Web implementation, and move up the chain toward strategy or out to other technologies such as mobile Internet or other interactive digital channels (e.g., TV, video on demand, and so on), this evaluation phase creates opportunities for you to demonstrate your commercial and strategic insight.

11.3.4   Performing to Standards

The Web is not known for having tightly controlled standards to which everyone adheres. There are governing bodies and organizations whose role it is to set standards and help people work more efficiently together, but market forces have usually prevailed over any official standards. Being a global, open-access network, the Internet is not inherently suited to standards.

However, the consumer market forces that have pushed standards one way or another in the past are increasingly tempered by commercial forces that recognize the need for setting some standards and protocols to facilitate e-business. In the early days of the Web, sites' success was measured in the number of hits they got. Hits were replaced by page impressions. Page impressions have, in many cases, been transplanted by unique users, which in turn have been superseded by registered users. Increasingly, there are metrics and valuation standards emerging that can be used to assess the performance of a Web business.

Having such standards is important in bringing some form of common currency to the Web. This currency makes it easier to ascertain value. If you have a notion of value, you can trade that value. You might want to trade content assets, traffic, user information, advertising, and so on. If you can show your site to be performing to standards, you have an advantage over competitors, as you have a degree of hard currency with which to trade. Standards also allow you to communicate the value of your Web site more effectively, whether it is to the press, to other potential partners, or to shareholders. As people begin to talk and understand a common language, trade is facilitated.

The next two sections look at some of the standards you might want to use in your evaluation phase. These will no doubt evolve, become more refined, and lead to entirely new standards (a Web currency, for example). Some of the standards described have reached a stage at which an independent audit is possible (e.g., log file analysis); others remain very intangible. You should aim to use a mixture of both, and define your evaluation methods to suit the particular site.

11.4   Quantitative Metrics and Analysis

This section and the one that follows look at different evaluation methods you might use to assess and review the performance of the site. This should help you develop metrics you can then use to benchmark and chart site performance. The sections are broken down into quantitative and qualitative approaches. A simple example of the difference between these two might be counting the number of emails the site is generating, as a quantitative measure, versus analyzing the content of those emails as a qualitative measure.

TIP   **Results count**

If everyone thinks the site you've created is no good but it delivers the traffic and the revenue. you'll be put on a pedestal. Equally, if it looks and works like a dream but delivers nothing, it is a waste of time and money. Think of the box office for motion pictures. A blockbuster generally generates more revenue than an artistic classic. This is all the more reason to make sure the client takes the marketing and maintenance of the site seriously, as it will reflect well on you.

Table 11.1, which follows, looks at some key metrics you can use for quantitative evaluation. The table includes details on how to obtain the metric, and considerations associated with it.

Data alone, without any form of analysis and interpretation, is useless. You have to know how to harvest the data you need, but your real opportunity to add value comes in your ability to then analyze that data.

Many of the metrics outlined in Table 11.1 are based on the analysis of log files produced by the Web server. It is unlikely you are going to want to wade through the log files yourself to analyze them. This could mean looking through hundreds of thousands of lines of text—not really a page-turner. There are a fair number of log analysis software tools on the market that can produce reports that cover the metrics we have discussed. See Appendix A for details on some of these tools. You will need to spend some time getting used to configuring these software packages. You need to set up when the reports should be run, whether they should be done in real time, and whether the software should run on the server itself or whether you are going to download the log files to analyze them locally. You also need to set up other parameters, such as files or directories that should not be included in any reports (such as blank or navigational frames), or users (such as robots, spiders, the client, and your development team) who should be stripped out.

Table 11.1 Metrics for quantitative Web site evaluation.

Metric	Description	Obtained
Number of hits	A request to the server for a file	Log files

Considerations
Now not considered valid currency, as one page can contain as many hits as you desire (e.g., by cutting one graphic into 100 files, you get 100 hits instead of one).

Metric	Description	Obtained
Number of page impressions	A request to the server for an HTML page	Log files

Considerations
Be aware that frames, proxy servers, and caching can distort the validity of page impression figures.

Metric	Description	Obtained
Number of unique users	Users distinguished by IP address or by cookies	Log files/database analysis

Considerations
Dynamic IP addressing used by ISPs can give you a falsely high number of users. Proxy servers, on the other hand, cause the number of unique users to appear lower than the real value.

Metric	Description	Obtained
Number of user sessions	A session spent on the site with no breaks in activity of longer than 30 minutes (usually)	Log files

Considerations
This will be defined by the session time-out you set on the Web server. This is usually set to a default of 30 minutes, but you could skew results by altering this (e.g., by shortening it to free up memory more quickly).

Metric	Description	Obtained
Average user session length	Average length of user session	Log files

Considerations
Where machines are shared, or due to a proxy server, it can be difficult to tell where one user leaves off and another takes over.

Metric	Description	Obtained
Top paths through site	Most common sequence of pages followed by users through the site	Log files

Considerations
Can become confused if frames are used. Possibility of "nonhuman" results (e.g., search engine spiders).

continued on next page

Table 11.1 (continued)

Metric	Description	Obtained
Top entry and exit pages	The pages most users enter the site at or leave from	Log files

Considerations
Useful to see if many people are following a particular link out of the site, or whether visitors appear to have a bookmarked page other than the home page.

Number of clickthroughs to and from site	Clicking on a link, particularly banner ads	Log files (often from ad server rather than Web server)

Considerations
Useful for gauging the appeal of a particular banner ad. Does not measure brand awareness or quality of clickthroughs (e.g., subsequent sales conversion ratios).

Top referring sites	The highest referring sites (i.e., sending traffic to you)	Log files

Considerations
Useful to see where the majority of your traffic is coming from.

Busiest periods	The points of greatest Web server activity	Log files

Considerations
Useful for load management, planning of downtime for upgrades, and so on.

Number and type of client/server errors	Details of client-side errors (e.g., scripts) and server-side errors (e.g., "500, 404 file not found," and so on)	Log files

Considerations
Useful for spotting missing pages and broken links, and for debugging Web server or other application errors. Many errors are not errors (e.g., some "404 file not found" errors are not broken links, they are caused when users have incorrectly guessed a URL).

User browser and operating system	Specifies what browser version and operating system the users have	Log files

Considerations
Useful to know how close the actual figures are to what you specified in your technical specification. Allows you to be more confident in future developments.

Table 11.1 (continued)

Metric	Description	Obtained
Geographic usage	Where site visitors have come from geographically	Log files

Considerations
Not very reliable as based on country domains. For example, many users will have a .com domain rather than their country of origin.

Site response times	How fast pages load and data is retrieved	Performance software

Considerations
Good benchmark to see how site performs over time with increasing traffic levels.

Server uptime	Percentage of time the site is available	Performance software

Considerations
Need to get this as close to 100% as possible. Particularly important if advertising is a key site revenue.

Number of registered users	Users who have logged onto the site, with details held	Database

Considerations
Requires users to register and log on. Good for capturing accurate user data, but could be seen as a barrier to site use.

Bespoke applications	Specialist reporting functions	Database analysis (e.g., of e-communications engine or CMS)

Considerations
Could include analyzing buying trends, sales conversion rates, customer life-cycle patterns, and so on. Very useful for targeted information.

Spend	How much it cost	Commercial records

Considerations
Can become less easy to quantify if you include the client's management time, and so on.

Revenue	How much direct revenue has been created	Commercial records

Considerations
Direct revenue should be easy to quantify; indirect revenue less so.

continued on next page

Table 11.1 (continued)

Metric	Description	Obtained
Cost savings	How much money has been saved	Commercial records
Considerations Can be difficult to put a reliable figure to.		
Number of sales leads or prospects	New customers coming via the Web site	Commercial records
Considerations Need to think about how to measure Web-generated leads as opposed to other leads (e.g., a different phone number on the Web site than for other business-generating sources).		
Search engine positioning	Where the site ranks in search engine results	Software analysis
Considerations You can use software or specialist e-marketing agencies to help with this. Some search engines will deliver quantity of traffic, but think also about the quality of traffic delivered, say, by specialist directories.		

TIP   **Log files**

The log files your Web server generates as users interact with the site are very valuable, as you can extract a lot of useful information from them. The following are some tips on how to manage log files:

- *ECLF or CLF?:* You can configure most Web servers to create common log files or extended common log files. You get a lot more information with the ECLF format, so in general go for this. However, bear in mind that ECLF log files are much larger than their CLF equivalent, and more CPU power is taken up creating them.
- *Large log files:* Although log files are only plain text, they can get very large; over 100 Mb a day on busy sites. Be careful about filling up your disk space! Log files are written to the C drive of the server by default. This could fill up very quickly, and cause problems with the proper functioning of applications. Consider writing log files to a larger nonsystem drive. Back them up and zip them up to conserve space. Storing log files by month is a common practice for month-by-month analysis and reports.
- *CPU demands:* Remember that running a log analysis tool on the server uses up a fair bit of CPU power. This could adversely affect the performance of the site,

and it might take several hours to run the report. Set the analysis tool to run automatically when the site is least busy. Many software tools allow for real-time log analysis. Although exciting to look at, remember the performance overheads this incurs.

- *Corrupt log files:* If the log file is there but the analysis software cannot read it, the log file might be corrupt. Try deleting the last and first 10 lines of the log file and rerunning the software. Often this corrects the problem.
- *Missing log files:* Are you sure they have not written elsewhere on the system? Have they written to their default location on the system drive? If they are really missing, there is not much you can do. You can make an assumption about the level of activity over the period where log files are missing by looking at similar periods in the past.
- *Misleading logs:* Be aware of how log files can be misleading. Many ISPs use dynamic IP addressing, which means that the same person could be logged in your log files with a different IP address each time, thus appearing to the analysis software as a different user. A corporate proxy server, on the other hand, will only register as one user, when in reality this may represent the usage of 1000 people. Pages cached by proxy servers or by the user's browser, and the use of frames, can give false levels of page impressions—one for the better, the other for the worse. Internal use and the activity of nonhumans (e.g., search engine spiders) should, ideally, be stripped out at the analysis stage.

Once you have harvested the data and then used a software tool to present it in a manageable form, you can begin your own analysis toward learning from the data. There are various approaches you might want to take. You could focus on user analysis. Using data captured on users, you can begin to build up demographic information to find out who exactly is using your site and why. You can then compare this with your offline customer base to see how the two tally. How many of your online users are also offline customers, and how many are new customers? Are your users connecting to the site largely from work or from home? How well have you captured the target market you defined at the outset of the project?

Rather than focusing on the details of users, you could spend more time analyzing how they, whoever they are, interact with the site. What paths do they take through the site? Where do they enter and leave the site? What pages do they stay on longest? Where in the buying process do people drop out? This is called clickstream analysis, which should help you spot usage patterns that allow you to optimize the performance of the site. For example, if you found that 50% of people dropped out of the buying process when they came to entering their credit card details, you might consider adding additional security guarantees.

You should also be able to analyze how site usage has been affected by real-world events, such as site marketing efforts or the client's company having won an award for their product. If there has been a big marketing drive, PR, advertising, or other promotion, has site traffic gone up notably? If you did an online advertising campaign, how many clickthroughs did you get to the site, and how much has this contributed to ongoing traffic levels? Other real-world events that are likely to have a large effect on traffic are public holidays such as Christmas. How much did sales go up in the lead-up to Christmas? How seasonally affected is the traffic? Is the site used more on the weekends or during the week? Why was there such a big traffic spike on that particular Monday?

A technical analysis of users' browsers and operating systems, together with other technical performance data such as errors and uptime, enables you to assess how successful your technical specification and implementation work has been.

TIP   User tracking

There are varying levels of user tracking you can employ. As a general rule, the more accurate the tracking mechanism, the more "user friction" is created; that is, the more effort is required of the user and the greater the barrier to site use. The following are the three main methods of tracking users.

- *IP address:* You can use the log files to see the unique IP addresses of site users. However, this is generally very misleading. As ISPs use dynamic IP addressing, and companies use proxy servers, there is no guarantee that a particular IP address represents a single person, or the same person each time.
- *Cookies:* Cookies are small text files that sit on the user's machine and store information on them, which can be passed back to the server that first set them there. Cookies act like flags for tagging a particular user, so that she can be recognized when she comes back to a site. However, cookies are machine specific. Therefore, if a machine has more than one user, your data will be distorted. Cookies can also be refused or deleted by the user.
- *Registration:* The user logs onto the site using some combination of user name and password. This uniquely identifies that person to the server, irrespective of

the machine they are at. This is the most accurate form of user tracking, but requires the most effort on the part of the user.

All of these analysis methods can then be further improved by looking at the results from a historical and contextual viewpoint. Once you have built up your information over several months, you can begin to build a historical perspective that shows you how the site is performing month by month. You can assess how the site is performing in relation to itself. The site will set its own benchmarks, which you can then use to set further success criteria and measure future performance. You should also set the site's performance in a context as far as possible. How are other sites in a similar sector performing? How long have they been around, and how much have they had spent on them? Are there any industry benchmarks that can be applied to the site to assess its performance in the context of its competitors?

Combine your knowledge of how the site is performing with competitor site analysis and you are very well armed to make development decisions and inform future site strategy. You should certainly be in a position to build a strong traffic strategy, including the most effective ways of attracting more people to the site, and you could build a strategy to improve customer retention and increase sales, all based on facts and observed behavior.

11.5   Qualitative Metrics and Analysis

It tends to be the quantitative data discussed previously that gets used first for site evaluation. This may be because it is something that is uniquely possible on the Web and therefore creates the most interest; it may be that it is relatively easy and inexpensive to implement; or it may be because it produces "hard" data—facts and figures that are less open to interpretation or susceptible to the vagaries of personal opinion.

However, many sites are beginning to turn to more traditional qualitative techniques to evaluate the success and performance of a site. This is in recognition of the fact that although mountains of quantitative data are very tangible it doesn't necessarily give you any answers or solutions. The data may tell you that site usage is dropping 10% month to month, but not why. There is also an increasing acknowledgement that the best Web sites deliver their value by having superior "intangibles." This includes items such as brands, customer service, and intellectual capital. If these intangibles are indeed becoming the most important element for differentiation and success, qualitative evaluation of sites is going to become just as important as quantitative. There is a perception that with the user-tracking powers of the Internet it is an all-seeing Big Brother, meaning qualitative evaluation is not needed, as the system can know more about the users than they do themselves. This is not the case. The following are some of the more important qualitative measures against which you might want to assess your site.

▶ Brand (mindshare, perception, relationship, and so on)
▶ User feedback (market research, and so on)
▶ Knowledge value (e.g., in-house skills and expertise acquired)
▶ PR value (press, awards, and so on)
▶ Data capture (for use in CRM, and so on)
▶ Competitive advantage

There are various methods you can use to help with qualitative evaluation. In some cases, it will be as easy as reading the emails users send from the site. You might want to conduct your own questionnaire on the site. You could hold focus groups, have online panels assess your site, or track down reviews and ratings the site has received online and offline.

Whereas the quantitative evaluation methods discussed can be implemented successfully by your development team and the client (the analysis part might require the skills of a consultant or strategist), qualitative evaluation is more likely to be carried out by a specialist market research company. They will be able to take a much more objective view, and will understand the techniques necessary better than you are likely to. Online techniques can be used in combination with offline techniques, and the market research agency will be able to advise you on the most effective combination for your client's site.

11.6 Summary

The following are significant points raised in this chapter.

▶ You need to review both the success of the project itself and the success of the site. The site will need to be reviewed and assessed on an ongoing basis.

▶ In order to perform a proper site and project review, you need to know what your success criteria are. These should have been defined in the project specification. Use these benchmarks to assess the success of the project and the site.

▶ Industry standards and sector benchmarks are beginning to emerge. These will help give you an objective assessment of the relative success of your site. However, they are not yet well established. You will need to benchmark the performance of the site relative to itself, over time, as well as compare it to competitor and industry research data you can find.

▶ Don't forget to use qualitative analysis as well as quantitative metrics and analysis in assessing the performance of your site. Traditional market and desk research techniques are equally valuable for the Web.

That brings us to the end of Part II, Method. The eight work stages we have gone through in detail are designed to feed into one another in a never-ending cycle of Web development. As soon as you get to this stage in the book, you should be going back to the beginning to start a new project.

Hopefully you will develop your own method, or a variant of the method proposed in this book, to suit your projects' and clients' needs. We will see how long this book's method holds up in the fast-evolving world of the Web, but there are enough fundamentals here that the book should continue to serve you for a while yet.

If you are tired of methods, specifications, theories, and details, you should find Part III, Case Study, a welcome change. It is all about real-world experiences. This includes an extended case study of a project I worked on, as well as comments from other industry professionals who have something useful to say on the subject of Web project management. If you've got comments you would like to make, please do so at the book's companion Web site at *www.e-consultancy.com/book*.

part III

CASE STUDY

chapter 12

Reality Bytes

Good Web project management relies entirely on planning ahead, foreseeing the obstacles that will undoubtedly be thrown in your path, managing expectations, and being realistic about timings and the eventual outcome. If you've thoroughly thought things through in advance then you should have built in an acceptable level of contingency and still be able to deliver on time. Lack of planning ultimately results in chaos, added expense, sleepless nights, or, worse, missed deadlines and a very unhappy client.

—Elin Parry, Online Manager, Channel 5, U.K.

e have looked at many techniques, and a suggested project method. But what about reality? Does it always go according to the book?

If you've spent much time in project management, you will know that the answer is definitely no. It is very important to have a project framework and a set of project management tools to work with, but no Web project is exactly the same as another, and there is no substitute for experience to help you recognize how to manage these differences and challenges as they arise.

This part of the book takes the theoretical foundations we have discussed so far and overlays them with a healthy dose of reality. There are two forms of reality included in Part III. One is an extended case study for a project I managed, and the other takes the form of quotes and comments from Web project managers, clients, and other Web professionals from around the world. These comments are interspersed in the text as appropriate. Part III concludes with answers to the question "What are the hallmarks of good Web project management and a good Web project manager?" The comments have been taken not just from project managers but from people who work with them. This is to try to provide an objective view of how we do our jobs well, and how we might do them better. I certainly find them very illuminating, often heartening, and sometimes amusing.

The case study is for Channel 5, one of the United Kingdom's five terrestrial broadcasters. In this case, the project involves a client/agency relationship with Channel 5, the client, and Wheel, the Web development agency. The information contained in the case study is taken from documents produced at the time, diary entries, and interviews with members of the project team. The case study consists of the following main sections:

▶ Project background and overview
▶ Eight project work stages
  · What happened
  · Lessons learned
▶ Summary

By breaking down the case study according to the work stages proposed in the method, you can see how the theoretical work stages map to practical work. For each work stage, there is an initial section that describes what actually happened. This is followed by "lessons learned," which is a combination of observations made at the time of the project and observations made more recently, with the benefit of hindsight. The summary takes a more holistic view of what lessons I took out of this particular project.

12.1   Project Background and Overview: *www.channel5.co.uk*

In late September of 1998, Wheel was first contacted by Channel 5 with an invitation to make a pitch for the job of creating Channel 5's Web site. They didn't yet have one, which was very late in the market, and they wanted to create a site that would extend their brand values online and help support their TV programming. As I had a background in TV production and a strong interest in the media sector, it was decided that I should be the project manager for this pitch.

Six months later, on Saturday, April 17, *www.channel5.co.uk* was launched, and heralded as a great success. It was launched on time, to the specified quality, and (at least for the client) to budget. Of course it was not as simple as that. The pages that follow outline some of the more important events and learnings of the project as it went through the eight work stages.

The following two tables should give you a better understanding of Channel 5 (Table 12.1) and an overview of the project itself (Table 12.2). Bear in mind that these are the details at the time; they have now changed as systems

Table 12.1 Overview of Channel 5.

Background	Channel 5 launched in 1997 as the United Kingdom's fifth free-to-air "public" broadcaster. With the TV license that every U.K. TV viewer has to buy, there are five "public" channels you receive for free. Channel 5 is to date the last of these channels to receive a license from the ITC (Independent Television Commission). Channel 5 was set up as an advertising-funded "modern mainstream" alternative to the other network TV channels.
Shareholders	Currently three large U.K. and European media conglomerates. The company is still privately owned, but is expected to list in the near future.
Valuation	$2 billion in March of 2000.
Core activity	Buying the rights to broadcast TV programs and selling advertising space around them.
Competitors	The four other "public" broadcasting channels: BBC1, BBC2, ITV, and Channel 4. ITV is the closest in content and target market. In addition, the many cable and satellite subscription channels.
Brand values	Extremely important to Channel 5 as a point of difference. Adjectives to describe these values: "brave," "irreverent," and "fast." Channel 5 is well known for its successful iconoclastic digs at its larger, slower, more bureaucratic competitors. Very successful marketing and PR on a comparatively limited budget. See Figure 12.1, the Channel 5 home page, to get a feel for the color, energy, and vibrancy that was used in the design to convey the brand attributes.
Market share	Just over 6% in 2000. Channel 5 has beaten its own targets and has been the only "public" channel to grow its market share over the last three years.
TV viewer demographic	Mass market. Daytime viewers tend to be older, female skewed, and lower demographic. Evening and weekend viewers tend to be younger, male skewed, and a higher demographic. High-profile programming (e.g., sports events and films) attracts large numbers of occasional channel viewers.
Number of staff/ locations	About 200, based in the United Kingdom (London and Manchester).
Revenue streams	Advertising is by far the most important.
Online activities	In 1998, almost none.

Table 12.2 *www.channel5.co.uk* **project overview.**

Brief/objectives	To create a site that extended the Channel 5 brand values (e.g., brave, irreverent, and fast) online. The site should support TV programming. It should stand out from the competition. It should experiment with e-commerce, but is essentially a marketing loss leader for the TV channel.
Schedules	The competitive bid process began in October of 1998. The final decision to go with Wheel as the development agency was made in December of 1998. The site had to launch just over three months later, in April of 1999, two years after the channel itself had launched.
Resources	Channel 5 had no dedicated resources for online. The marketing department was managing the process, working with Wheel and some other partners. The Wheel team involved 12 near full-time members at its busiest point, as well as a number of external freelance specialists as required.
Cost	The budget over year 1 for Wheel was $500,000. $200,000 was spent in the three and a half months up to launch, and the rest as maintenance and ongoing development costs. The site also benefited from some free promotional airtime on the TV and a separate online marketing budget.
Technical overview	The IS arrangements were left to Wheel. The site was hosted on two 450-MHz dual processor Compaq Proliant servers, with 512 Mb RAM each, running NT 4, Service Pack 4. One server ran IIS4 as the Web server; the other, MS SQL Server 7 as the database application server. The servers were hosted at Telehouse, London, by UUNet, an external ISP, as part of their facility-managed service. The site was quite quickly getting over 40,000 unique users per month, and creating over 1 million page views, with large traffic spikes caused by PR and TV promotion.

and content have evolved, the site has expanded, and the technology has been upgraded.

12.1.1 Project Clarification

Preproduction			Production			Maintenance	Evaluation
Project clarification	Solution definition	Project specification	Content	Design and construction	Testing, launch, and handover	Maintenance	Review and evaluation

During this work stage, Wheel worked with Channel 5 to understand and define what a proposed Web site might achieve, both for the site's users and

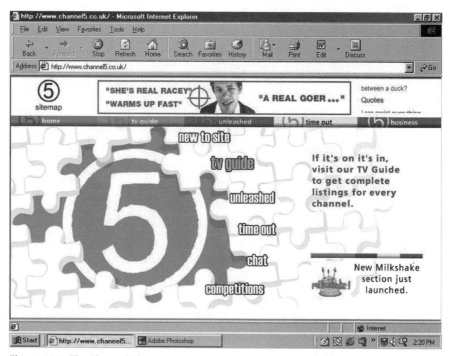

Figure 12.1 The Channel 5 home page.

for Channel 5 from a commercial standpoint. Wheel was involved in a competitive bid, so it was important for Wheel to convince Channel 5 that it was the agency that best understood the potential of the Web, and had a high level of insight into the environment and industry in which Channel 5 operated.

What Happened

An initial meeting was held internally at Wheel to put together a small team of people who would respond to the invitation to bid. At first, this was limited to a board director, an account manager, and myself, as the project manager.

The next few days were used getting a better understanding of Channel 5, their business,

From a marketing perspective, in many agency relationships (advertising and PR, for example) the most important person is the account manager. In my experience, this person plays less of a role in Web development, where the skills of the project manager come to the fore. This is because there is a greater amount of day-to-day involvement with technical requirements, and also because there is a great deal of work to be carried in pre- and postimplementation phases. **—Dave Robertson, Marketing Development Manager, Autoglass, U.K.**

the industry, and the competitive landscape. A brainstorming session was also held with 10 people from across the company, to flesh out some initial ideas and thoughts as to how Channel 5 might exploit online opportunities. This helped us create both some impressive "teaser" ideas, as well as a list of questions we wanted to put to Channel 5. An initial client meeting was duly arranged.

At this stage, Wheel was still bidding against other agencies to try and win the Channel 5 business. This meant that we did not have that much time to spend with the client, and we needed to make an impression in a short period of time. This was done partly through general credentials presentations; partly through the people that Channel 5 met and the relationship Channel 5 felt they could have with them; partly through our enthusiasm, understanding of their industry, and initial ideas; and partly through the seriousness and thoroughness we exhibited in our questions.

> Having a Web strategy places you half way towards team motivation. It demonstrates that you are dedicated to the future of the site, and it provides goals for the team to work towards. Even better is to get the team involved closely in the development of such a strategy. **—Katie Streten, Web Site Manager, The Science Museum, U.K.**

We had three meetings with Channel 5, during which time an important knowledge transfer and relationship-building process was initialized. We established that commercial returns were not important for the site, whereas points of difference from the competitors and strong brand values were very important.

A budgetary figure of $500,000 for the year was mooted by Channel 5 as what they wanted to spend. There seemed to be little room for negotiation on this. The time frame, as ever, was "as soon as we can," with anything past three months deemed too long, and almost too late to be worth doing.

> Accurate budgeting: Oh boy, budgeting is the hardest thing to do. Always double the estimations made by programmers and designers. Always triple your own estimations for project management hours. Increase the result by 20% and you might not go over budget … **—Peter Boersma, Information Ergonomist, Satama, Amsterdam, The Netherlands**

We were dealing exclusively with the marketing department, so there was understandably less interest in the commercial aspects, no interest at all in the technical aspects, and a high level of interest in any branding and publicity elements. A big launch idea was already under discussion.

Our main point of client contact was the head of marketing, who reported directly to the marketing director. Although the marketing director did not get very involved, there was a high level of commitment and project sponsorship from the client. At Wheel, the account director was also a board director. The Channel 5 account was particularly important to Wheel for the high levels of publicity it would attract.

> It's very important to have a proper and thorough Web strategy at the outset of the project. Otherwise, when it comes to the marketing of the site, you will find that it can become pretty fragmented and thus less effective and more costly. **—Isaak Kwok, CEO, Interactive Ink, Singapore**

In the absence of any written or defined Web strategy, the project brief we created for this phase also served to crystallize the strategy we intended to follow. This boiled down to providing existing Channel 5 viewers with additional Web-only content to enhance and support existing programs, but also to provide a site that contained content to attract non–Channel 5 viewers. The Internet demographic and Channel 5 TV viewer demographic were quite far apart at this time, so we felt it important to cater to the Internet user as well as the

> Budget for budgeting and never browbeat the quoter. My unfailing experience is that the first quote—the one that makes the client faint—is right. The result is that it ends up costing the developer what it should have cost the client. **—Matt Flynn, Director, Wheel, U.K.**

Channel 5 viewer. If we could attract people to the site, we could then convert them to watching the TV channel.

The project brief, doubling as a pitch document, contained a budget and timeline for the entire first year that fit the budget and timeline put forward by Channel 5. It also contained some initial ideas on content, along with an outline site map, a few example Web pages, a communications brief describing our message to the target market, and a breakdown of the team that would be dedicated to the project. An appendix to the project brief contained the usual credentials, method, terms and conditions, and so on.

Lessons Learned

The following are lessons learned from the Channel 5 experience that have implications for Web project management in general.

Try to meet a representative of all departments you will be working with. It would have been good to get the IS department involved earlier. This would have helped us better understand Channel 5's IS capabilities and in-house skills, particularly related to the Web. It would also have better prepared us later in the project for the working processes they favored.

Make sure you look into, and understand, the content sources. As you will learn when we get to the content work stage, content became more of an issue than we had counted on. Channel 5 did not have any editorial staff, so could not create their own content. The rights Channel 5 bought for the TV programming were only primary broadcast rights, and Internet rights were not included in any photo shoots. This meant that none of the TV-related content was usable without lengthy rights negotiations.

Don't believe anyone who says they don't have a commercial interest. It made quite a change to be working on a site that genuinely appeared to have no intention of paying for itself other than in the brand extension and reach value it created. Not brochure-ware, but supercharged, online "brand-ware." However, within three months of launch, the site started creating new revenues through advertising, and other projects appeared (intranet, online image library, press information distribution, e-commerce, and so on) that had a much more commercial slant. Elements of business-to-business began to creep in where it had been purely business-to-consumer before. We would have done better to take the future commercial needs of the site into greater account at this early stage.

Try not to allow yourself to commit to fixed budgets and schedules at this stage. This is easier said than done, especially if you are trying to win important business. As a project manager, you should be fighting not to commit until you know all of the variables and can be confident about your costs and timings. As a salesperson, however, you want to get the business almost at any cost, with short-term losses set off against longer-term gains. In this case, we agreed to fixed costs and schedules up front, before the full solution was defined or project specified. This is not the way to do things, though commercial forces often mean that this is how it happens. We were running the risk of going over budget internally, or staying up 24 hours a day to get the work done. In fact, we did go over budget internally, but did not work overly long hours.

12.1.2   Solution Definition

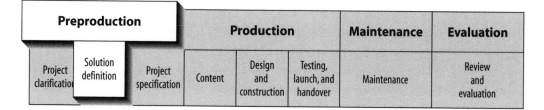

During this stage, a prototype was developed in order to road test and demonstrate a proposed solution. Wheel also put forward technology, content, and resourcing solutions that best met the budgetary and other project parameters.

What Happened

The bidding process for this project was somewhat atypical. Following the submission of the bid document, Channel 5 decided they wanted to go ahead with the project and were fairly sure they wanted to work with Wheel. However, they wanted to do some further planning and build a small prototype to see just how some of the ideas we had put forward would come to life on the screen. Channel 5 paid a nominal fee to Wheel to obtain this. This benefited both sides, as Channel 5 remained uncommitted to the full budget if necessary, and Wheel was able to further develop the ideas and get paid for doing so. It also allowed for both sides to see how the working relationship would pan out.

Regular meetings were set up: a progress meeting once a week on Tuesday between Wheel and Channel 5, and another full-team meeting once a week on Friday internally at Wheel. This gave Wheel time to prepare for the client meetings on Tuesday.

It was decided the prototype would be a flat-file HTML mockup. This meant the files could run on any machine with a browser and did not require a Web server. In order to show as much of the design work as possible in a compressed development period, the screens were single JPG files with image map hot spots for links. The site at this stage used DHTML to impressive effect, but only worked in IE 4. Download times were not an issue, as the site was running locally. This also meant that sound effects could be used.

Dynamic content was feigned by demonstrating a few predetermined search and interactive examples. As a demo for the marketing department, this worked extremely well, as a lot of interactive content could be developed and demonstrated in a short space of time.

In order to re-create the experience of the prototype online, it was decided that Flash would need to be used. Only Flash could offer the immersive and high-impact media experience we were after, and yet keep file sizes to a minimum and retain the quality necessary. See Figure 12.2 for an example of an interface we created in Flash. You don't see the animation and interactivity on the page, but if you can imagine everything reacting to your mouse on rollover, you should be able to see how this page would not have been possible using animated GIFs; the file size would have simply been too large.

There was neither the budget nor the time to do a non-Flash version of the site, so the brave decision was made to go Flash only. Looking at the target market, the likely penetration of the Flash plug-in in that market, and referring back to the Channel 5 brand values, the decision seemed reasonable. It fit

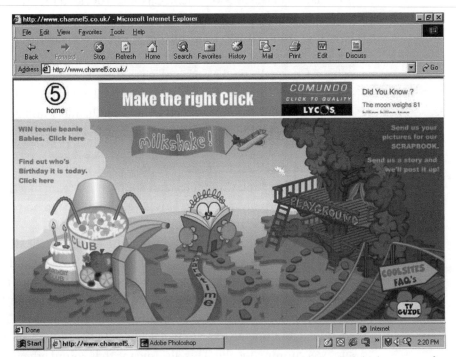

Figure 12.2 Flash allowed us to create fun, interactive environments, such as this home page for a kids section of the site.

with the Channel 5 brand values to create something innovative and compelling as an experience and not be afraid to require users to get the plug-in in order to access that experience. At the launch of the TV channel, there had been press and public criticism that you couldn't always get Channel 5 on your TV. Were we opening ourselves up to the same criticism on the Web?

Not only Flash but multiple frames were allowed as part of the design, which did indeed stand out from competitors' sites, which seemed very dull by comparison. Using many frames has its disadvantages (see Section 6.2.9), but we recognized the implications of what we were doing and decided the advantages outweighed the downside. In the long run, the large number of frames would actually prove to be a bigger issue than we appreciated at this stage.

The technical specification was created and we made sure the IS department at Channel 5 saw it and signed it off. As it meant very little to our marketing contacts, we felt it important that the IS department take responsibility for ratifying the specification at the client end. With the decision on Flash and the use of frames, it was all the more important that what was being proposed was clearly understood.

Once the technical specification was signed off, the account was set up with the chosen ISP (one Wheel had worked with successfully often in the past) and the two servers ordered. There was a lead time of 20 days to get the servers configured and installed. Even with these 20 days, the servers were still available three months ahead of launch date. Although this meant paying hosting fees on servers that were not being used by the general public, it did allow us to show work in progress on the actual servers, install all of the necessary software in good time, and test in the live environment as we went.

Domain names were investigated at this stage. Fortunately, the key master domain channel5.co.uk had already been registered by Channel 5. We were able to register some other relevant .co.uk domains (such as c5.co.uk, as Channel 5 is often referred to as C5), but all relevant .com domains had been registered and there seemed little hope of getting them.

This did not matter too much, as the Channel 5 site was targeted very much at the U.K. market.

The challenges posed by the lack of content began to become apparent. Wheel proposed that a team of freelance writers be commissioned to create the initial content. We also took on two TV researchers to help develop some

264   Chapter 12   Reality Bytes

of the ideas. Almost all content had to be created as original content, to avoid intellectual property rights issues. In the contract with Channel 5, Wheel assigned all IP rights to the client.

As content resources and budget were tight, it was proposed that one of the key applications, the multichannel TV listings guide, be sourced from an existing Web provider and housed within the Channel 5 frame set. Figure 12.3 shows you the interface for this application. The drop-down boxes allowed users to select a TV channel, a day, and a time. The search results would then be displayed in the central area, with the pages pulled from another site into the Channel 5 frame set. Channel 5 would get the application for free, the provider would get the page impressions, and the user would be none the wiser. This model was further used to cover some other site applications where source data was missing.

Although Channel 5 did not want to increase their head count, Wheel made the case that a Webmaster would be needed to keep the site up to date,

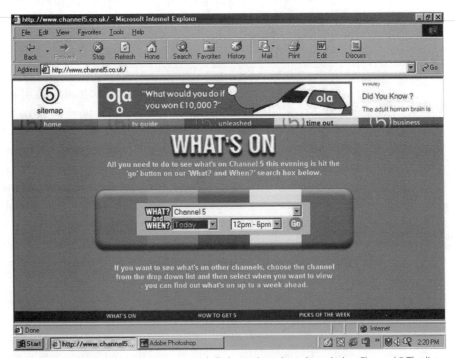

Figure 12.3 The TV listings engine covered all channels and was branded to Channel 5. The listings data was supplied by an external provider.

answer emails, moderate chat forums, and so on. As Channel 5 had no experience in recruiting such a person, Wheel suggested they recruit a Webmaster on Channel 5's behalf.

Lessons Learned

The following are lessons learned from the Channel 5 project solution-definition work stage that serve as general project management guidelines.

Always keep your target market and site objectives in mind. If you do this, it becomes much easier to make decisions. The decision to create a Flash-only site would have been much more difficult to make if we had not been targeting home users, used to entertainment sites, and with "brave" and "irreverent" as core brand values. There was little negative feedback from people who wanted a non-Flash version, as the vast majority of site visitors had the Flash plug-in. However, it is difficult to know how many site visitors we lost thanks to having only a Flash version of the site. We can be sure we lost quite a few when the site was first launched, and probably increasingly few as the plug-in became more commonplace with ongoing browser updates. Under the circumstances, the loss of some users was a sacrifice we were prepared to make.

Make sure the client understands what you are proposing. You may have several client contacts, each of whom will be better prepared to talk to than their colleagues on certain subject matters. Make sure you get the relevant people to take ownership and responsibility for signing off your decisions. If you can do that, there is no room for the client to revoke a decision on the basis that they never understood the implications of what you were suggesting in the first place. Getting the client team used to taking this type of responsibility early on in the process is also very effective.

> It is important to recognize Web sites as a way of increasing your general target audience; for instance, encouraging more overseas visitors/clients and to design sites that speak not only to your familiar audience, but also to those you want to attract. Your audience's capabilities should inform your Web site design. There is no point creating a Flash-based site if the majority of your visitors do not have Flash and are unwilling or unable to upgrade. It is better to provide a gracefully degrading site than a cutting-edge site. **—Katie Streten, Web Site Manager, Science Museum, U.K.**

Don't delay in registering necessary domain names. If they haven't already gone, they soon will. It seems almost impossible to think of any .com name that hasn't already been registered. If the client has a well-known brand and registered trademark, you have a good chance contesting ownership of a domain name if someone else has registered it. However, if you can avoid the trouble, all the better.

Recruitment is a time-consuming and costly business. Recruiting good people is one of the most difficult things in the Web industry today. There is a lot of demand and not enough supply. The earlier you can start building the necessary team, the better. Be careful of agreeing to recruit on your client's behalf unless it is paid for; a recruitment consultant certainly wouldn't do their job for free. In the case of Channel 5, looking for and interviewing innumerable potential Webmasters took far more time than we had ever anticipated, and in the end it was decided we would be better off training someone within Channel 5's marketing department.

It's never too soon to do things that will inevitably have to happen anyway. If there are things you know are going to have to happen at some point in the project, come what may, do them as soon as possible. This way, you don't have to worry about them further down the line, when you can count on having enough else on your plate. Setting up the server, switching IP addresses as necessary, and installing all of the necessary software in good time was a huge benefit in the case of Channel 5. The entire process can take about four days of man-time. Not what you want near the deadline.

Be aware of the expectations a prototype can set. You should be careful to manage clients' expectations regarding prototypes. Explain any differences in the methods, timings, and outputs of the actual site development process versus what you have done for the prototype. In the case of Channel 5, what we created was less a prototype and more a "sales" demonstration, whose spectacle aimed at showing off the sorts of things that might be achieved. This sales-driven approach can be very dangerous, as you can build up expectations that cannot then be satisfied. With Channel 5, we were in danger of allowing the client to think that full-screen motion video was (1) realistic over a 33-kps modem, (2) easily knocked together in a couple of days, and (3) would work for all users without any need for testing.

12.1.3   Project Specification

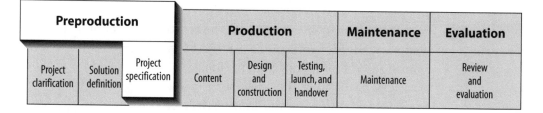

Preproduction			Production			Maintenance	Evaluation
Project clarification	Solution definition	Project specification	Content	Design and construction	Testing, launch, and handover	Maintenance	Review and evaluation

Following on from the prototype and the proposed solutions, it was now time to specify exactly how the site would be created. The scope of the work needed to be controlled, as there were other projects and ideas emerging. The project specification would form the basis of the contract between Wheel and Channel 5.

What Happened

The project brief/bid document was reasonably long and detailed and, for the purposes of the marketing department, sufficient by way of a project specification. As long as the ideas materialized, it mattered less to them how exactly this happened. As time was tight, it would have been easy to go into the content and design and construction phases using this project brief as our guiding document.

However, two things happened that actually helped us in the long run by forcing us all to spend more time focusing on the project specification. First, Channel 5's IS department became properly involved for the first time. As they had been out of the loop thus far (apart from signing off the technical specification), and used to working to certain software development methods, they wanted to see a project specification. This would help them see what had been agreed, where the project was, and

If you can build it on paper you can probably build it on time. Programmers *love* a good spec, and hate bad ones. Nothing makes a programmer more righteously indignant than to be able to say, "How can I build this when you haven't even decided how it works!"

I like to define good functional specifications in this way: Let's say I were to give Joe Developer a functional spec and a disk containing the media assets, and then shove him in a closet with a laptop, six pizzas, and a cell phone. A week later he emerges with an Alpha version of the code that looks and behaves pretty much as I had envisioned it, and he's only called me twice. Then I know I've written a great spec. **—Janet Kirker, Vice President, Project Development, Global New Media, USA** who was to be accountable for what. As ever, it was interesting to see the various methods, ways of thinking, and tensions that can arise when IS meets marketing. However, both sides had a lot of value to add. The IS team helped force a clarity and specificity onto the creative and communication ideas that were already on the table. And so the vital project specification was born. It soon became known as "the Bible."

The second thing that helped form the project specification was the decision that the commercial contract between Channel 5 and Wheel would be based on the project specification. This meant that the project specification defined a set of deliverables, and a schedule that Wheel had to meet or risk losing fees, even incurring penalties. There is nothing like a contract of this sort to focus the mind. It forced us all to think even more carefully about what exactly we were committing to,

> Legal and contractual issues: Get a good lawyer and use them. Nothing is ever standard enough for you to understand. If the client doesn't require a contract or won't sign one, go somewhere else. It won't be worth it in the end.
>
> **—Jay Goldbach, Corporate Webmaster, Harcourt Inc., USA**

how far we were prepared to commit, with what assumptions and escape routes. There was a lot of goodwill in the negotiations, but it did mean that the project specification became all the more important as a document.

One area that was perhaps not clearly enough defined was the success criteria by which the project would be judged. As the site was billed as a brand-extending marketing loss leader, it was difficult to attach many hard measurement criteria to the site, such as e-commerce revenue and sales volumes. As we were not sure of Channel 5's level of marketing commitment (in terms of above-the-line marketing expenditure, TV promotion, and so on), it was also difficult to accurately predict levels of traffic to the site. User data was to be captured through the site, but again it was difficult to set success criteria against this data. As the fees were not linked to performance, and as there was a lot of goodwill, this did not matter too much at the time. However, as the site has evolved and matured into a more commercial entity, it would have been useful to very clearly demonstrate how the original site met and exceeded its objectives as initially defined.

Another area that could have done with more definition at this stage was the site updates and maintenance section. At this stage, we were not sure what the ongoing deliverables would be month to month. The focus was so much on the launch that it was easy to put off these issues. We knew how

much budget we had left over the year, and
what team this could buy us. However, as we
were putting so much time and effort into
making the launch a great success, there was a
danger we were setting expectations for Channel 5 and the site users that we could not then
maintain in the long run.

Finally, this phase was notable for the number of other "parallel" bits of work that seemed
to be cropping up. This might be referred to as
the infamous "scope creep." As other departments at Channel 5 became involved, there
were further ideas and wishes (many of them
very good), which were submitted to be part of the overall project. For example, Figure 12.4 shows the screen that allowed journalists password-protected access to special programming information. Although this did not fall

> Resource planning: Over-
> estimate. Remember the
> Scotty Principle: on *Star
> Trek*, Scotty was always
> able to repair the ship in
> much less time than he
> originally forecasted. This is
> because he knew to give
> outside numbers, not what
> could happen under ideal
> circumstances. **—Jay Gold-
> bach, Corporate Webmaster, Har-
> court Inc., USA**

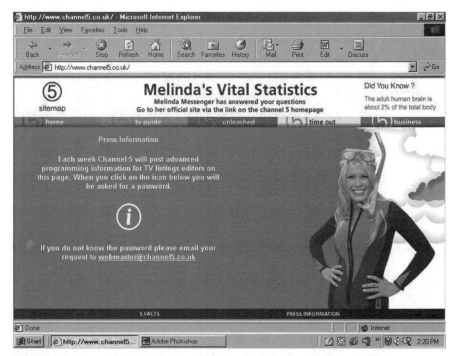

Figure 12.4 Password-protected areas of the site allowed selected members of the press to access special information.

strictly within the business-to-consumer project specification, it was a good idea and did not take too much additional work to create. A video presentation of the prototype was also required for the Channel 5 shareholders. This required voiceover artists, a camera crew, scriptwriters, and so on. As it was for the shareholders, it was very suddenly a high-priority (and unscheduled) piece of work. However, in the run-up to Christmas, this video presentation was dropped as suddenly as it appeared.

Rather than saying no outright to these further pieces of work, we began to define them as "incremental projects." Doing this allowed us to cost and specify the projects separately. It also allowed us to assign priority levels to the various projects. It is much easier for a client to make decisions when faced with cost and deadline implications that can be weighed against priorities.

Lessons Learned

The following are lessons learned from the project specification work stage of the Channel 5 project.

The project specification takes longer than you think, and requires revision throughout the project. As this document is a synthesis of the entire project, there is a lot of time and effort that needs to go into it. The document might be in Word, but also contain Excel spreadsheets, graphics, project schedules, database schemas, PowerPoint data-flow diagrams, and so on. By the time you have mastered how to integrate numerous file formats into a single document, maintain page numbering, and control portrait and landscape layouts as necessary, you will probably find that the document needs to be changed again. It isn't worth spending all of your time working on this document, but it is worth setting aside a few days at the beginning of the project to break the back of it, and then setting aside several hours a week to update the document where necessary. If you are unable to continue with the project for any reason, this document will serve as a blueprint for whoever takes your place. The template project specification available at *www.e-consultancy .com/book* gives you something to work from.

Make sure the onuses of any contract are fairly balanced between client and developer. You should ensure that it is not only you, the development team, who carries all of the responsibilities set out in a contract. Consider including the following stipulations:

▶ Stage D will use only the deliverables produced by stages A through C. If the client wants to change something from a previous delivery, the entire process has to be rolled back to that point. Despite going several steps backward, this will mean an increase in overall budget.

▶ The client should be clearly responsible for any delays caused by their own failure to deliver content, requirements, feedback, or sign-off in a timely manner.

▶ You might also include some type of financial cost the client can't escape without being responsible and committed. These might include nonrefundable downpayments, opt-out penalties, reversion of content and design rights to the developers without a major balloon payment if the client wants to back out of the deal, and so on.

These types of contractual agreements need not be seen as hostile to the client. They are designed to help focus the client's attention and help them ensure they are committed to the project. If this is not the case, the project will suffer. In the general pattern of office life, the things that scream loudest get prioritized. Anything that can be ignored without financial impact to the company will get shuffled down into the pile of things that need to be done, and never be seen again.

The bottom line is that the more critical the project is to the client, even if only for financial contractual reasons, the more committed they will be. Assuming that the development team is equally committed, you have the essential starting ingredients for doing a really good piece of work.

Don't ignore the postlaunch activities just because they seem less important now. This is very easy to do in the hectic run-up to launch, but if you are not clear about what you will be doing in the postlaunch maintenance phase, you may find that life becomes even more complicated postlaunch. In most cases, the maintenance costs for a given body of information will be more than the cost of initial generation. The development costs are a one-time cost, but maintenance is an ongoing expense, and if it's not clear how it is going to be controlled from the outset, it can balloon.

> The project manager must understand that any definition of success must include tangible results for the company, whether that be new revenue streams, increased market penetration, or more efficient distribution. —**Andrew Bibby, Director of Projects, Razorfish, USA**

Be careful of the expectations you are setting in the initial development phase. Will you be able to maintain them, and be paid for them, once the launch has come and gone? As a rule of thumb, site maintenance over a year is likely to cost twice the original launch costs. Is the client aware of this?

Defining success criteria is important for the long term, not just the short term. In the short term, having success criteria is invaluable as a yardstick against which project performance can be measured. Reminding yourself of what it is the site is hoping to achieve is also very useful, and greatly aids decision making. However, don't forget that in the longer term the site will change, the strategy will evolve, and the decision makers will have different priorities. In these cases, it is important to be able to demonstrate why, at a point in time, particular success criteria were chosen and how they were met. If you cannot do this, you risk the new dismissing the old as a failure and, worse, as something that has always been a failure.

> Defining success criteria can be difficult, as often clients don't like to admit that they don't know what they're trying to achieve. Help them to love even modest targets! —**Matt Flynn, Director, Wheel, U.K.**

What you call things is more important than you might think. In the example of Channel 5, the effect of calling additional, unspecified work "incremental projects" was much more powerful than I would have imagined. It didn't sound too negative (as "additional" projects or "side" projects might have); in fact, the word *incremental* even suggested a sense of growth and progression. At the same time, it was clear that this work was over and above what had initially been discussed. By separating this work into discrete projects, the work became more defined, and could be costed for and prioritized. As people got used to referring to this work as the "incremental projects," their rightful place in the chain of priority was more easily found. Don't forget that when you are not with the client they will still be talking about the project internally, and may be discussing the project with superiors who have only just become involved. Establishing a common language to refer to project elements helps everyone communicate more efficiently, and there is less room for misunderstandings. "Hot spots," "incremental projects," "the Bible," "rolling action list," and "the master plan" became accepted project terminology with Channel 5, and each, like a currency, had a value that helped the project team trade priorities.

Have a system in place for managing the infamous "scope creep." Scope creep, where the client asks for work that was never originally agreed to or specified, happens in every project. You need to have a way of dealing with it that does not simply dismiss good ideas and additions but at the same time protects your ability to deliver against the original specification. The volume of scope creep is roughly equal to the developer's willingness to accommodate it at no extra cost.

One tactical means of dealing with scope creep is to keep a suggestion box for ideas people come up with in mid-process, or ideas that come in with new stakeholders. You announce that the new ideas are good, but that it's not practical to incorporate them into the current production schedule. Nothing on the Web stands still, though, so once the current release goes live, it will almost immediately need to be updated. At that point, fresh ideas will be worth their weight in gold, so you're putting the ideas "in the bank" until then.

Instead of fully integrating the new ideas into the current project, you can make minor adjustments to make the site compatible with the new ideas in the next development phase. This will often bring important issues to light regarding the site's present design, and smooth the way for sensible development in the future.

12.1.4   Content

Preproduction			Production			Maintenance	Evaluation
Project clarification	Solution definition	Project specificatio	Content	Design and construction	Testing, launch, and handover	Maintenance	Review and evaluation

During this work stage, we realized the magnitude of the challenge that content would pose us: the rights issues surrounding TV are even more fiercely contested than usual. In many cases, this meant creating original content for which we then had the rights.

What Happened

One of the largest problems we faced was rights issues surrounding the use of TV-related content. As Channel 5 only owned the primary broadcast rights to the TV shows and had not, until this point, included Internet usage rights in any photo shoots, almost every piece of content we assumed we could use needed rights clearance. In many cases, this also included fees. These rights fees had not been foreseen in the budget, nor were they included in any of the assumptions accompanying the budget. Fortunately, Channel 5 was happy to pay these costs, but it was a lesson learned.

Some of the strongest content we were working on relied on TV shows that were imported from the United States: the soap opera *Sunset Beach*, for example. Getting rights clearances for U.S. material, particularly where large studios were involved, was a very involved, complex, and time-consuming business, with no guaranteed outcome. In the case of *Sunset Beach*, we were kept hanging until two weeks before launch, on the assurance that we would be able to go ahead with the content we had developed. One week before launch, the content had to be pulled down; the U.S. studio's site saw us as competition.

The sound effects we used on the site were much easier to source and pay for in terms of copyright. They came from a large sound effects library Wheel had paid a one-time rights fee for, including Internet rights. The music clips we wanted to use (for some downloadable games) were less easy, however. The thought of trying to get permission to use a well-known pop music track, with all of the levels of authority this entails, was too much to be worthwhile. The time and budget was not there to commission original music. In the end, we managed to source some music Channel 5 had commissioned for on-air promotional purposes and owned the rights to.

Even audio clips from Channel 5 celebrities were not as straightforward to use as you might think. Several of Channel 5's presenters have strong charac-

> From Channel 5's point of view, legal and contractual issues are paramount. Television is a particularly litigious industry; therefore, it is critical that all rights for every single program featured are cleared in advance of publication on the Web site. We've learnt some harsh and costly lessons when trying to pre-empt clearance on a program, so it's worth building in that extra time from the very beginning to save everyone time and expense. **—Elin Parry , Online Manager, Channel 5, U.K.**

ters and are well known for their voices, commentary, and phraseology. We offered users the option to download sound files they could then use to customize the system sounds on their PCs. Once again, however, unexpected time delays and costs were incurred, as the celebrities' agents required a fee be paid for the use of this content.

Creating all of the new content from scratch proved to be a very labor-intensive process. For example, we had invented a game called "Fantasy 5," where users could pick a team of characters from a Channel 5 program, through which they scored according to categories such as Romance, Violence, and Catchphrases. In the Romance category, each time your character was involved in a kiss, your team scored 5 points; a bed scene, 20 points; marriage, 50 points; and so on. Figure 12.5 shows you the home page for this game. You can see characters from the TV soap opera *Days of Our Lives* on the right, and down the left the navigational icons to help users play the game. We felt this was a strong idea, as it was based on a fantasy games format users would recognize from the popular Fantasy Football, Cricket,

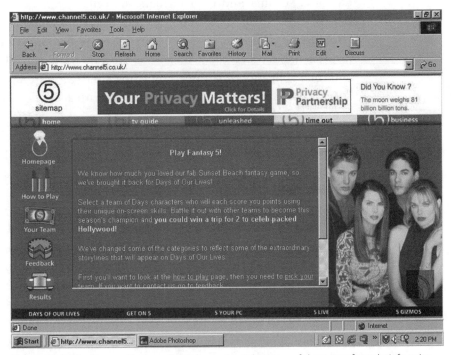

Figure 12.5 The Fantasy 5 game allowed users to pick a team of characters from their favorite TV soap opera.

Rugby, Golf, and other sports games. It was also fun, and it involved users in both the Web site and the TV programming. Indeed, it turned out to be a great success. Writing the rules and terms and conditions, developing the gaming engine and logic, and getting the rights clearances on the characters' photos required both a lot of creative and entertaining writing, as well as clear-headed logic and game usability testing. Once the game had launched, of course, somebody had to do the scoring, which involved a fair amount of TV viewing, as well as respond to the many users' queries.

Content generation was not the only challenge. In a few cases, Wheel was reliant on Channel 5 to provide the content. An example of this was the area code and transmitter data needed to drive an application, allowing users to enter their area code in order to find out what sort of signal strength they should be getting for Channel 5. The function also told users where their nearest Channel 5 transmitter was, and who their local cable and satellite installation providers were. This database contained over 3 million records and was accurate to street level. We very carefully designed and scoped the database schema and data formats in conjunction with Channel 5's IS department. Fortunately, when the data arrived it did adhere to the agreed structures and formats. However, it arrived six weeks late. Although this took us perilously close to the launch date, the data imported into the database and the application functioned fully first time, without any errors. A tight specification helped ensure that a mission-critical application was ready as planned.

Despite the pressures of content creation, gathering, and formatting, we were able to add a few nice touches that improved the content experience for the user. For example, we introduced a character who would appear whenever technical help might be needed. This character was a monkey in a lab coat, who appeared in various random postures of thought and consternation. This fitted the brand values well, and made the technical help parts a little less dry. The technical help monkey also appeared in the place of the usual error messages. For example, the "404 Page not found" error message was made much more friendly and explanatory by the appearance of the monkey, who also provided a link back to the home page. Adding a Channel 5 icon (favicon.ico) to the root directory also meant that if using certain browsers you bookmarked the Channel 5 site, you would see the Channel 5 logo in the bookmark. Easy, but a nice touch.

Finally, as well as the rights issues we had to deal with, there were a number of legal hurdles the content needed to overcome. As a condition of its broadcast license, Channel 5 is governed by the Independent Television Commission (ITC). This means that Channel 5 needs to employ compliance lawyers who sign off all of the station's content. This extends to the Web site as well. Any material that might be deemed defamatory or obscene would incur the wrath of the ITC. Any promotion of the site on the TV that could not be shown to be offering the viewers program-related content on the Web was also frowned upon. For content that was "brave" and "irreverent," you can imagine that it sailed pretty close to the wind. The lawyers also needed to disclaim any content on the Web site that came from site users (e.g., discussion forum postings). The discussion forums needed to be monitored on a very regular basis, in order to satisfy the legal requirements. And finally, of course, there were data protection issues. The laws in the United Kingdom governing what you can and cannot do with personal data are much more strict than in the United States. Every data capture point had to carry appropriate data protection guarantees, opt-out possibilities, and data guardian contact details at Channel 5.

Lessons Learned

The following are lessons learned from the content work stage of the Channel 5 project.

Don't leave yourself open to escalating content costs. Good content is expensive. There are costs involved in creating it, licensing it, and syndicating it. The number of people and organizations that sometimes need to be involved for rights purposes can be very large, and the process can take a long time. Make sure your budget and the cost assumptions that go with it explicitly cover these eventualities. Unless you are an expert in the rights negotiation field, it is probably best to leave the responsibility for resolving rights issues, and meeting any attendant costs, to the client. In the "good old days" of the Web, rights issues were less of an issue. Today, they are big business and need to be taken very seriously by any commercial Web enterprise.

Don't take legal responsibility for the site. Unless you are a legal professional who charges for expertise in intellectual property, do not take any responsibility for the legal issues that might attend your client's site. As a project manager, you should understand, be aware of, and make sure issues are covered, but you cannot be expected to take full responsibility for things such as this. The legal issues can be very complex, especially when multiple jurisdictions are involved. You should make clear in your project specification that legal issues and associated costs will be handled by the client.

Try to stay clear of creating too much content yourself. It can be good fun getting involved in creating content, writing copy, and creating graphics. However, as a project manager you should be spending the majority of your time monitoring and facilitating the work of others, checking on progress, and planning ahead. If you become too involved in the content creation process, you risk losing sight of the bigger picture, and you may be doing things you are actually not very good at!

Demand content early, and assume it will come late and in the wrong format. Late content, incorrect content, no content—content is the single biggest headache for developers working with clients. There is no option other than to try to leave as much leeway as possible to accommodate the inevitable problems encountered with content delivery. Make very clear the implications of content delivery delays. Prioritize content that only the client can deliver you, content that forms part of mission-critical functions, and content that

> If the client is supplying the content, then be prepared for a long wait, and don't be afraid to chase, as often this task gets put on the back burner in relation to the day-to-day running of their business. If you're a contractor, this can adversely affect your cash flow. **—Simon Waldron, Director, Office Wizard, U.K.**

resides in more complex formats (e.g., databases). Ensure the specifications you give for content format are agreed to by the client and are abundantly clear.

Think how you can add value in small ways, and let the client know what you've done. You should be able to use your superior knowledge of the medium to think of ways you can add value to the content proposition. The Channel 5 examples of bookmark icons and customized error pages are just two examples of ways this can be done. Personalization touches, or how email is used, might open other avenues for small but effective added-value features. Make sure you let the client know what you have done; otherwise, they may never appreciate it.

12.1.5 Design and Construction

Preproduction			Production			Maintenance	Evaluation
Project clarification	Solution definition	Project specification	Content	Design and construction	Testing, launch, and handover	Maintenance	Review and evaluation

At this work stage, the project team had grown as large as it would get, and there were multiple partners involved. The main challenge was ensuring everyone continued to work to the project specification, and that any new work or changes were properly controlled.

What Happened

One of the distinguishing aspects of this work stage, as it really got under way, was the number of people that needed to be briefed and kept on track. The Wheel team had grown to 10 people who were working almost exclusively on the project. At Channel 5, there was one person working full-time on the project, two others about half-time, and a whole host of others as required. As new people joined the team, the project specification became all the more invaluable as a means of bringing them up to speed on what was happening. By this time, the project plan (which had over 300 individual items) had been printed out onto eight sheets of paper and mounted onto boards so that everyone could see what had been done and how much was still left to do.

As well as the Wheel and Channel 5 teams, there were, in total, 18 other companies involved in the process. These companies ranged from specialist technology providers, TV production companies providing content, payment providers for the e-commerce, four online content suppliers, and many specialist providers, including a company that specialized in vintage car magazines. These partners were based all over the United Kingdom, and several were from the United States. Managing the input of this many partners to fit in with the schedule required a lot of time be set aside for meetings and phone calls.

As the scale of the number of man-hours per day spent on the project grew, so too did the need for a structured and methodical document and content management process. Managing the large volume of digital and hard assets became increasingly critical, so that team members could find what they needed as soon as possible. If a crucial content asset or document cannot be found for three hours, and the time of 10 people is wasted, you have lost almost a week's worth of time. In this case, we had a lot of hard assets (including tapes, CD-ROMs, 35-mm slides, and photos) that Channel 5 had loaned us for the design and construction of the site. All needed to be returned, as some were unique copies. This meant that rigorous asset tracking and management was necessary. Everything was stored according to the site map: digital files on a networked file server, and hard assets in a row of cupboards with labeled shelves. One of the assistant producers on the project was charged with guarding and controlling access to the cupboards—a challenge not made any easier by moving floors twice during the project.

During this work stage, there were so many things going on that I could not begin to describe them all. However, the following gives you a taste of what this work stage involved.

▶ Holding page put up on live server. Domain names all pointed to this page. Meta-tags (especially keywords and description) added, and page submitted to search engines to begin to filter through.

▶ Merchant account set up for e-commerce, Verisign secure server ID obtained, and credit card purchases tested with NetBanx. This was all necessary to accept credit card transactions over the Web, a necessity for the shopping area of the site. Figure 12.6 shows you a screen taken from this part of the site. You can see some of the Channel 5 merchandise that was on sale through the site.

▶ Webtrends installed and configured on live server. Log file analysis to run every night, giving traffic statistics.

▶ Channel 5 opened up their merchandise cupboard, to the team's delight. Towels, vodka, notepads, sweaters, and candy galore.

▶ Technical difficulties with forcing PDF files to download, and not launch in the browser window across all browsers. Problems with getting desktop

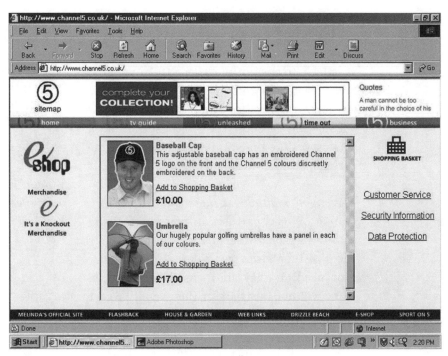

Figure 12.6 The shopping area of the Channel 5 site.

themes to download and self-extract reliably across multiple operating systems, meaning different installation instructions and programming needed for each.

▶ Half-hour internal team meetings now happening every morning for briefings and progress updates.

▶ Talk to ISP to ensure they are aware of launch date and can provide bandwidth as needed.

▶ February 17: first meeting to talk about the launch.

▶ February 22: Channel 5 ask Wheel to do their intranet asap, as well as the Web site . . .

Lessons Learned

The importance of the project spec increases as a team grows and new members join. The more people working on a project, the more important the project specification is as a point of reference. With only a few people in a team, it is much easier for everyone to know what is going on and what they

need to be doing. In a large team, and particularly during the design and construction work
stage, the project manager may not always be
available to spend time with a team member
for a briefing. In this case, the project specification serves well as an initial brief. As new
people join the effort, the project specification
also saves the project manager a lot of time
bringing the new team member up to speed.

Managing multiple partners is very time con-
suming. Project partners are often performing
quite a specific role in the project, usually
because they have a particular talent or service
you need. As they are focused on this task,
they will not be aware of the overall project
issues and how their work fits in. There is a
danger that if the partner is not clearly briefed
and kept up to date, a lot of time and effort on
their part may be spent in vain as they work at
a tangent to the actual requirements. It does
not actually take that long to check in on how
partners and suppliers are doing, but it is often
time that is not accounted for. When the number of partners grows significantly, you can
suddenly find yourself spending a consider-
able amount of time managing them. If the project looks like it will involve
multiple partners, make sure you are clear in your costs and timelines who is
to be coordinating their work and, if it is you, that sufficient time is allocated
to do this.

> Production meetings can very literally mean the difference between success and failure. Before the meetings, I make sure each member has a current copy of the project schedule, which sets the agenda. We review the schedule, task by task, and see where we are on key milestones. If a task is slipping against the target completion, we work together as a team to figure out how to bring it back on track. Because people are usually anxious to get out of the room and go back to the safety of their workstations, it's tempting to breeze over some critical issues. That's where the project manager comes in. It's our role to *really listen*, and ask the tough questions when necessary. **—Janet Kirker, Vice President, Project Development, Global New Media, USA**

It is important to structure document and content management from the out-
set. On a smaller project, you may not need formalized document and asset
management procedures. A shelf and a file directory will probably suffice.
However, on larger projects, the sooner that a recognized storage, retrieval,
and backup system can be implemented, the better. In the long run, this will
produce significant time and cost efficiencies, not to mention averting the

frustration that can come with wasted hours of trying to find something you are sure is there somewhere but just can't lay your hands on. Source control becomes more vital for programming teams, and file naming conventions become more important for the entire team. Time can be squandered if team members unwittingly work from an old version of a document. It is easy to postpone thinking about document and content management until further into the project, but the longer you wait, the more time you will eventually lose.

Prioritize forms and applications. Where you are working with numerous external companies and using many software applications, there will be a lot of forms, applications, and paperwork that needs doing, be it licensing, contracts, registrations, or other applications forms. Any e-commerce venture will necessitate a fair amount of paperwork as arrangements between banks, secure services providers, merchants, distributors, and payment providers are put in place. The technology may not be that complicated, but getting all of the forms correctly filled out and signed by the right people can take a long time. There is no shortcut to doing this work, and unless it is done, a mission-critical part of the project can be held up. Make sure you put enough time in up front to ensure that these applications are in progress before you get too caught up in the nuts and bolts of implementation.

The importance of staying focused when new things crop up. Although new ideas and new initiatives should not be discouraged, there is a grave danger, particularly with Web projects, that you never complete one idea satisfactorily before a new one is under way. You will spend a lot of time delivering nothing. As new ideas come up, they need to be identified and flagged as new ideas, and fit in where possible with the existing project plan. In rare cases, these ideas can change the course of the entire project, but usually they will be bits and pieces that aim to add value. If these can be worked in without disrupting the flow of the project, fine. If not, perhaps they should be handled by a separate project team, or become part of a phase 2 implementation.

Knowing when to spot unnecessary risks: There are so many built-in risks when creating a Web site that you always have to keep your eyes open to when you are sinking in the swamp of too high expectations. Take something real and manageable and take it to market. **—Andrew Bibby, Director of Projects, Razorfish, USA**

12.1.6   Testing, Launch, and Handover

Preproduction			Production			Maintenance	Evaluation
Project clarification	Solution definition	Project specification	Content	Design and constructio	Testing, launch, and handover	Maintenance	Review and evaluation

The Channel 5 site launch date was set in stone. It could not be moved or postponed because the TV schedule had been arranged to help promote the launch of the site. This was definitely a "hard" launch; the lever would be pulled, the site would go live, and press and TV promotion would immediately ensue. This meant we had to be confident that the site was properly tested.

What Happened

We had set aside two weeks for testing the site. We were as adamant as we could be that for the two weeks prior to launch we would not be adding to or changing content but would be concentrating on ensuring that what was there worked as specified. In this case, we did not use an external testing company. Although we had been testing the site throughout the project, this was the first opportunity to go through it in rigorous detail and systematically address any problems.

We carried out cross-browser, functional, and user acceptance tests. We had five operating systems, five supported browsers, and two screen resolutions on which to test the site. This meant going through the site 50 times. We began by logging comments and errors to a testing matrix devised in Excel. However, we soon found that this worked better in Access, so we developed a proprietary bug-tracking database. This type of testing and bug fixing is

Testing: Do it yourself, but don't stop there. Set up browser labs, perform usability tests with real-world situations. Try to break it. Let a child try it (depending on the content) and let an executive try it. If both can use it, you're in good shape. Get an outside dial-up account so that you can see how the site is performing on a modem. Have friends or acquaintances that are in different geographic locations test your site for you occasionally. **—Jay Goldbach, Corporate Webmaster, Harcourt Inc., USA** all the more intensive, as fixing one bug may create two more that weren't there beforehand. We had to conduct a fair amount of regressive testing—in which we tested areas that had already been signed off as fully functional—to ensure that new errors were not creeping in.

The testing was made somewhat easier as a result of our decision to use Flash throughout the site. Unlike the potential cross-browser vagaries of client-side scripting (e.g., JavaScript), either the Flash content worked in all browsers or it didn't work in any. This was a great help, as the interactivity and functionality we had developed using Flash would have been very complex and difficult to test if done using HTML and scripting.

> Always evaluate interfaces and design with your audience. This doesn't have to be a complex procedure; it can take the form of asking an audience sample to look at printouts of proposed designs. Questioning them as to how they would find particular segments of information or what they would use to navigate usually throws up problems or queries that had not even been considered. —**Katie Streten, Web Site Manager, Science Museum, U.K.**

A fair amount of time was spent proofing the copy on the site for grammatical accuracy and spelling. Errors of this type are not fatal, but they do not give a good impression, especially for a first launch. We needed to go through the entire content of the site once again for the legal department to ensure the site did not raise any compliance issues. To help the compliance lawyer do this, we created hard copies of the site's content where possible. With over 300 static pages alone, you can imagine that this was a time-consuming task.

One area of testing, it turned out, we had not pursued vigorously enough was load testing. We ran load testing scripts on the site, and encouraged multiple users to simultaneously stress test particular applications to see how they performed. Under normal circumstances, and up to what seemed like a very high level of predicted usage, the servers performed fine. However, the circumstances that actually occurred turned out to be far more extreme than we had anticipated.

> Crisis management: However big the crisis, the cause is always the same. Crisis occurs when tasks are being identified quicker than they can be actioned, creating an avalanche effect. So at the root of any crisis lies a series of tasks. It's very easy to lose sight of this, and to try to implement "bigger" solutions. The reality is that if you can identify clearly the component tasks, distribute them appropriately, and communicate the plan honestly, you don't need to panic. —**Matt Flynn, Director, Wheel, U.K.**

In the midst of the testing, there were, despite our best efforts, many last-minute things to do. Two core site applications, the TV listings application and the zip-code database, only came online a week before launch, delayed variously by commercial negotiations and late arrival of content. Figure 12.7 shows you what the interface to the zip-code database looked like: a simple enough search interface, but with a very large amount of data sitting behind it. The "Sunset Beach" section of the site had to be pulled down for legal reasons, so the content and applications developed needed to be redeployed elsewhere in the site.

In the week before launch, I no longer used my Outlook Calendar but instead carried around large boards with a handwritten "to do" list. The next stage of priority was to write things on the back of my hand. You'll know you've gone too far if you need to resort to tattooing action items on the inside of your eyelids.

The site was set to launch on a Saturday, to coincide with TV programming and on-air promotions. We had created a special cartoon character

Figure 12.7 The zip-code engine, accurate to street level, told users exactly how to tune in to Channel 5.

that appeared on-air to promote the Web site. The deadline could not be missed, as the TV programming schedule had been set and could not sensibly be changed at short notice. We actually set the site live on Friday evening, though it was not announced anywhere. This gave us the chance to check the site one final time. It also gave us the chance to check that the statistics package (Webtrends) was running as expected, so that we would get reports following the actual launch day. We also made sure the ISP knew what was happening.

Although I had nerve-related nightmares the night before the launch, the launch day itself was eerily calm—like the lull before a storm, when the birds go quiet, or perhaps the eye of the storm itself. By this point, there is a certain sense of calm made possible by the knowledge that now it is too late to do anything more.

We spent most of Saturday alternating between watching Channel 5 on TV and checking that the Web site was still up and watching the log files balloon in size to several hundred megabytes. The server performed slowly at times, and even toppled over once. Fortunately, we were on hand to immediately restart it, meaning that there were only about 3 minutes of downtime. However, clearly we had underestimated the levels of traffic. The traffic over the first few days was driven by the four prongs of huge free PR (including the infamous page 3 of *The Sun*, the United Kingdom's mostly widely read national newspaper), large-scale on-air promotion, an email marketing campaign to a large interested user base, and various online awards, including the Shocked Site of the Day award on the Macromedia site. Figure 12.8 shows the home page of a TV celebrity named Melinda Messenger, who appeared often on Channel 5 and was well known as a former glamour girl. This area of the site attracted huge press interest and caused large traffic surges. The traffic spikes calmed down after the first week, but we had seen the true effect not so much of overall volume of users but sudden spikes in the number of simultaneous users.

As Wheel had an ongoing relationship with Channel 5, the handover was minimal. We returned all of the relevant content assets as required, made sure Channel 5 had copies of the latest project documentation, and continued to help train Channel 5's internal Web team on how to update the site. Task lists and rotas were created for the Channel 5 team to ensure that all site sections were being updated as required. As well as developing new content, Wheel also spent some more time creating administrative functions to help the

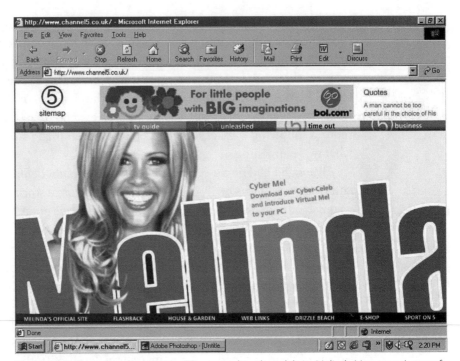

Figure 12.8 The national newspaper PR surrounding the celebrity Melinda Messenger's part of the site created huge traffic spikes.

maintenance team update the site with a minimum of technical expertise. And, of course, we celebrated the launch of the site—once with the Wheel internal team only, and once with the entire client/agency project team.

Lessons Learned

The following are lessons learned from the testing, launch, and handover work stage of the Channel 5 project.

Treat the day before final testing begins with as much importance as the launch date. You really need to try to put as big a stake in the ground as possible to prevent ongoing additions and changes from compromising your testing time. The client needs to see the testing deadline as the final deadline. In reality, some things will still have to be done (such as legal changes), but the more time you can concentrate on the primary task of testing, the better. If you allow yourself to be beaten down on testing time, you may gain favor in the short term but it will quickly be forgotten if the client gets inundated by customers complaining that the site doesn't work.

Design your technical infrastructure to cope with spikes of simultaneous users rather than with a general volume of traffic. In essence, this means that you will always be speccing the systems far higher than you might otherwise. However, you only have to read the numerous reports on e-businesses that couldn't cope with the Christmas upsurge in demand to realize how important it is to be able to manage traffic spikes. Handling large volumes of traffic spread over time is not such a problem, and it is relatively easy to design systems that will be more than adequate. Knowing how to handle sudden demand, from a technical and operational view, is increasingly important. Burstable bandwidth, load balancing, redundant systems, and mirror sites help combat sudden traffic surges. However, these solutions are not cheap, and for some e-businesses demand can be adequately predicted and controlled such that they may not be necessary. Get good load testing software to help you with your benchmarking, and don't forget to warn your ISP before launch.

Don't commit to launching at a specific time. Or if you do, launch it earlier, without telling anyone. If you have built a launch campaign around launching not just on a particular date but at a particular time, you are exposing yourself to all sorts of nasty risks—not least the Internet itself. Not that long ago, the entire United Kingdom lost its Internet connectivity. Not a good moment to have been launching a site. The ISP might lose connectivity for a few hours, and there is little you can do about it but pull your hair out. Don't launch on a Friday, either. You only risk having to come in on the weekend to sort out ensuing minor issues, which are all the more difficult to resolve, as it is more difficult to reach people and get things done during the weekend than during office hours. Wednesday would seem like a good day.

However much you plan, there will always be a last-minute rush of things to do. Don't tell anyone you have allocated time for last-minute alterations. In fact, tell them you won't do them. But be realistic and allow time to fit in those inevitable tasks that appear from nowhere and are presented as more urgent than life itself. Resign yourself to working on the weekend before any major launch, for similar reasons. There *will* be things to do, and if you write off the weekend in advance, at least you won't be disappointed when it happens.

Be ready with your viewing statistics. Understandably, the first question the client will ask postlaunch is "How did we do?" Fair enough question. Make sure you have an answer. Also, prepare to be continually asked this question. Make sure you have costed for Web reporting as part of your maintenance fees, if appropriate. It doesn't take much to run log analysis software on your client's log files, but it can take a lot longer explaining and interpreting the results you get. Applying business and marketing intelligence to this site data is an important, and often overlooked, element of site maintenance and evaluation.

12.1.7   Maintenance

Preproduction			Production			Maintenance	Evaluation
Project clarification	Solution definition	Project specification	Content	Design and construction	Testing, launch, and handover	Maintenance	Review and evaluation

The site had many areas that needed regular updating, such as the TV listings information for the press, the discussion forums, and other supporting TV program information. Users' phone and email enquiries also needed to be answered. The introduction of advertising to the site added an additional revenue stream (to the existing e-commerce), and a special Internet night on the TV channel further boosted interest in developing the site.

What Happened

The number of regular meetings, which had reached one a day, was scaled back to a once-weekly progress update. By now, Channel 5 had two members of the marketing department who were almost exclusively dedicated to the Web. Indeed, one had become "online manager" and took responsibility for managing the site on a day-to-day basis at the client end. As the skills and experience at Channel 5 grew, they were able to take more and more of the maintenance work back in-house. This left Wheel to concentrate on developing new content areas, new ideas, and key new pieces of functionality.

With the team that remained, it soon became clear that we were not going to be able to support the users' demand for content by producing it all in-house. In order to have access to greater depth and breadth of content—

particularly in specialist areas such as gardening, extreme sports, wine, and weddings, to name a few—we began to make deals with partners. This started off as simple content-for-traffic deals, but evolved to include more strategic partnerships that included deal elements such as airtime-for-equity (Channel 5 promotes the partner on air for free in return for an equity stake in the partner) and cross-platform (TV, Web, and mobile phone) content provision. Channel 5 greatly benefits from its speed and flexibility of decision making in these negotiations.

There were two key changes that greatly impacted on the site during the maintenance phase. First, from being a marketing loss leader, the site became seen as a means of creating new revenue, principally through advertising and e-commerce. Advertising would be in the form of banner ads shown at the top of the page. These were to be sold and served by 24/7 Europe, an external sales house. E-commerce would be in the form of in-house sales and fulfillment (largely merchandise) and partnerships with e-commerce providers of books, CDs, wine, videos, DVDs, and so on. This tactic had limited success in the short term, as it became clear that as the site had not been originally set up either as a publishing venture (with ad revenue as the key driver), or as a shop (with e-commerce the key revenue stream), it fell somewhat between the two. Rectifying this situation had no overnight solution, and needed to be built into the new content as it was created. Striking the correct balance between retaining the character and difference of the online brand experience while ensuring the site performed to its new business targets became the daily challenge.

> I would say the most common project management mistake is, on a new account, to take a passive role regarding development life cycle best practice in order to gain favor with the customer in the short term but at the unintentional expense of compromising the architecture and maintainability of the site in the long term.
> **—Julian Everett, Lead Developer, USWebCKS, U.K.**

> Updating a site: Most clients don't want to pay for this, or assume that someone in-house can do it. It reflects badly upon you if this is not true. Spend a few extra minutes with the stakeholders and be sure that you know what their ongoing requirements are so that you can recommend a regimen for them to follow once you're gone (or working on another project). This should include not only keeping content up to date, but checking links, functionality, and search engine placement at least weekly. **—Jay Goldbach, Corporate Webmaster, Harcourt Inc., USA**

The second major change was the success of Internet Night. This was an entire evening of TV dedicated to the Internet. All of the programs, and the main film, were about various aspects of the Web. The TV heads of programming, whose job it is to commission programming that will draw the sizes of audiences that satisfy advertisers, had been somewhat nervous about the Web and whether it was mainstream enough to be commercially viable on TV. Internet Night dispelled these doubts, as it was both a ratings success and a commercial success. All of the advertising was for Internet companies (mostly for dot coms) and so fit the programming very well. Following the success of Internet Night, the site, and the Internet in general, suddenly became seen as a much bigger opportunity than previously, as it had "proved itself" to the core business. The goal of integrating Web and TV became much more achievable.

The commercialization of the site and increased access to the TV channel were the two key factors affecting the maintenance phase. However, the following are a number of other notable elements that formed part of this period.

▶ *The online manager took an active part in the site's discussion forums.* She was able to give the official view of the TV station. Her postings appeared in a different color than other users, so she was clearly identifiable. This different color isn't visible in Figure 12.9, but the indented bulleted item from "webmaster" is her posting. This was an important point of difference from similar sites, where users' questions tended to go unanswered. This human interaction helped build the community feel of the site. However, it is worth noting that this type of activity, although very effective, is also very time consuming. It is easy to underestimate the time needed to answer users' enquiries.

▶ *Another element that can take up a lot more time than you might expect is the statistical reporting on the site's performance.* We were producing reports on a daily basis using log file analysis software running on the server. Once configured, the software automatically produced reports every night. See Appendix A for further details regarding such software. TV ratings are the lifeblood of a TV channel. As the site took on a more commercial focus, the Web ratings gained a similar importance. Increasingly detailed analysis of traffic flows, retention rates, spikes, and usage trends was required. The extent of the work involved in this had been underestimated. By training Channel 5 to manage and interpret the results internally, however, the Wheel development team was able to

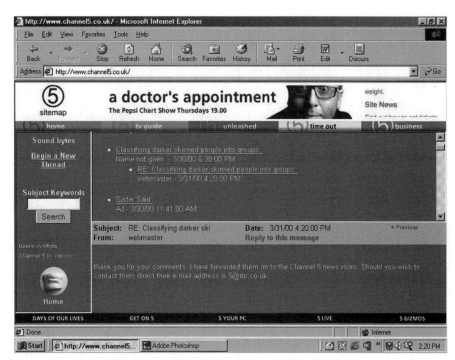

Figure 12.9 The online manager at Channel 5 took part in discussions to help answer users' questions and build a sense of community.

ensure its energies were once again focused on developing new content and functionality.

▶ *Technically, we were greatly aided by Generator in updating the site, in particular the Flash content.* Generator, from Macromedia, is server-side software that allows for dynamic graphics generation, including (but not limited to) Flash files. This allowed us to create templates that, once the data source was updated, automatically output new graphics files. This was very important in facilitating the maintenance process. Generator had been one of the reasons we had felt more comfortable about deciding to go with Flash in the first place. Fortunately, we were now seeing the benefits.

▶ *Data and security became more of a concern in this phase.* There were many unauthorized attempts to log in to the administration parts of the site, fortunately all unsuccessful. However, there were a few instances of denial of service attacks in which the servers were bombarded with requests until they could take no more. In one case, this meant the servers were down for an entire weekend. Unfortunately, there was very little we could do about these malicious attacks. However, we were glad that a daily tape backup of the entire site was made each day by the ISP (part of its SLA), and we were able to recover lost data.

Lessons Learned

The following are lessons learned from the maintenance work stage of the Channel 5 project.

Don't underestimate training costs. The demand for skilled and experienced people in the e-business marketplace outstrips the supply. This means that it is often easier to train someone with an existing knowledge and experience base. You should not underestimate the time and cost that can be involved in this. Pin down in your budgets and project specification whether or not you will be expected to perform training—and if so, to what degree.

The importance of being clear about your business expectations. The way a site is designed, built, and maintained will clearly be affected by the nature of the site and its target market. The business needs of the site also have a profound effect on the way a site should be constructed. If advertising revenue is fundamental to site success, for example, you would want to ensure that pages loaded as fast as possible. User data capture would also be a priority. This would enable you to sell more, and better targeted, advertising, increasing both volume of sales and profit margins. The site would need to be structured in a suitable way for both user and advertiser, the data would need to be captured and mined as effectively as possible, and the graphic design/technical infrastructure would need to allow for very fast page serving.

Don't forget that the Web may still only be a small part of your client's business. Just because the project means everything to you, and may represent a big piece of business to you, it is quite possible that the Web project is of less importance to the client. Clearly this is not true for dot coms, but for established businesses the Web is more likely to be a complement to their existing core business than the actual business itself. Most larger companies realize that the Web will account for more and more of their business in the future, but they still need to concentrate on improving their current core business performance. What this often means is that the more you can help the core business through the Web, the more acceptance and support the Web projects will get. This also tends to kick off a larger process, of cultural and business change.

Change user names and passwords regularly. Unfortunately you should assume that someone will try to hack into your systems. They may only be doing it out of curiosity, but it could cause a lot of damage. You should have suitable security features in place to make it as difficult as possible for an unauthorized user to access your site. User names and passwords are one area of potential weakness. They should be alphanumeric and changed regularly. The longer that user names and passwords are in circulation, the more people tend to know them. You may forget that there are freelancers or part-time staff who know passwords to access the systems remotely. As long as you change the details regularly, you can much better control who has access to what.

Data capture and log file analysis are one thing, but intelligent interpretation and application of this data is quite another. All Web servers can produce log files showing site activity, and it is not difficult to run a software analysis package on these log files. Likewise, it is not difficult to store users' email addresses, personal details, and other data if they give them to you. However, to gain any real insight from these data sources into who your customers are and how they are using the site, you need to do quite a bit more analysis that applies your understanding of the business, the site, the marketing, and the real-world events that will have shaped the data. At a basic level, you will need to be able to interpret for the client such things as "it is not surprising that index.html is the most popular page, as this is the site's home page." At a more advanced level you might be segmenting site users by demographic, psychographic, buying-habits, and

As investment in the Internet increases, so does the level of accountability. To secure a constant or increased level of investment, it is essential that you are able to demonstrate an acceptable level of return on investment, however that may be defined for your purposes. This could be in terms of traffic levels, repeat visits, sales, or all of the above. Both quantitative and qualitative evaluation is necessary to ensure that you are achieving these targets and fulfilling the needs of your users. Promotion of your Web site may attract a significant number of first-time users, but if you're not retaining those users, then you need to understand why. **—Elin Parry, Online Manager, Channel 5, U.K.**

other types of categories. Make sure the client understands what is possible, and knows what level of reporting they want, and how much this will cost to set up and then maintain.

12.1.8 Review and Evaluation

Preproduction			Production			Maintenance	Evaluation
Project clarification	Solution definition	Project specification	Content	Design and construction	Testing, launch, and handover	Maintenance	Review and evaluation

In this work stage, we reviewed the project itself, how Wheel and Channel 5 had worked well together, what might be improved for the future, and the highlights and lowlights. We also reviewed the performance of the site against the expectations set out at the beginning of the project.

What Happened

The client/agency team relationship throughout was excellent. Both sides worked very well together to form a project team that was committed to delivering the best it possibly could with the time and resources available. Both client and agency learned a lot from each other as the interactive channel expertise of Wheel met the marketing and broadcasting strengths of Channel 5.

It was agreed that the site met its objectives as originally set out. External plaudits, in the form of press coverage and awards nominations, helped show the impact the site had made. Site users were also very helpful in pointing out what they felt had been done well and what could be improved. It was also recognized that although the site had met its original objectives, it needed to move on if it was to continue to succeed. More people were becom-

> As the project evolves, the definition of the critical success factors must also evolve. I don't mean we lose sight of our original ambitious goals, but rather that we keep pushing the boundaries on what we hope to achieve for a business. **—Andrew Bibby, Director of Projects, Razorfish, USA**

> A full debrief and project write-up is vital to ensure the same efficient methods/shortcuts are used in the future, while the same problems are avoided.
> **—Carrie Brech, Director, Noop, U.K.**

ing involved at board and shareholder level. This opened new opportunities and brought with it a need for further reporting, presentations, and business justifications. The increased interest from the programming department also meant that the potential scope of and funding for the site could be dramatically widened.

We agreed that we needed to update the site content even more regularly than we were doing, to keep users coming back to the site. This would mean expanding the site's editorial team. We also felt that we could do more to make intelligent use of the user data we had. A level of interpretation and application had already been achieved and had been successful. We could build a stronger relationship with the site users to help improve the service the site offered them.

We learned a lot about the Web/TV dynamic. On the Web site, we saw that overall traffic was growing steadily, but there also tended to be big spikes of usage, a percentage of which would then be retained. This reflected very closely the viewing trends of the TV channel. The most common way for the Web site's users to come to the site was from something they saw on the TV channel (41%). The users the site got from the TV tended to belong to a younger age group, with a higher than average percentage of students. The site was mainly being used from home, and week-

> Site evaluation is really challenging. It is very hard to benchmark a site, and there are still very few acceptable standards for commercial Web evaluation and usage. Project evaluation should be easier, but only if you set out your requirements for evaluation at the start of the project. It's no use trying to do this after the project is complete, because you have nothing to measure against. The performance of Web sites, and therefore Web project managers (both client and agency), will increasingly come under the microscope. It is therefore entirely relevant that due consideration is given to these areas early on in a project's life. It is also very important that ongoing evaluation and suggestions are provided by the project managers to keep awareness high. It is your responsibility to deliver the project, and that doesn't stop at implementation. **—Dave Robertson, Marketing Development Manager, Autoglass, U.K.**

end site usage was higher than weekday usage (not true of most sites). The site's busiest periods, in common with other sites, were at lunchtime and early evening. Users' browsers and operating systems were skewed toward the very latest versions, as we had expected. The geographic spread was surprisingly wide, with many users living in areas that couldn't even receive the TV channel via their aerial. We saw concrete examples of how the Web was helping to increase TV viewing time: several people playing the Fantasy 5 Web game commented on how they watched *Sunset Beach* more as a result. Overall, we concluded the following:

▶ The site had met its initial objectives but needed to move on.
▶ The project team had worked very effectively together.
▶ TV was the most effective way to drive traffic to the site. (See, for example, Figure 12.10, the kids' TV presenter, which promoted the site on-air, which worked in conjunction with a cartoon version of the presenter the kids could find on the site.)
▶ More customer insight and relationship building was needed.
▶ Editorial resources were needed to further boost frequency of site updates.
▶ Increased marketing, partnerships, interactive TV, and WAP would be actively explored.

Lessons Learned

The following are lessons learned from the evaluation work stage of the Channel 5 project.

Customers are an e-business's greatest asset. Many of the lessons learned given for this case study are not new lessons learned, and many of them may read like obvious truths. However, in many cases it is good to have to relearn lessons, or at least constantly remind yourself of what was learned on a previous project. Putting your customers at the heart of your online proposition seems to be just one of those obvious truths that needs to be repeated as often as possible. It is a constant source of surprise that users are actually real people with real views and opinions. It is easy to think of users as statistics. However, with an interactive medium such as the Web, users have a voice and a presence stronger than ever. They can be your best friends and worst enemies. Respect users' opinions and comments. Accept that they expect the highest standards. If you can't give them the highest standards, they *will* go elsewhere.

Offline is still the best way to get people online. This may change, and may not be true for every type of site, but currently, traditional advertising and marketing methods generate more awareness and traffic for Web sites than online methods. That is not to say that online methods do not have a place in the marketing mix—they certainly do—but for volume and exposure you can do a lot worse than, say, a TV advertising campaign. Of course this is very

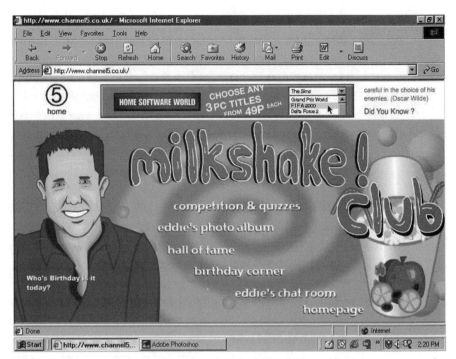

Figure 12.10 Tie-ins to the TV programs, such as this kids' page hosted by a cartoon version of Eddie, the TV presenter well known to the kids, were effective ways of keeping users within the world of Channel 5, both TV and Web.

expensive. However, it does work, as Channel 5 has proved on numerous occasions (not just with its own site), and it explains why the dot coms in particular need such large marketing and advertising budgets.

You can never stop improving your site offer if you want to survive. I am loath to repeat the clichéd "the competition is only a click away" phrase, but with new competition, low barriers to entry, big money, and new technologies flooding the market, you simply cannot afford to stop improving your site offering. Users will continue to be loyal to you as long as you service their needs. If they feel, or perhaps hear from a friend, that their needs can be better served elsewhere, you are likely to lose them. Conversely, if you do improve your site such that it exceeds what the competition can offer, you can very quickly gain a lot of customers.

Don't blow all of your marketing money at once. Some start-ups have been guilty of spending their entire marketing budget in one big initial push. This gets them some visibility and traffic in the initial stages. However, it doesn't leave anything to spend on ongoing marketing efforts. Although Channel 5 was not guilty of this, it was nonetheless clear that marketing efforts had to be sustained, even increased, in the face of fierce new competition if the site was to continue to attract new users. Do not think that you can acquire a lot of users at the beginning who will then stay with you forever and get all of their friends to come to your site as well. It can happen, but rarely. A big launch push is a good idea, but make sure there is budget, resources, and energy left over to continue the battle thereafter.

It's better to do a few things really well and keep them updated than spread yourself too broad and thin. Users don't give you a second chance. If you cannot offer them something compelling, or if you disappoint them on first visit, it is unlikely they will come back. Rather than trying to be all things to all people and doing a lot of things to mediocrity, you are better off doing a few things extremely well and building from there. Users may forgive you for content they don't know about, but not for content that is there but cannot compete with similar content they can get elsewhere. Make sure you know why your content has a unique point of difference from the competition, and is therefore uniquely appealing to a user. In the case of Channel 5, we were able to do this using the brand values to infuse the tone and nature of the content with a voice and character users could not get elsewhere.

12.2 Summary

It's always easy to see how you might have done things differently in hindsight. It isn't ever only about how things might have been done differently, of course, but about how things worked well. You also begin to see that there are factors that affect projects that are beyond your control, and you gain a deeper insight into how e-businesses, the marketplaces, and the industry themselves are evolving. The following are the key things I took out of the Channel 5 project experience.

▶ *The power of TV:* However evangelical you are about the Web, the TV is still the ruling force in most households, and if you are targeting a mass market, this is unlikely to change for a while yet. The success of interactive TV shopping in the United Kingdom confirms the confidence bred of familiarity that the TV gives people. In a modern "wired" society, where share of customer time is paramount, the impulse buying TV promotes will be a huge asset.

▶ *Frames and plug-ins:* Although the decision to go with a Flash-only version of the site could be vindicated—in as much as it fit the brand, enabled us to do what we wanted creatively, and meant we could use the majority of the budget for a single site version—the use of so many frames proved problematic. From a design, and even usability, point of view, a large number of frames is not always a problem, though it does adversely affect load times. From a programming point of view, it makes things unnecessarily complicated, but again this is not the key issue. The two main reasons fewer or no frames would help are (1) ease of update and (2) ease of statistical reporting. As the site gets bigger, point 1 becomes more important. Point 2 is not just about more accurate page impression figures but about allowing for a better understanding of where people have been in the site, the paths through the site they have followed, and so on.

From a commercial point of view, targeted advertising is easier if you can refine targeting to page level. Frames complicate updates and targeting because for every screen the user sees there are several HTML pages that need to be pulled together. Some people go as far as to say there is never any excuse for frames. If you look at the world's largest and most successful sites, you will see very few, if any, that use frames. In some cases (e.g., inline frames for use on an intranet application for which you know what browser the users have), frames can be justified, but you should start on the premise that you will not use frames unless convinced otherwise.

▶ *Data capture versus data application:* The key point to note here is, as mentioned earlier, the difference between merely capturing data and what is then done with that data. In order to make data capture a sensible and worthwhile exercise, you need to know what you are then going to do with that data. In order to understand your customers better and improve the service you are offering them on the site, a data strategy needs to be thought through in the preproduction phase and built into the project specification. In this way you can be sure to extract the maximum value from the site and its users. Intelligent use of metadata (data about data) and content tagging, for example, can help inform important site decisions. As more digital channels become available (e.g., TV, Web, and mobile phones), the ability to understand how your customers are interacting with your business becomes more important.

▶ *The importance of commercial relationships:* It is very difficult, perhaps impossible, for any site beyond a certain size to compete without having at least several important commercial relationships. These relationships might be with fulfillment companies, co-marketing or affiliate marketing partners, content providers, e-commerce providers, technology partners, and so on. It is very difficult to excel in all of these areas, so in most cases it will be sensible to do well what you do well and not bother to compete where you can't. In this respect, the strength of the Channel 5 brand, and its market awareness and the relationships the company already had in place within the industry, were a great asset. These are things that start-ups usually lack. As e-business becomes bigger business, the ability to "talk at the right level" and "sit at the right table" (and any other phrase that means people will actually take you seriously) become more important. Having the right commercial relationships helps.

▶ *Assume nothing can be a success for very long:* Don't get complacent, as only those sites that continually reinvent themselves to improve their offering will thrive. New standards, new competition, and new technology mean everyone should stay on their toes.

▶ *New team members help bring fresh ideas:* As new team members were involved in the Channel 5 project, it was clear how their fresh input and insight helped kick-start new initiatives and processes. It is easy to feel as though you "own" a project if you have been involved with it for a fair time. However, you can become entrenched in your ways of thinking, and refreshing the project team with new members helps give a new perspective on things. Large companies tend to change their advertising agency every couple of years for precisely this reason. This is something that interactive developers should learn from.

▶ *The future?:* Faced with broadband Internet, third-generation WAP phones, intelligent agents, interactive TV, and global competition, to name but a few, it is a potentially bewildering time for any company venturing into the interactive world, let alone for a broadcaster forced to emerge from the protection of a government license. Making sure the right strategy is developed, the right partners are selected, and that customers are put first will be key to future success. For a Web project manager, the future remains challenging but incredibly exciting, with almost unlimited opportunity for personal and career development.

appendix

A

Resources

A ll of the resources detailed here are available on the book's companion Web site. The URL for the site is *www.e-consultancy.com/book*.

Not all of the content on the Web site is replicated in the book. For example, the glossary of terms is available on the site but not here, as it is much easier to add to and keep up to date via the Web. The content duplicated here (such as the reading list and useful URLs) will be kept up to date on the Web site, so it is worth visiting. In particular, the template documents and other files are available only on the Web site. Table A.1, which follows, shows you what resources are available and where to find them.

Table A.1 Location and description of resources associated with this book.

Resource	Description	In book?	On Web site?
Example documentation	A template project specification. Feel free to use and modify to develop your own version.		✓
Bookmark/ favorite files	Download these files to your browser and you will get all online resources mentioned in the book, bookmarked and categorized for you.		✓
Purchase and comments links	Links to where you can purchase the book online and leave your comments for others.		✓
Useful URLs	Recommended sites to help you with your work.	✓	✓
Recommended reading list	A list of the books for Web project managers.	✓	✓
Glossary of terms	A database of Internet terms and definitions.		✓
Discussion forum	A threaded discussion forum in which users can ask questions and give answers.		✓
White papers and reports	A database of white papers and reports freely available on the Web.		✓
The story behind the book	An account of how the book came to life, how it came to be published, and what was easy, what was difficult, and what I'd do next time.		✓
Quiz	A quiz with questions about the Internet to test your knowledge. Helpful knowledge tips with each answer.		✓

Useful URLs

You can download a bookmark file (for either Netscape or IE) from the *www.e-consultancy.com/book* site, which contains all of the sites listed in the following material, categorized as you see them here.

What the bookmark file does not contain, however, is any explanation of what the site is about, which you will find here. In the case of the software section, I have not included a review of the applications' features, as they will no doubt have changed by the time you read this.

The reasons for choosing the resources found here are simple: these are the sites that project managers I have talked to use on a regular basis to help them do their jobs. No doubt you will recognize some of the sites, and will hopefully get good use out of the ones you don't yet know. The resources are broken down into the following structure:

- ▶ News and Information
- ▶ Research
- ▶ Software
  - · Site Visitors' Analysis
  - · Search Engine Submission
  - · Project Management
  - · Performance Analysis
- ▶ Other Useful Resources
- ▶ Search

News and Information

VNUnet

www.vnunet.com
Describing itself as "your computer connection," this site contains a wealth of IT information and news. Features audio, downloads, special reports, and many European language versions.

ZDNet

www.zdnet.com
"Where technology takes you." It could take you a fair way if you ever got around all of the content on this site—from free software to MP3 downloads to buying guides to news and reviews. Make the most of the Ziff Davis empire.

Earthweb

www.earthweb.com
"The IT industry portal." Includes a whole load of useful sites under its umbrella (e.g., gamelan, jars.com, and developer.com). Most useful for programming-related content.

Clickz.com

www.clickz.com
A good source of information on e-marketing, advertising, metrics, and commerce. Articles with attitude.

Internet.com

www.internet.com

"The e-business and Internet technology network." Not a bad URL to go with that ambition. Twelve channels covering everything from the technical to resources to venture capital.

Red Herring

www.redherring.com

"The business of technology." Online version of well-known publication. Best for financial, corporate, IPO, and investor type news and comment. Gives you an insight on what the movers and shakers are up to.

Business 2.0

www.business2.com

"The magazine of business in the Internet Age." Online version of popular Internet business publication. Some very useful reports and commentary on what is shaping the networked economy.

The Industry Standard

www.thestandard.com

"Intelligence for the Internet economy." Builds on the publication to offer some very useful content, along with articles and news, such as recruitment, metrics, and events and conference details.

Wired

www.wired.com

News that can be delivered not just by email but to your handheld device. Business, culture, politics, and technology. Other useful sites you can get to from here include Webmonkey and suck.com.

Research

International Data Corporation

www.idc.com

"IDC delivers dependable, relevant, and high-impact data and insight on information technology to help organizations make sound business and technology decisions. IDC forecasts worldwide IT markets and technology trends and analyzes IT products and vendors, using a combination of rigorous primary research and in-depth competitive analysis."

Media Metrix

www.mmxi.com

"As the worldwide leader in Internet and Digital Media measurement, our mission is to help clients achieve their business objectives and support the growth of Internet advertising and e-commerce." Particularly useful for worldwide site rankings information.

Datamonitor

www.datamonitor.com

"At Datamonitor, we are Market Analysis Experts. We don't just deliver top quality data, we interpret it, combining an insider's market expertise with the objectivity of an outsider to give you the best possible insight into your competitors' strategies and tactics." Good news service and breakdown by global markets.

Iconocast

www.iconocast.com

"We are the *definitive* source for facts, figures, trend analysis and insider information in the Internet marketing industry." Popular email list, with 50,000+ subscribers.

CyberAtlas

cyberatlas.Internet.com

Acquired by Internet.com in 1998, "CyberAtlas is the Web marketer's guide to online facts . . . CyberAtlas gathers online research from the best data resources to provide a complete review of the latest surveys and technologies available."

Zona Research

www.zonaresearch.com

"Superior market analysis and strategic consulting for the Internet industry." You need to be a client to get full access to their reports, but you can get a fair amount for free.

Durlacher

www.durlacher.com

"Durlacher Corporation Plc. is a research-driven investment and securities group focused on emerging technology and media . . . increasingly widely recognized for the depth of its expertise in the European technology, convergence,and media markets." Some good reports for free as files; small charges for hard copies. Durlacher is quite heavily involved in start-ups.

Jupiter Communications

www.jup.com

"Jupiter Communications Inc. is a leading provider of research on Internet commerce. Jupiter's research, which is solely focused on the Internet economy, provides clients with comprehensive views of industry trends, forecasts, ,and best practices." The research services are paid for by subscription, but if you sign up, you can get some good content from the site for free.

Nua Internet Surveys

www.nua.ie

"World's no.1 resource for Internet trends. Over 200,000 readers." Great for quick-fix facts and figures on worldwide Internet usage.

Forrester

www.forrester.com

"Helping businesses thrive on technology change . . . Our research spans consumer, business-to-business, and technology marketplaces. Forrester offers comprehensive analysis of the global Internet economy and its impact on society and business." Forrester organizes its research into various "lenses" covering pretty much everything you could want. Guest registration allows you limited access to free content.

Internet Advertising Bureau

www.iab.net

"The first global not-for-profit association devoted exclusively to maximizing the use and effectiveness of advertising on the Internet." Research, events, and news on Web advertising. Could be very useful if advertising revenue is key.

Software

This section covers sources of software and software-related products and services.

Freeware, Shareware, and Software Sources

The following are two of the leading sites that will help you obtain the software you are looking for, much of it for free, or at least free for evaluation purposes.

CNET's Download.com

www.download.com

No surprises what this site offers. A great place for obtaining software.

Softseek

www.softseek.com

"Your source for shareware, freeware, and evaluation software." Says it all.

Site Visitors' Analysis

The following are some of the industry's leading software vendors that specialize in providing intelligence on how your site is being used, and by whom. Some of these software applications feature site personalization whereby the content of a site is dynamically served to suit a particular user profile.

Macromedia and Andromedia's Aria

www.macromedia.com

Accrue Insight (or Vista)

www.accrue.com

Webtrends

www.webtrends.com

Microsoft Site Server

www.microsoft.com

NetGenesis's NetAnalysis

www.netgenesis.com

Engage's I'PRO

www.engage.com

Search Engine Submission

The following software vendors have created applications that take a lot of the work out of submitting sites to search engines, and help monitor the performance of a site in search engine results.

WebPosition

www.netpromote.com

Topdog

www.topdog.com

Submit-it
www.submit-it.com

WebPosition
www.webposition.com

Project Management

I use Outlook and Microsoft Project as my two key project management software tools. However, there are other software applications out there, such as the following, many of which have evolved from software development methods.

Work Management Solutions
www.workmgmt.com

Project Scheduler
www.scitor.com

Microsoft Project
www.microsoft.com

WebProject
www.wproj.com

Performance Analysis

Performance analysis software tools (offered by the following, and others), some of which can be run online for free, are designed to assess, monitor, and manage the performance of a Web site. This will include checking for broken links, ensuring server uptime, checking file sizes, monitoring server response times, load and stress testing, and so on.

Website Garage
websitegarage.netscape.com

Netmechanic
www.netmechanic.com

WebLoad
www.webload.com

MasterIT
www.cai.com

Segue–Silk Product Family
www.segue.com

Mercury Interactive Corporation
www.merc-int.com

Other Useful Resources

The following are sites I use on a regular basis to perform a variety of functions, as described.

Webmonkey
www.webmonkey.com
A great general resource for Web developers, covering all aspects of development.

Whatis.com
www.whatis.com
The ultimate glossary of Internet terms.

Moreover.com
www.moreover.com
"The world's largest collection of Web feeds." Over 250 categories of news feeds at last count.

iSyndicate
www.isyndicate.com
"The Internet Content Marketplace." Aggregating content from over 800 providers and syndicating content to about 200,000 Web sites.

Search Engine Watch
www.searchenginewatch.com
News, tips, and more about search engines. In fact, all you need to know about search engines.

InterNIC Registration Services
www.networksolutions.com
If you need to know whether a domain has been taken or not, and by whom, use the WHOIS lookup on this site.

Jakob Nielsen's site useit.com

www.useit.com

World-renowned Web usability guru. Listen and learn.

egroups.com

www.egroups.com

A great tool for running communities of interest, and it's all free. Very useful for project management of virtual teams separated by geography or time differences. Includes file archives, calendars, group email functions, databases, voting engines, and so on.

Search

Everybody gets used to using his or her own personal selection of search engines. The following are mine.

DevSearch

www.devsearch.com

"The Web Developer's Search Engine." Good for tracking down specific development sites.

Ask Jeeves

www.askjeeves.com

If you get tired of Boolean operators, you can relax with this natural language search engine, which aggregates results from other major search engines.

Google

www.google.com

If it's speed you want, this one is about as fast as it gets.

Alta Vista

www.altavista.com

Trusty old favorite number 1.

Yahoo!

www.yahoo.com

Trusty old favorite number 2.

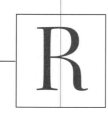

appendix

B

Recommended Reading

R ather than provide a long list of books, I have debated long and hard and managed to reduce my recommended reading list to six books. These are the books I have learned most from, and that I think every Web project manager should read. As new books come out, they will be added to the *www.e-consultancy.com/book* site.

The Mythical Man Month: Essays on Software Engineering, Frederick Brooks, Addison-Wesley Publishing Co., July 1995, ISBN 0-20183-595-9

Generally regarded as a classic text on programming project management, this book is a must read for anyone working with programmers on Web sites. Although originally released as long ago as 1965, the book is still very powerful today, and has more recently been updated with four new chapters outlining Brooks's most recent experiences.

Rapid Development: Taming Wild Software Schedules, Steve McConnell, Microsoft Press, July 1996, ISBN 1-55615-900-5

Renowned for its section "Classic Mistakes Enumerated," which should make any software project manager wince with recognition, this is a very thorough and insightful read at 647 pages. Read it yourself, and then try to make your clients read it.

Designing Web Usability: The Practice of Simplicity, Jakob Nielsen, New Riders Publishing, December 1999, ISBN 1-56205-810-X

More wise words from Web usability guru Jakob Nielsen. Opinionated but at least, in my view, right. A lot of real-world examples to back up his arguments. Two things that are of particular interest: (1) when is the sequel to this book coming out, giving the "hows" to accompany these "whats"? (2) I'll be interested to see how Jakob reacts to broadband Internet when it happens. You should try to ensure your designers read this book.

Secrets of Successful Web Sites: Project Management on the World Wide Web, David Siegel, Hayden Books, 1997, ISBN 1-56830-382-3

Despite overblown titles—of which this is nothing compared to other Siegel books (*Killer Sites, Futurize Your Enterprise*)—and despite a fairly design-led approach, there can be no denying that this makes good reading. It is easy to understand and follow, and, as you might expect from someone obsessed with typography, looks good on the page.

Collaborative Web Development: Strategies and Best Practices for Web Teams, Jessica Burdman, Addison-Wesley Publishing Co., August 1999, ISBN 0-20143-331-1

Very good on communication, team, and client issues. Deals also with planning and process issues as well, making this a very effective all-around guide to Web development, which is of great use to project managers.

Philip and Alex's Guide to Web Publishing, Philip Greenspun, Morgan Kaufmann Publishers, 1999, ISBN 1-55860-534-7

Whereas Siegel feels like a designer at heart, Greenspun is definitely in the programming camp. He teaches at MIT and runs his own Web development firm, so he certainly knows what he is talking about, even if he loses me in some of the code sections. What is most refreshing about this book is the strong written style, the common sense gained through experience, the deep understanding of database-driven sites, and the wonderful photos ... And Alex the dog, of course. Find out for yourself.

Index